The Best Ways to Teach Primary Science

The Best Ways to Teach Primary Science

Research into Practice

Using Learning Progressions to Help Become a More Effective Teacher

Michael Allen

Mc Graw Hill Education   Open University Press

Open University Press
McGraw-Hill Education
8th Floor
338 Euston Road
London
NW1 3BH

email: enquiries@openup.co.uk
world wide web: www.openup.co.uk

and Two Penn Plaza, New York, NY 10121-2289, USA

First published 2016

A catalogue record of this book is available from the British Library

ISBN-13: 978-0-33-526186-4
ISBN-10: 0-33-526168-8
eISBN: 978-0-33-526187-1

Library of Congress Cataloging-in-Publication Data
CIP data applied for

Typeset by Aptara, Inc.

Fictitious names of companies, products, people, characters and/or data that may be used
herein (in case studies or in examples) are not intended to represent any real individual,
company, product or event.

Printed and bound by CPI Group (UK) Ltd, Croydon, CR0 4YY

Praise for this book

"This book makes a major, evidence-based contribution to teaching science in the primary school. It provides a solid grounding for busy teachers to access and use research findings to enhance their professional development and practice. Each chapter provides comprehensive coverage of a science topic, including: revision of subject knowledge; research findings on children's ideas; learning progression; suggested ways to teach, and research exemplars and lesson outlines. This book is a valuable resource for student teachers and for teachers with many years of experience. It is an indispensable addition to every primary teacher's bookshelf and every university education department."

Rob Toplis, recently Senior Lecturer in Science Education,
Brunel University, UK

"This is a great 'why to...' and 'how to...' book. Michael Allen's use of progressive understanding underscores both the unfolding stories of primary science alongside children's developing grasp of the key ideas involved. His work is based on a wealth of research that provides the basis for the 'why to...' in curriculum organisation and planning. This is then brought to bear on considerable professional experience and classroom practice to provide the 'how to...' for teachers, covering a range of important topics in primary science. An excellent compendium of rationales and resources."

Mike Watts, Professor of Education, Brunel University, UK

Contents

Acknowledgements

Thanks go to the amenable folk at Avanquest Software UK for their kind permission to use images from the software package *100 000 Clipart and Web images (Volume 2)* in several of the figures.

1

Introduction

Rationale

The teaching profession is currently undergoing a period of substantial change in England in reaction to a series of government reforms to education. Whether these changes are judged to be positive or otherwise is perhaps less relevant than recognizing that teachers need to adapt to survive in the demanding, seemingly ever-changing climate of educational reform. What impact these reforms will have on the teaching profession is difficult to predict, although it is certain that teachers will be significantly more accountable for their own performance in the classroom. With this in mind, becoming a more effective teacher will be facilitated by a new shift towards valuing teaching methods that have convincingly been shown to help children learn better.

The rationale behind this book is to ease the transition for teachers who want to improve their practice by looking at what others have found really works for them. Part of this involves removing barriers that exist between teachers and educational researchers, who devote their careers to exploring new and effective ways to teach. The ultimate aim is to encourage teachers to become more research-literate so that the profession itself can drive forward the research agenda, which is currently not the case, and will help shape the future teacher to become a more professionalized, enabled and informed educator.

Theoretical perspectives of children's learning in science

As with all school subjects, it is helpful for teachers if they are able to antici-
pate what their children will be thinking during science lessons. Experience is
important here, since the better you know your children and the more you have
taught science, the clearer you will be about what to expect. Although this is
vital, adopting an evidence-based approach does not mean relying solely on your
own experiences; to supplement them, the thoughts and experiences of others
are essential. The literature contains a considerable amount of information sum-
marizing how children learn science, taken from the viewpoints of a variety of
different theoretical traditions. This section will briefly summarize these traditions in order to provide context for the information presented in the remaining
chapters of the book, which detail children's scientific ideas.

Children see the world differently to adults. They are not born with the same
mental faculties that they will possess once they have attained full maturity;
instead, these faculties gradually improve as brain tissue develops, and also as
they learn more through their interactions with the world. Because children's
psychology gradually changes over time, it is beneficial for teachers if they are
aware of how these changes impact on learning in the classroom. The ways in
which science is taught to different age groups needs to vary so that children's
thinking is taken into consideration. Jean Piaget (1972) proposed that children
pass through clearly defined stages of cognitive development determined by
age and that certain types of thinking are not possible before these stages are
attained. Piaget's theory became popular both in the fields of psychology and
education, with many curricula being designed around his findings (e.g. Adey
et al., 1989). However, Piaget's methodologies and conclusions have been seri-
ously challenged since it was found that if tasks are presented in certain ways,
children are capable of mental operations at much younger ages than Piaget had
stipulated (for a summary, see Goswami, 2014).

More contemporary views assume that cognitive development is more
experience-mediated than age-mediated (Eimas, 1994). As learners learn
more about the world around them through practice and accumulated knowledge,
their abilities develop accordingly. Children and adults do not use different mental processes as Piaget and others had suggested; instead, they use the same types
of processes, and the reason that adults perform better is the increased amount
of source information that is available to them. This constructivist view of development sees the vital experiences as being linguistic and cultural, including exposure to teaching, with children steadily building up their mental faculties bit by
bit over time instead of them appearing abruptly once a certain age is reached.
As young minds are developing, due to this lack of experience, they exhibit certain types of behaviour, such as anthropocentrism (looking at the world from

an entirely human perspective), teleology (end-point driven reasoning) and egocentrism (a tendency to see things only from one's own viewpoint). These emergent ways of thinking appear repeatedly in the current book and are reasons why children's ideas can differ from the scientific view. To illustrate, a common anthropocentric theme is ascribing the cause of events to human action. Blake (2004), for example, reports that some children think that humans are responsible for volcanic eruptions.

The work of the Russian psychologist Lev Vygotsky has had a significant influence on science education in recent years. He argued that children learn when they interact socially with other people, particularly when they cooperate in practical ways (Vygotsky, 1978), which is one reason why his theories have particular relevance to science learning. However, in the opinion of some writers, the fashion for citing his work has led to misinterpretations of his original meanings together with a wholly uncritical treatment of Vygotskian theory (Miller, 2011). Often linked to Vygotsky's work is the influential conceptual change movement that originated in the early 1980s, triggered mainly by a seminal paper by Posner et al. in 1982. These events signalled the rise of constructivism in science education, whose tenets include that learners best construct science ideas if: (1) they interact socially in groups performing hands-on experiments; (2) they are able to formulate coherent theories that make sense to them; (3) they are given autonomy for planning and carrying out their work; and (4) they are allowed to test competing hypotheses (Jofili et al., 1999). It has since evolved into a socio-cognitive research paradigm where individuals' performances are considered alongside potential social factors that were present when studies were carried out. Constructivism has stood the test of time and remains the dominant paradigm in science education, although lately conceptual change assumptions have been challenged by proponents of the 'knowledge-in pieces' movement, who contend that instead of constructing complete, coherent theories, learners usually hold small bits of science knowledge that do not always connect with each other, are unstable and easily liable to change (diSessa, 2006).

One recurring outcome from the multitude of conceptual change studies is that children frequently construct ideas that do not agree with conventional science, ideas that have been variously called misconceptions, alternative conceptions, naïve science and children's science. Smith (2010: 557) reminds us that these are often powerful default states of mind, 'shortcuts or rules of thumb' that children construct when they are attempting to make sense of the world around them. They are 'hardwired' into the developing brain and can be very difficult for teachers to change because the child sees them as quite valid representations of the world (ibid.). Sometimes teachers can believe that they have been successful in dealing with a child's misconception but it reappears later as the child reverts back to their default position over a period of time. It has long been known that children can happily believe a misconception alongside its scientific version of the idea and adopt one or other as the situation demands (Claxton, 1985). This is one reason why children are sometimes inconsistent when answering scientific questions. However, some writers see misconceptions as a positive sign that science learning is progressing along desirable lines. Swan (2001) views them as a necessary stage of cognitive development, while Ault (1984) argues that they are an indication of an engaged, imaginative and perceptive learner.

In summary, there is a well-established body of research that has explored what children think when they are being taught science in the classroom; however, teachers are not normally aware of this work (Tracana et al., 2012). The current book aims to help address this discrepancy by presenting a comprehensive account of how children learn the different areas of primary science, alongside effective methods of teaching that have taken children's ideas into consideration. This work is presented specifically in the context of how children's thinking naturally develops over time, and these *learning progressions* are considered in the following section.

Learning progressions

When they are first introduced to a piece of scientific knowledge during a lesson, children do not necessarily leave the classroom holding a final, complete and finished version of that knowledge. During their schooling children construct mental models that in the early years are simple and unsophisticated. As they become more experienced, they build on these basic concepts, constructing progressively more complex ideas as they learn more science and their cognitive faculties develop. These advancements in thinking are *learning progressions* and represent how ideas unfold over time (Plummer and Krajcik, 2010). They offer a map of the routes that can be taken to reach the final destination of the successful learning of a scientific concept (NRC, 2012). Duncan and Rivet (2013: 396) have defined learning progressions (LPs) as follows:

> Embodying a developmental approach to learning, LPs describe paths by which students might develop more sophisticated ways of reasoning over extended periods of time ... LPs begin with consideration of learners' prior knowledge and build toward targeted learning goals through carefully designed instruction. These progressions define intermediate levels in students' understanding, derived, where possible, from research on student learning.

Using learning progressions to inform the planning of teaching is a relatively new innovation that first emerged in mathematics education during the mid-2000s in the United States and is currently in the process of becoming embedded in US curricula as part of the Next Generation Science Standards (NRC, 2012). An important premise is the familiar constructivist principle of using the prior knowledge of children as a starting point for teaching – to assume that a learner arrives at school as a blank slate is a myth. Children's starting points often reflect an incorrect understanding of science and they do not usually progress to full scientific understanding in a single conceptual leap. Instead, there are often intermediate steps, or *halfway houses* that tend to be more correct than the starting points but still do not represent acceptable scientific ideas (Alonzo and Gotwals, 2012). Learning progressions are also referred to in the literature as learning trajectories, developmental trajectories, developmental progressions or progress maps.

The LP approach requires that teachers plan sequences of lessons based on the assumption that it is likely that children's thinking will pass through a predictable succession of steps. These lesson sequences ensure the correct elements of models are retained and incorrect elements are rejected (Suzuki et al., 2015). Core features of the LP approach are that learners construct ideas by using scientific enquiry, and that they are firmly grounded in research on how children learn science concepts. In contrast to learning progressions, science in schools is usually taught as a stepwise sequence of concepts that has been written by curriculum experts and bear little relation to the order in which children naturally construct them (Alonzo and Gotwals, 2012). In addition, instead of taking a traditional curricular approach where more facts are simply added over time in a cumulative way, learning progressions are dedicated to deeper, more complex learning.

Early on in a sequence, teachers elicit children's ideas to assess which stage of the learning progression children are presently operating at in order that work can be selected for them that is appropriate for that stage. For instance, if elicitation shows that a child is at the upper reaches of a learning progression, learning can be taken from this point and their thinking stretched accordingly. Children operating at the upper levels tend to use ideas consistently across different contexts and have a robust grasp of concepts. At intermediate levels they use ideas less consistently, with the situation becoming more complex in that the same child may display ideas from different stages on the learning progression. As a rule of thumb, it is important to ensure that the concepts lower on the learning progression are secure first before focusing on intermediate concepts, not least because fundamental ideas are likely to be the longest and so most firmly held. The general aim is to arrive at the scientific concept by making certain that the early and intermediate steps have been navigated successfully.

It is, however, essential to bear in mind that a child's learning is not always linear. A learning progression does not represent a precise order of concepts that every learner will pass through; thus any learning progression is not 'written in stone', it is merely hypothetical, even when based on credible research (Plummer and Krajcik, 2010). As stated, if incorrect ideas are held early on in the progression, then this will clearly affect successful progress to the scientific idea. It is therefore vital to ensure these simpler ideas are in place before more complex ones are introduced – that is, concepts should be taught in a particular sequence in order to provide firm foundations on which to build scientific understanding.

A core principle behind using a learning progression is that when teachers plan a lesson or series of lessons, they *sequence scientific concepts so that they reflect the same order as they appear naturally in children.*

A glance at the LP tables in this book will show that science ideas therein relate to a specific age category. However, this does not mean to say that teachers should be rigid in restricting teaching these ideas to certain age brackets. The fact that concepts in learning progressions are to be found in certain age groups does not mean that this represents the limit that children of that age are capable of understanding. Teachers are clearly aware (and studies repeatedly show) that there is nearly always considerable variation of ideas within any single age group and that children are at different stages of learning. It is therefore possible to position children from the same class at different points on a LP continuum. Because of this, the age categories as denoted on the LP tables are of secondary value; indeed, they have been labelled 'typically'. It is the *sequence of ideas* that is important and should govern planning. During their planning, teachers should not feel that learning progressions restrict their creativity because they appear to be too prescriptive – they are only prescriptive in that concepts need to be introduced in a certain sequence. Otherwise, teachers have full autonomy and can be flexible as to exactly how the sequence is taught. The following chapters of this book suggest a variety of activities and teaching sequences that have taken learning progressions into consideration ('best ways'), together with one detailed example that research has shown to be highly effective in teaching scientific concepts ('research exemplar').

The fact that there are intermediate steps on a learning progression means that teachers can build halfway houses of conceptual support where progress to the scientific idea can take place in a piecemeal way. These middle stages of development show partial understanding of a concept that is 'not quite right', but provide a convenient jumping-off point for further understanding. Of course, this can only be done if the intermediate step is not too far removed from the scientific concept, and the reader needs to be aware that just because a concept or fact appears on one of the LP tables, this does not mean that it must be taught. Instead, the learning progressions denote the direction in which learning naturally progresses in order to inform planning. The LP tables sometimes show that there is little progression in learning throughout the primary years, with the same idea appearing more or less unchanged throughout the primary age range. This signals ideas that are strongly held and represents scientifically correct as well as incorrect ideas.

A learning progression can also be used as an assessment tool to measure the current attainment of individual children; for instance, the LP tables can help teachers identify the cognitive stage at which each of their children is currently operating. As stated, for children who are at the upper reaches of the progression, teachers can capitalize on this by building on the firm base of their scientifically appropriate constructions and extending their learning. Learning progressions are less about assessing whether a child 'has got' a particular idea (endpoint mastery) and more about the progressive detail – how far along they are on their conceptual journey. In England, children's progression is on the agenda in the form of recently introduced lists of knowledge statements that children need to have in place at the end of each Key Stage. The previous system of assessment involved 'levels', which resemble learning progressions in that there is a gradual increase in complexity of ideas with age. However, the old levels system differs markedly from learning progressions, which instead are firmly embedded in conceptual research that explains how children learn science, and also include incorrect ideas. Levels were a top-down system of how curriculum experts believed a subject should be taught; learning progressions are bottom-up because they are constructed from learners' experiences (Alonzo and Gotwals, 2012).

Despite its apparent strengths, the LP approach currently has limited validity. The National Research Council (2012: 315) in the USA notes that 'because [research and development] on learning progressions in science is at an early stage, many aspects of the core ideas and their progressions over time with instruction … remain unexplored territory'. Because the movement is at an early point of its evolution, there are presently only a small number of studies that show the effectiveness of LP approaches. Despite these gaps in the research base, the learning progressions show early promise: 'they offer a productive starting

---

Ten things to know about learning progressions

1. Learning progressions represent how children's ideas unfold naturally over time.
2. Children's developing ideas often do not reflect correct science, but sometimes they do.
3. Most children pass through a predictable sequence of cognitive steps during a particular science topic.
4. A minority of children's thinking proceeds in completely different directions to those indicated by a learning progression.
5. Teachers plan lessons by considering the sequence in which scientific concepts will be taught, so that they reflect the same order as they appear naturally in children.
6. Halfway house concepts are useful jumping-off points for deeper learning.
7. Concepts in a learning progression are not tightly bound to a specific age, although they may be more associated with one particular age group than another.
8. Teachers can use learning progressions to assess their children's current levels of understanding.
9. Unlike most science curricula, learning progressions are 'bottom-up' because they are intimately interlinked with children's real experiences.
10. Learning progressions map out in detail children's conceptual journeys, not just mastery of a specific endpoint.

Figure 1.1 Ten things to know about learning progressions

place for developing standards, curricula, and assessments' (Duncan and Rivet, 2013: 396). In the future, researchers will be able to assess the long-term impact of LP-driven curricula, with the best data coming from longitudinal studies, which examine progression in the same children over a period of years.

The value of incorporating research findings into primary teaching

The idea of evidence-based practice has recently come to the fore in English education. The movement initially emerged during the 1990s in medical fields where the emphasis for deciding the best treatment for patients moved away from established traditional methods that appeared to work anecdotally, towards looking to see if there was any research evidence to show whether a treatment actually worked (DiCenso et al., 1998). These two viewpoints might appear to be referring to the same thing – effectiveness of treatment – but anecdotal or folklore evidence based on personal experience can be weak when larger populations are taken into account. To give a hypothetical example, a physiotherapist finds that by applying daily massage when treating a patient's fractured arm, the arm recovers in a relatively short period of time. The physiotherapist continues with this treatment over a period of years with several patients and is satisfied that it works. Subsequently, a research team interested in arm fractures decides to test a number of different methods of rehabilitation, including daily massage, with a sample of 2000 patients. Their findings show that patients receiving daily massage recover no more quickly than those in a control group who receive no treatment.

A preference for approaches that have been objectively verified by research instead of traditional ways of working is now beginning to take hold in non-medical fields, including education. There are long-established issues in England and elsewhere of attainment gaps between groups of learners; for instance, in most school subjects boys lag behind girls in performance, and children from less affluent families consistently have lower educational outcomes. These attainment gaps have not been dealt with adequately despite a raft of government interventions such as the National Strategies in the early 2000s. Writers like Ben Goldacre (2013: 9) have argued that what is needed is a reassessment of 'what works the best' in the classroom. Through careful experience, all teachers know that certain ways of presenting ideas to children help them understand the material. But because of barriers between teachers and researchers, teachers are almost never aware of those really effective approaches that have been tested objectively, often using large numbers of children. This disparity lies at the heart of why I think it is important to promote in more systematic ways evidence-based practice in schools.

Like others, Goldacre – who is a medical doctor – believes that randomized controlled trials (RCTs) are the only way to show effectiveness. Indeed, quantitative research outcomes such as found with RCTs are easily measured and can be more readily understood by laypeople than other, more qualitative approaches. Methodologists such as Gorand (2013) mention the trustworthiness of findings with regards to causal, quantitative research and link this to statistical methods. Ironically, however, trustworthiness judgements are themselves subjective and not absolutely measurable, as they depend on the reader's opinions, with different people (even of the same theoretical tradition) holding potentially different views of whether a piece of research is trustworthy. I agree with Goldacre that evidence needs to be convincing, but this does not, as he suggests, always have to be linked to statistical warrants. That said, it is generally easier to show whether an educational approach is effective if we measure the statistical performance of one group of children against another by means of written or verbal tests. Indeed, a good many of the studies described in the following chapters have adopted this approach.

This book has taken a wider view of evidence-based practice in the classroom. A primary teacher is an autonomous professional who makes informed choices about how to deliver science to the children in her class. Ideally, she will understand enough about learning theory to know the particular ways her children think about science concepts and how those concepts may progress over time (because knowledge and understanding are not static entities). She will be aware that these changing concepts lie at the heart of lesson planning. For instance, the sequence in which ideas are taught over the course of a single science topic must be compatible with the core ideas children hold. Any alternative ideas that children construct should be anticipated and addressed. Children's ideas are related to their cognitive development and so the ages at which ideas typically appear is vital knowledge for teachers. Only after these considerations can appropriate activities be planned and presented in the classroom, with this *research-informed* process being part of an overall evidence-based approach to teaching. Each chapter of this book was created to enable teachers to more easily undertake these procedures by first presenting detailed research evidence that summarizes the ideas children have about science concepts and how they change over time, in the form of learning progressions. This information is followed by a series of suggested activities that teachers can carry out and are linked closely to the learning progressions. The final section of each chapter is aligned with a more tightly bound definition of evidence-based practice as advocated by Goldacre and others, and offers an in-depth description of a single teaching method that 'really works', together with practical information so that teachers can try it out with their own class.

If teaching is to become a real evidence-based profession, then practitioners need to maintain the status of autonomy and actively use the literature themselves to habitually seek out information about how children learn, which includes methods that research has shown are efficacious. As stated, barriers exist that prevent school teachers from accessing research findings, not least a lack of time to devote to scouring the literature. In the next section, some approaches are suggested that will help overcome specifically access issues. Some teachers may eventually choose to become part-time researchers themselves, undertaking their own studies, sometimes in cooperation with university departments, currently an emerging area (BERA, 2014). In the short term, educational consultants who conduct INSET in schools need to use evidence-based approaches when determining material to convey to teachers, which would clearly mean that they would need to become research-literate to some degree.

Tips on using the research literature

Since the late 1970s, educational researchers have examined the factors that affect how schoolchildren learn science. Broad areas under study have included looking for learners' ideas that do not correspond with accepted, 'textbook' science (misconceptions), approaches that help them best learn science, and attitudes towards school science. This body of knowledge is the *science education literature*. This literature has focused mainly on secondary pupils, in part because the researchers themselves are largely serving or ex-secondary science teachers, although many studies have also sampled other age groups, including primary children, pre-schoolers and university students.

The science education literature is a vast resource: as a rough guide, the ERIC database (*Education Resources Information Center*) retrieves nearly 200,000 titles in response to the keyword 'science'. Despite this wealth of material, the literature is and always has been underused by the people for whom its findings are the most relevant – practising teachers in schools. There are valid reasons for this underuse that centre on availability. It is very difficult for practitioners in schools to obtain research articles without incurring a cost, as access is generally limited to university students and academics. Therefore, an aim of this section is to encourage practitioners to search for and acquire articles of interest by means of circumventing the barriers that impede access.

First, where are the best places to find research articles? The most straightforward approach is to search the literature by visiting the websites of the different science education journals (there are not that many, see below) and scroll through the titles of current and past issues to identify any material of interest. Although a little time-consuming, this approach will give you a good overall feel about any 'hot' topics and themes that researchers are currently interested in. An alternative starting point is to use the ERIC database, a free online service where a keyword or phrase can be searched for and then hits filtered out according to age range, type of journal, authors, and so on. An alternative web resource is *Google Scholar*, where again keywords can be entered and articles retrieved, although filtering out non-education hits is more difficult. You can use a standard search engine such as *Google, Yahoo* or *Ask.com* to search the entire web, which sometimes is a more fruitful route than *Scholar,* as webpage targets are not as restricted and so sometimes can find things that *Scholar* has missed. There are online literature databases such as *ProQuest, Scopus* and *Web of Science* that have useful filtering-out mechanisms so you can narrow down your search, although these tend to require users to have university logins or hold a corporate account.

Once you have found an article you would like to read, the next step is to access it. The majority of journals will allow you to read and download an article for no cost, but first require you to log in via an inter-institutional login system such as *Shibboleth* or *Athens.* This is fine if you are a member of an institution that subscribes to the journal such as a university or local government agency, but otherwise you will need to make a payment in order to secure access (which is often no small sum). One way to circumvent this is to find out whether the article is available elsewhere online, which usually means the original authors' webpages at their own institution. Such availability is becoming increasingly common, with a tendency in higher education towards open access of published material, and a quick search in *Google Scholar* will show whether or not the article is directly available for download in PDF or HTML format. If not, it is accepted practice to email the authors directly and request the article. *ResearchGate* is a worldwide social networking website for researchers and has the capability to find authors and make direct requests for material.

The literature contains two general types of article: original research studies and secondary sources. Classroom practitioners unfamiliar with reading journal articles may find the latter type of resource more easily digestible because the former sometimes assume basic or even advanced knowledge of research-related concepts involving methodology and theoretical principles. Secondary sources often review a variety of primary sources and offer a synthesis that is more immediately useful in the classroom. Journals aimed specifically at practitioners such as *Primary Science* in the UK and *Science and Children* in the USA contain activities that are 'classroom ready', although they lack some of the background detail that primary teachers may be interested in, such as learning theories that underpin certain approaches. For looking at recent trends in science (not science education), see *New Scientist* or *Scientific American.*

The literature contains studies that summarize research of varying quality – note that publication is not necessarily a good gauge that a study has been carried out according to accepted rubrics or standards. The journal that an article appears in is, however, a fair indicator. If a research journal uses a peer-review system, then it tends to publish work of more value that those that do not. The quality of different journals can be compared against one another in several ways. A journal's *impact factor* is a number that measures how often articles from that periodical are cited, which shows how often they are read by other researchers. League tables exist (e.g. the SJR world rankings) that take into account impact factor and other variables. Reputation is also important but can be an unreliable measure because it can be influenced by nationalistic or regional affiliations, such as researchers from one country insisting their journal is better than others. When all of these indicators are taken into consideration, four journals emerge as being the most prestigious science education periodicals: *Journal of Research in Science Teaching, Science Education* (both US based), *Research in Science Education* (Australia/New Zealand), and *International Journal of Science Education* (UK). This does not mean to say that other journals are not worth looking at – most will contain good articles – it is just that their quality is variable because the acceptance criteria tend to be more relaxed.

How this book is organized

This introductory chapter has hopefully set the scene and provided a feel for the focus on using research to inform teaching, particularly how children's ideas progress naturally from simple to more complex versions. There follows twelve further chapters, each of which deals with a discrete area of science; for example, Chapter 2 covers *Animals including humans*. Each chapter begins with a brief summary called *Refresh your subject knowledge*, which provides background information about the scientific concepts under consideration. This is important for the subsequent discussions, as it will help you differentiate between children's correct and incorrect ideas. The next section in each chapter, entitled *Children's ideas about ...*, provides a summary of the findings of research studies carried out over the past 35 years or so that have focused on children's science concepts. Many of these studies are cross-sectional, which means they have sampled children of different age groups, showing how their ideas develop over time. These changing ideas are collated in *How learning progresses* tables, which summarize them in a more concise way. You can use the tables as a basic reference when planning lessons and return to the main text for more detail about children's ideas. The data in the tables are categorized by the ages of the children in the various studies, although as explained earlier in this chapter, the age boundaries should be taken as fluid because it is likely that within your class there will be a range of ideas that span the learning progression. It may seem from the tables that some age groups have more knowledge than others, but it is often the case that the age group with the least number of entries has been less well studied by researchers. Note that some of the statements in the tables for a particular age range are contradictory – this reflects the different ideas that children of the same age might have, indicating alternative routes on the learning progression. It is anticipated that student teachers in particular will find the information within *Children's ideas about ...* and the LP tables useful to inform their assignment writing, as these offer a synthesis of the important conceptual research.

The penultimate section in each chapter is *The best ways to teach ...*, which gives an extended account of the types of classroom activities you could try so that the children are able to construct appropriate science concepts. The reason they are termed 'best' ways is because they are research-informed, being presented in accordance with the learning progressions data so that the sequence of delivery matches the natural order in which children arrive at scientific ideas. The core rationale is that early, incorrect ideas must be addressed in order to provide a firm foundation upon which to build later scientific concepts. The activities are largely enquiry-based pedagogies, which are hands-on and engaging and constitute a mix of traditional and newer, more innovative approaches. The activities are placed under subheadings according to the English Primary Science National Curriculum Programme of Study statements, hereafter called simply POS (DfE, 2013). The POS is a statutory body of knowledge that is required to be taught to children attending state-maintained schools – that is, to children of all abilities – and as such is set at a simple level. Children of above-average ability will be capable of learning ideas that are beyond the POS and schools have always recognized this, extending teaching above and beyond the minimum that is required, and the activities in this section reflect this view.

Each chapter ends with a single *Research exemplar*. This section provides a detailed description of one study that has conclusively shown children make significant improvements in their learning when they are taught in a particular way. They are mostly intervention studies, where one group of children are taught one way and a second group a different way. The learning progress of each group is normally compared before and after the intervention to determine whether one approach was better than the other. In line with the evidence-based principles of the book, because one of the most robust ways to show whether an approach really works is by comparing children quantitatively in this way, many of these studies have employed statistical analysis. That said, a number have adopted qualitative methodologies that have not utilized statistics. The approach is described in sufficient detail that you should be able to reproduce the method with your own children, if you wish to. Linked with this section are *Lesson outlines*, which are teaching sequences that summarize the approach. Note that research studies that have used computer simulations as the intervention have been avoided due to accessibility issues – the software is generally only available through purchase or is bespoke and has been designed by the researchers to demonstrate a theoretical point. The aim of this section is to present a single, credible example partly in that hope that it will inspire readers to use the literature to find and implement more pedagogies that really work in the classroom.

I would like to end this introductory chapter with a discussion of a few of the important assumptions that guided and limited the writing of the book. First and foremost, each chapter is not a proper meta-analysis where specific quantitative rules would have had to be adhered to. Instead, studies are presented more as a narrative, a string of related findings collated together to form a synthesis, the aim being to give teachers as wide a view as possible of how children's ideas commonly progress when learning a science topic. The book has been written more for classroom practitioners and less for theoreticians. The result, it is hoped, is that each chapter offers a systematic review that is comprehensive, though not exhaustive (no single volume could be), in that it covers the main ways children conceptualize a particular area of science. The *How learning progresses* tables mix together findings from a wide variety of studies from all over the world, and so it could be claimed that some ideas are culture-specific and so irrelevant to other cultures. If this potentially is the case, then it has been denoted in the main text. The overriding factor here is the commonality of human cognition – that there are more similarities regarding the human mind than dissimilarities, regardless of culture. There is also the fact that studies have used different methods to obtain their findings, and the assumption is made that the findings themselves are more important than the method used. Where in a small number of cases it is thought that the method may have influenced the findings, then this is discussed (e.g. limited sample size). Finally, the book has mainly sourced articles in the English language, which further limits its overall scope. Note that for brevity, Anglicized terms have been used throughout (e.g. *primary school/primary children*) even with international studies where different terms are applicable (e.g. *elementary school/elementary children*).

2

Animals including humans

The phrase 'animals including humans' in the primary science programme of study (POS) denotes concepts of animal physiology, essentially focusing on how life processes such as digestion and blood circulation work. Although the word 'animal' is prominent, the curricular emphasis is firmly on human physiology. As is the case with all living things, animals require certain conditions for their life processes to function adequately. To the basic physiological needs of oxygen, water, food and warmth can be added psychological needs such as having adequate shelter, feeling safe and the need to reproduce the species.

Human nutrition has figured large in English primary curricula not least because of its link to growth during childhood, and of late to healthy living, partly driven by the rise in levels of obesity in affluent countries, including the UK. Aside from promoting the advantages of healthy eating, which has traditionally been covered in PSHE (Personal, Social and Health Education) curricula, children are taught the basics of the physiology of digestion. After food has been eaten, the various parts of the digestive system 'do their best' to extract as much nutrition as possible. This is achieved by physically breaking down food into smaller bits to increase surface area (by the chewing of the teeth and the churning of the stomach) so that chemicals called enzymes can be mixed in and start to chemically split large food molecules into smaller, simpler food molecules. These smaller molecules are then absorbed mainly in the small intestine and enter the bloodstream, which distributes them around the body to all cells. After these food molecules have been absorbed, what remains leaves the small intestine and enters the large intestine where excess water is absorbed, with the waste eventually being removed from the body during defecation (egestion).

The circulatory system, essentially the blood, the heart and blood vessels, not only plays an important part in digestion but is vital for transporting a variety of useful materials around the body, including oxygen and hormones, as well as waste materials such as dissolved carbon dioxide gas and urea. Circulation is linked intimately with the respiratory system. As air is taken into the lungs, oxygen dissolves into the bloodstream, which delivers this necessary substance to all cells in the body. At the same time, cells dump waste carbon dioxide into the blood, which returns it to the lungs to be excreted in expired air. Driving this whole process is the heart, which pumps rhythmically to push blood around the lungs and the rest of the body. It is important to note that in humans the circulation systems that supply the lungs and rest of the body are two completely separate loops – the double circulation.

The skeleton of a vertebrate animal (one which has a backbone) lies in the interior of the body below the skin, and is called an *endoskeleton*. In contrast, many invertebrates have *exoskeletons* on the outside of the body, forming part of the skin itself. A skeleton gives an animal's body support by providing a frame on which to hang organs and tissues. They also have a protective function because they are hard and enclose vital soft tissues that might be easily damaged, such as the brain. Skeletal muscles attach to the skeleton and contract to allow an animal to move, thus without a skeleton, movement would be impossible. Other muscles lie in the body's interior and play central roles in keeping vital organs working. For example, cardiac muscle causes the beating motion in the heart and smooth muscle pushes food through the digestive system.

Children's ideas about animals including humans

What makes something 'alive'?

Before learning about living organisms, children need to have some idea about what being alive actually means in a scientific sense. Before something can be judged to be alive, it needs to be capable of all seven processes of life: *movement, respiration, sensitivity, growth, reproduction, excretion* and *nutrition* (MRS GREN). However, children under the age of 10 years tend to think artefacts such as cars and robots are living things (Piaget, 1929; Inagaki and Hatano, 1987). From an early age, anything thought to be moving in a conscious, voluntary way is usually classified as being alive (Opfer and Siegler, 2004) and so young children misclassify artefacts because they think they are capable of moving by themselves. This is despite the fact that children as young as 5 years understand that animals are capable of the life processes of growth, nutrition and reproduction (and death) while artefacts are not. Self-initiated movement appears to be *the* governing life process when children judge whether something is alive (Margett and Witherington, 2011) and this is thought to be one reason why 5–9 y/o children are reluctant to classify plants as living (Opfer and Siegler, 2004; see Chapter 3 for more on children's ideas about plants being living things).

Nurettin et al. (2009) argue that there is a progression in thinking where children first grant living status to humans, then to animals and finally to plants. However, Gelman and Opfer (2002) found that preschoolers attribute anything with eyes and moving legs (self-initiated movement) as living things; in fact, when they realize some living things do not have eyes, they also begin to attribute living thing status to eyeless artefacts. By 10 years, it appears that most children have accepted that plants and animals are alive but artefacts are not (Opfer and Gelman, 2001). These ideas link directly to POS year 2 where children are required to understand whether something is living, dead or has never lived.

What do animals need to survive and grow?

Related to ideas about why something is 'alive' is what a living thing needs for continued survival. In a recent study into children's ideas about animal needs, Myers et al. (2004) informed a sample of American primary children that a particular animal was unhappy and asked them to suggest what the animal would need to make it happy again. The most common needs children stated were physiological – food, water, rest and air. Other frequent responses were ecological or psychological – animals need somewhere to live, a place to hide or shelter, another species to prey on, and the company of members of the same species (especially as 'friends'; Myers et al., 2004: 550). Less frequent suggestions were the need to reproduce, the freedom to play or exercise, and legal protection from harm by outlawing hunting or living in a wildlife reserve. There were developmental patterns, with the 8–11 y/o mentioning more physiological and habitat reasons than younger children.

Endreny (2006) confirmed this preoccupation with physiological needs. She asserted that even from preschool age, children are aware that animals need food in order to grow. In a study of a small sample of English primary children's ideas about growth, Russell and Watt (1990) asked them what happened over time as they observed and recorded the growth of caterpillars. The most common observation was increased size, and around a quarter mentioned the caterpillars' feeding behaviour. When questioned about what things the caterpillars needed to grow, there were age-related differences, since food was mentioned by three-quarters of 10–11 y/o but less than half of 5–9 y/o. Air or oxygen was cited by nearly a third of 10–11 y/o. There was a tendency to think the caterpillars grew at one particular time, such as when they sleep or eat, although these responses might have been triggered by parents telling their children that eating all their meals and getting to bed early will help them to grow. The importance of understanding animals' needs may have wider repercussions, since some authors conclude that if children develop an interest in the needs of individual animals, then this will be linked to a more caring attitude for the environment as a whole (e.g. Myers et al., 2004).

Nutrition and digestion

Despite children understanding that an animal needs food in order to grow, their ideas about how the body deals with ingested food are frequently at odds with correct science. Garcia-Barros et al. (2011) note that learning about the physiology of nutrition is difficult for children because it requires an understanding of how the digestive, circulatory and respiratory systems work in unison. However, they only begin to think about their body systems all working together to keep them alive at around 10 years (Caravita and Tonucci, 1987). This considered, it is perhaps not surprising that they construct simpler models in attempts to make sense of digestion. Contento's (1981) sample of American 5–6 y/o had a vague view of what happens to food once eaten. Although they understood it was broken down into smaller pieces and went to the stomach, they thought it remained there unchanged. Contrastingly, when Osborne et al. (1992) asked English primary children to draw what happened to food inside the body, 5–7 y/o commonly drew the body as an empty container containing bits of food located throughout, including within arms and legs, known as the *hollow bag model*. Cubero (1998) also found this model prevalent with Spanish 8–10 y/o. Children from 8 years upwards did not tend to think the body was a hollow bag, instead drawing one or two tubes leading from the mouth to where they judged the stomach to be, frequently in the middle of the abdomen at the level of the navel (Osborne et al., 1992). This is below the anatomical location, which lies at the bottom of the left rib cage. Few children understood what happened to food beyond the stomach. Carvalho et al. (2004) found that when Portuguese 5–6 y/o drew the stomach, some had no connections to the mouth. Similarly, the location of the intestines is not well known by younger children, such as the Spanish 4–7 y/o of Garcia-Barros et al. (2011).

Teixeira (1998) asked a small sample of Brazilian primary children to eat a bar of chocolate and then draw on paper the journey it takes through their bodies, naming relevant organs and describing what happens to food at those organs. All children in the 4–10 y/o sample understood the basic idea that food placed inside the mouth travels through the interior of the body down to the abdominal area, which they referred to as the tummy (mainly 4 y/o), stomach or intestines (mainly 10 y/o). The fact that food leaves the body through an orifice (usually called the bottom) was well known by most 6–10 y/o, but not by 4 y/o. The hollow bag model was apparent as the 4 y/o also drew the abdomen as a largely empty space containing bits of chewed-up food. A common idea was that food leaves the stomach and accumulates in the legs, which causes stretching of the body and an increase in height. When the child bends over at the waist, some of this food ends up in the arms, having the same effect on growth. Children aged 6 years drew the abdomen in similar ways to the 4 y/o, but the older children drew a more accurate digestive system that resembled a continuous tube.

Regarding the fate of food, primary children are almost never aware that food is transformed into simpler forms during digestion (Gellert, 1962; Contento, 1981). Osborne et al. (1992) found that they generally thought the reason for eating was simply to stay alive, grow, get stronger or stay healthy. None of the responses indicated the knowledge that foods provide energy or act as raw materials for growth and repair. Although many knew that food was broken down into smaller pieces, there were no sophisticated models of digestion that included the breaking down of food into more simple components that are then capable of being absorbed and distributed around the body in the blood. The authors note that this would require an understanding of the particulate nature of matter, which is problematic since particle theory has never been a part of the English primary curriculum. In a similar way, Rowlands' (2004) sample of English 10 y/o thought that digestion was merely a mechanical process that distributed food to different parts of the body and did not appreciate that foodstuffs are chemically broken down. Some of Teixeira's (1998) 6 y/o were aware that ingested food provides the body with nourishment but because they held the hollow bag misconception they did not see the need for a circulatory system to distribute the nourishment. Even the older 8–10 y/o children who knew that digestion was a process that breaks down food to derive nourishment still thought the smaller bits of food retained their identity inside the body. No child mentioned that food is chemically changed into something different.

Younger children have difficulties correctly linking the food that they eat with the products of defecation. The 4 y/o in Teixeira's study tended to think that all ingested food never leaves the body (the *fixed container model*) and is not transformed, keeping its original identity despite having been chewed into smaller pieces. In contrast, many 6 y/o believed all food leaves the body during defecation, which the authors suggest may be due to a perceived need to preserve quantity – what goes in must come out. The 8–10 y/o thought that some of the food stays inside the body while the rest leaves. Gellert (1962) found that primary children thought that defecation occurs to prevent them getting too full or to stop them bursting, and had little idea that it was the egestion of waste products no longer required by the body. Cakici (2005) interviewed Turkish 10–11 y/o and discovered that many correctly understood that some parts of digested food were egested from the body while other parts are sent around the body via the blood. Similarly, Garcia-Barros and colleagues' (2011) 4–7 y/o sample generally did not understand that faeces and urine leaving the body were products of digestion and excretion. However, nearly all 7 y/o drew the digestive system as one tube from mouth to stomach, connected to two tubes leaving the body – one for faeces, the other for urine. Giordan and Vecchi (1988) also found that both children and adults thought that solids and liquids entering the digestive system take two different pathways.

Learning about teeth in school is part of promoting dental hygiene. In addition to health education reasons, knowledge about animal dentition during science lessons can be related to carnivorous, herbivorous and omnivorous diets in the sense that a variety of animals have different teeth. Teeth are shaped to do particular jobs, for example, carnivores often have prominent canines to stab and kill prey, while herbivores possess large molars to chew and grind down plant material. Given the relative importance of a scientific knowledge of teeth, there is a surprising lack of research about children's concepts in the science education literature, although there is some material that has a health education theme. For instance, Mafra et al. (2015) found that although a small sample of Portuguese 9–10 y/o were aware that their teeth plaque carried leftovers from meals in the form of food scraps, it came as a surprise to learn that microbes were living inside their mouths, inhabiting the plaque.

There is currently little research available about children's ideas of the digestive organs of non-human animals, although a recent study did find that Spanish 4–7 y/o were able to locate an area they called the stomach or tummy in drawings of a dog, duck and fish (Garcia-Barros et al., 2011). There are studies about children's ideas of what constitutes healthy eating but these have been positioned more in the health education genre and not science education, and the interested reader is referred to this literature for further information.

Skeletal and muscular systems

Dempster and Stears (2014) state that the three body systems that young children recognize most are the digestive, respiratory and skeletal systems because they are perceptually aware of the familiar physiological functions of eating and breathing, and can readily feel their own bones. That said, primary children often represent bones inside their body as cartoon-type bones – that is, 'dog-bone' or dumbbell-shaped structures (Osborne et al., 1992). Focusing on their knowledge of skeletons, Tunnicliffe and Reiss (1999) asked English children to draw what they thought was inside their bodies and found a typical progression of learning with age. Many 4–5 y/o drew bones as simple circles or lines, although some drew no bones at all. Older children (6–11 y/o) tended to draw bones as 'dog-bone' shapes randomly distributed throughout the body, although many did place at least one type of bone in its correct location. More advanced models such as a general vertebrate organization with skull, backbone, limbs and ribs were rare. However, as with all types of free-recall research, children's actual knowledge may have exceeded what the authors reported, as in the absence of probes children will present only the first few ideas that come to mind. That said, when Óskarsdóttir et al. (2011) explicitly asked Nordic 6–8 y/o to draw bones on human body blanks, they represented bones in the same way as Tunnicliffe and Reiss's (1999) 6–11 y/o.

Although bones contain living tissue, Caravita and Falchetti (2005) found that half of Italian 8–9 y/o thought that bones were not alive at all, because they never move or that their function is merely to act as a support for the body and nothing else. In contrast, practically all 10–11 y/o gave correct responses and knew that bones were living parts of the body. For those children who knew that bones are alive, a commonly cited reason was because they are able to grow or repair themselves. There is a notable lack of research regarding children's ideas about the exoskeletons of invertebrates such as insects and crustaceans, which is surprising given the importance of these structures in primary school topics about 'mini beasts' and animal classification. In a rare study, many of Prokop and colleagues' (2008) Slovak primary children incorrectly drew invertebrates such as the stag beetle with internal bones instead of exoskeletons. In an earlier study by the same team, when asked to draw skeletons of different animals, children drew the fish skeleton the most accurately, probably because of familiarity with filleting a fish during meals (Prokop et al., 2007b).

The literature contains little material pertaining to primary children's concepts of the muscular system, although most of the primary children in Osborne and colleagues' (1992) study named arms and legs as places in the body where they had muscles, with few other locations named. As was the case with bones, the authors linked this to muscles that children are able to directly perceive – the biceps and triceps (arm), quadriceps (thigh) and gastrocnemius (calf). Dempster and Stears (2014) looked at South African children's drawings of their own internal body structure, finding that muscles were the least represented of all the organ systems. In their study of Italian primary children, Caravita and Tonucci (1987) found that when drawing muscles on diagrams, the children did not link them with bones at skeletal joints, an idea that is important for understanding how skeletal movement occurs. Some children also did not know that the meat they consume at mealtimes is actually an animal's muscles. From the responses of Caravita and Falchetti's (2005) Italian sample, it would seem that at least some primary children think that muscle is living tissue (while bones were considered non-living).

Circulatory system

This topic is newly introduced to the English POS, so perhaps unsurprisingly there has been little research activity concerning primary children's blood circulation concepts aside from a few studies that focused largely on anatomical ideas. Gellert (1962) concluded that the heart was the first internal organ that primary-aged children became aware of because they can perceive it beating, although they only realized that its role was to pump blood around the body at age 10–11 years. Children aged 5 years and upwards from Osborne and colleagues' (1992) primary sample knew that the heart beats, although as in Gellert's study they did not know that it acts as a pump until age 9 years. Reiss et al. (2002) found that 6 y/o from 11 countries nearly always included the heart in diagrams of what is inside their bodies. The correct shape of the heart is not well known by primary children, with over two-thirds of Osborne and colleagues' (1992) 5–11 y/o drawing it as a valentine shape; this tendency has also been observed in other countries, including Spain (Garcia-Barros et al., 2011). The favoured valentine shape can have further repercussions on circulatory understanding. When

Arnaudin and Mintzes (1985) asked American 10–11 y/o to draw the interior of the heart, the most common depiction was of a vessel with three chambers, which fitted best with the valentine heart outlines that the children had drawn (the three-chambered model actually resembles an amphibian's heart; the mammalian heart has four chambers). The precise location of the heart is also a cause for confusion, with most 5–7 y/o situating it in the abdomen, and nearly all 8–11 y/o locating it (incorrectly) in the left side of the chest (Osborne et al., 1992).

The function of blood is less well known, although children from age 5 years were aware that it keeps you alive, with a few understanding that it travels around the body (Osborne et al., 1992). Some 5–7 y/o explained the mechanism for how blood moves as being driven by body movements: 'it moves around when you wriggle' (6 y/o, Osborne et al., 1992: 34), suggesting a view that the blood is not contained by blood vessels but is free to splash around inside a hollow body. Some older children did mention that blood was found in veins, although none named arteries. When asked about the heart's function, nearly three-quarters of 10–11 y/o mentioned that it was a pump, although some ascribed additional but incorrect functions such as it cleans, stores or makes blood. Explanations of the circulation system as a whole reflect a single circulation where blood travels: heart → body → heart → body and so on, with no mention of the additional pulmonary loop that extends to the lungs – that is, the double circulation (Arnaudin and Mintzes, 1985). Descriptions of blood were largely kept to simple accounts of it being a red liquid; few children had any knowledge of red or white cells, or the fact that blood is a mixture of cells suspended in a clear liquid called plasma. When asked what blood does, a high proportion of children gave vitalistic responses such as it keeps you alive/going (Osborne et al., 1992).

Respiratory system

The respiratory system is not explicitly mentioned in the POS but because it is closely connected with blood circulation, simple ideas are taught in primary schools, such as when you run, you breathe more quickly. Several studies, such as Reiss and colleagues' (2002) international study of 7 y/o, have indicated that together with the digestive and skeletal systems, the respiratory system is one of the organ systems that is most understood by young children. Despite this, Gellert (1962) found that hardly any 5–7 y/o had heard of the lungs though by 10–11 years they could begin to explain that an exchange of gases takes place in the lungs that is associated with providing oxygen to the blood. Garcia-Barros et al. (2011) concluded from the drawings of 4–5 y/o that they were not able to identify the lungs or any other part of the respiratory system, and cite Gellert's finding of primary children thinking that air breathed in remains inside the head, suggesting that they might also hold the view that air circulates freely inside all the body and so does not require a dedicated organ system.

Osborne et al. (1992) note that the position of the lungs within the body is not well known by primary children, with some believing that they lie in the abdomen, probably due to the perceptible rise and fall of this part of the body that occurs during breathing. Similarly, a proportion of Brinkmann and Boschhuizen's (1989) Dutch primary sample related the stomach to breathing. Surprisingly, despite acknowledging that the lungs are organs of the respiratory system, Spanish 5 y/o still thought that the stomach was the only organ required for breathing, drawing pictures of a single 'bag' in the abdomen linked to the outside by a tube to allow the passage of air. They appeared to equate the need for air as analogous to the need for food and drink, with the stomach being the site where all of these collect (Garcia-Barros et al., 2011). In the same study, 6–7 y/o tended to include two lungs in their diagrams, although sometimes they were connected by tubes to the stomach, which is an intermediate model, though some 7 y/o drew just lungs without the stomach. Tracana et al. (2012) found similar ideas with Portuguese primary children when asked where air goes once it is breathed inside the body. The 6–7 y/o drew a variety of scientifically incorrect diagrams, including air circulating freely inside an empty body, or air going to a single organ in the abdomen/stomach. A minority drew lungs, either one or two lungs but with no connecting tubes to the outside, or one lung with one connecting tube. In comparison, nearly all 8–10 y/o correctly depicted two lungs connected to the outside by one tube (sometimes lungs had connecting bronchi). A different model was offered by about a third of Arnaudin and Mintzes' (1985) American 10–11 y/o, who drew air entering the body through the lungs then passing directly to the heart via further air tubes, although a similar number could offer no explanation about the fate of inspired air.

In a Spanish study partly about the respiratory and digestive systems of the dog, duck and fish, Garcia-Barros et al. (2011) found that very few 4–5 y/o drew the fish's gills, whereas all the 6–7 y/o did so. They concluded that the children had less knowledge of the respiratory system of non-human animals compared with the digestive system. Slovak primary children tended to incorrectly draw lungs inside the bodies of invertebrates such as crawfish. Instead of lungs, invertebrates have simpler respiratory systems. In insects, for example, instead of being transported by blood, air circulates freely around air channels to supply body cells (Prokop et al., 2008).

Reproduction

Animal reproduction is taught in the context of life cycles of varied complexity. Mammalian life cycles are the most familiar to children and are the simplest, with parents giving birth to live young which then grow and in time reproduce to produce new offspring. Amphibians such as frogs, on the other hand, have complex life cycles that involve metamorphosis, where different stages show diverse morphologies (egg → young tadpole → tadpole with legs → immature frog → adult frog), as do insects (egg → larva → pupa (chrysalis) → adult insect).

In common with other sections in this chapter, research into primary children's ideas about animals other than humans in the context of life cycles is sparse (Cinici, 2013), although a handful of studies have examined ideas of insect metamorphosis. Shepardson (1997) found that American 6–7 y/o held one of three models of an insect life cycle. With the first model, just the adult stage exists, which simply grows larger with age and no metamorphosis occurs. The second model involves larva → adult, and the third larva → pupa → adult; no children saw any need for an egg stage. However, Barrow (2002) interviewed a small sample of American 6–11 y/o, many of whom were puzzled about how moth larvae (mealworms) could change into adult moths, with one 7 y/o stating: 'I have never seen a baby insect' (Barrow, 2002: 59). Unlike Shepardson's sample, Barrow's children did not mention the pupa stage, the common model being egg → larva → adult. The 6–7 y/o were unable to name any stages of the insect life cycle, even the adult phase (Barrow, 2002). Note that aspects of reproduction other than life cycles are included in Chapter 4 in the context of inheritance.

Animal classification

How animals are classified into a biological taxonomy is related more to ecology than to physiology but nevertheless has been included in POS year 1 within *Animals including humans*. In year 1, children are expected to be able to name examples of animals from each of the five vertebrate classes (fish, amphibian, reptile, bird and mammal) and compare their structures, which will involve some knowledge about why particular animals are classified as they are. Children naturally tend to classify animals differently to the accepted taxonomic system that we teach in primary science. Researchers from a variety of countries have looked specifically at this issue and their findings are listed in Figure 2.1. This section will summarize this research, whose references are listed below the figure.

Both children and adults relate the term *animal* to large, four-legged mammals usually found in the home, zoo or farm (Bell, 1981). Invertebrate animals such as insects are not usually thought to be animals because they do not resemble this common archetype. Bell also found that half of 10–11 y/o mistakenly used life processes criteria (MRS GREN) to determine whether something was an animal. Another reason for errors in classification is mutual exclusivity of groups – something cannot belong to two groups at the same time (e.g. a shark is not an animal because it is a fish). There is evidence to suggest that 3–4 y/o actually classify animals more correctly than older primary children because they have not yet been exposed to the common archetype, and their performance later falls off as they become older (Allen, 2015). Humans are often not considered animals for semantic reasons – an 'animal' is bestial and uncivilized – or religious/cultural belief that gives humans an elevated position above other animals.

When children are asked to categorize living things into sets of their own choosing, they tend not to create sets that resemble the scientific taxonomies that we introduce in primary school. For instance, Kattmann (2001) found that German 9–11 y/o sorted animals into categories based mainly on habitat (e.g. aquatic, terrestrial) or locomotion (e.g. fliers, creepers). In POS year 1, when

Ages (yrs)	Animal 5–7	Animal 8–9	Animal 10–12	Fish 5–7	Fish 8–9	Fish 10–12	Amphibian 5–7	Amphibian 8–9	Amphibian 10–12	Reptile 5–7	Reptile 8–9	Reptile 10–12	Bird 5–7	Bird 8–9	Bird 10–12	Mammal 5–7	Mammal 8–9	Mammal 10–12	Insect 5–7	Insect 8–9	Insect 10–12
Ant													✓	✓	✓				✓	✓	✓
Bat																x	x	x			
Beetle	x	✓	✓																✓	✓	✓
Butterfly	x	x	x										✓	x	x				✓	✓	✓
Centipede																			✓	✓	✓
Crab						✓		✓	✓												
Cricket											✓	✓									
Dog	✓	✓	✓														✓				
Dolphin						✓												✓			
Duck	✓	✓	✓																		
Earthworm	x	x	x						✓		✓	✓	✓						✓	✓	✓
Eel					x	x						✓									
Fish	x	✓	✓	✓	✓	✓															
Fly													✓	✓	✓				✓	✓	✓
Frog	x	✓	✓					✓	✓		✓	✓									
Human	x	x	x													x	x	x			
Jellyfish					✓	✓															
Kiwi													x	✓	✓						
Leech								✓	✓		✓	✓									
Lizard									✓		✓	✓									
Mackerel					✓	✓															
Mouse																		✓			
Ostrich													x	✓	✓						
Owl													✓			✓					
Penguin								✓	✓				x	x	x		✓	✓			
Pterodactyl													✓	✓	✓						
Seagull															✓						
Seal									✓								x	x			
Shrimp	✓	✓			✓	✓															
Snail	x	✓	✓			✓					✓	✓									

Figure 2.1 How children classify animals

Ages (yrs)	Animal 5–7	Animal 8–9	Animal 10–12	Fish 5–7	Fish 8–9	Fish 10–12	Amphibian 5–7	Amphibian 8–9	Amphibian 10–12	Reptile 5–7	Reptile 8–9	Reptile 10–12	Bird 5–7	Bird 8–9	Bird 10–12	Mammal 5–7	Mammal 8–9	Mammal 10–12	Insect 5–7	Insect 8–9	Insect 10–12
Snake	√	√	√					√	√		√	√					X	X			
Sparrow													√	√	√						
Spider	X	X	X														X	X		√	√
Squid	X	X	X	√	√	√															
Starfish					√	√															
Tiger	√	√	√													√					
Turtle	√	√	√	X	X	X		√	√		X	X									
Whale			X													√					
Woodlouse																			√	√	√

Key
√ Child thinks the animal belongs to this group
X Child thinks the animal does not belong to this group

*References
1. Tunnicliffe et al., 2008 (Malta)
2. Chen and Ku, 1998 (Taiwan)
3. Trowbridge and Mintzes, 1988 (USA)
4. Bell, 1981 (New Zealand)
5. Trowbridge and Mintzes, 1985 (USA)
6. Ryman, 1974 (UK)
7. Braund, 1991 (UK)
8. Yen et al., 2007 (Taiwan)
9. Yen et al., 2004 (Taiwan)
10. Prokop et al., 2007a (Slovakia)
11. Shepardson, 2002 (USA)

Figure 2.1 (continued)

we introduce the biological taxonomy of the five vertebrate classes, common misclassifications arise. Children correctly think that most fish have elongated, streamlined bodies, fins and a tail, live in the sea and can swim. However, as can be seen from Figure 2.1, species such as crabs and shrimps are sometimes wrongly classified by children as fish simply because they are aquatic, while starfish and jellyfish are thought to be fish because they have 'fish' in their names. Eels are fish but because they do not resemble the archetype, they are often misclassified as reptiles because they look like snakes.

Amphibians inhabit both aquatic and terrestrial habitats, have complex life cycles, and are able to breathe in air and underwater. Children often think that anything that lives in water and on land such as a seal or a penguin is an amphibian, even if they know that these animals cannot breathe underwater. Reptiles are vertebrates with scaly skins, although invertebrates such as earthworms and snails are sometimes classified as reptiles because children think a reptile is something that crawls or wriggles on the ground. A common bird archetype is something that flies, has noticeable wings, feathers and a beak, although children can incorporate butterflies and bats into their bird set on the basis of flight alone. For the same reason, younger children believe flightless birds such as the ostrich and kiwi are not birds. Older primary children classify mammals according to whether they are furry or provide milk for their young and include dogs and dolphins, while 5–7 y/o classify mammals more or less randomly. Penguins are thought to be mammals because children mistake chicks taking shelter in their mothers' feathers as milk feeding (Yen et al., 2007). People correctly classify species such as ants and beetles as insects because they are small, have jointed legs and crawl around a ground-dwelling habitat, or if they are harmful to humans (e.g. they bite or sting) (Shepardson, 2002). Insect misclassifications include woodlice (crustaceans), centipedes (myriapods), spiders (arachnids) and earthworms (annelids), all of which are non-insects.

The best ways to teach animals including humans

<u>POS Year 1 – Animals including humans</u> (identify, name, and draw and label the basic parts of the human body and say which part of the body is associated with each sense; identify that humans and some animals have skeletons and muscles for support, protection and movement; identify and name a variety of common animals, including fish, amphibians, reptiles, birds and mammals)
<u>POS Year 2 – Living things and their habitats</u> (explore and compare the differences between things that are living, things that are dead and things that have never been alive)

	Typically 5–7 years	Typically 8–9 years	Typically 10–11 years
Concept of living	Anything with eyes and moving legs is alive. Anything capable of self-directed movement is alive. Animals and artefacts are alive; plants are non-living.	Anything capable of self-directed movement is alive. Animals and artefacts are alive; plants are non-living.	Anything capable of self-directed movement is alive. Animals and plants are alive; artefacts are non-living.
Animal survival needs	Animals need the company of members of the same species.	Animals need food, water, rest and air, somewhere to live, a place to hide or shelter, other animals to prey on.	Animals need food, water, rest and air, somewhere to live, a place to hide or shelter, other animals to prey on. Starts to think about the reproductive needs of animals.
Animal growth	Animals need food to grow; growing takes place only at particular times (e.g. during sleeping).	Animals need food to grow; growing takes place only at particular times (e.g. during sleeping).	Animals need food to grow, which makes them stretch or get bigger; growing takes place only at particular times (e.g. during sleeping).
Why do we eat?	To stay alive, keep healthy, to grow.	To stay alive, keep healthy, to grow.	To stay alive, keep healthy, to grow.
Anatomical location of the stomach	Circular organ in the abdomen, about the level of the navel.	Circular organ in the abdomen, about the level of the navel; a tube connects the mouth to the stomach.	Circular organ in the abdomen, about the level of the navel; a tube connects the mouth to the stomach.
The fate of ingested food	Food goes to the stomach and remains there unchanged, or food enters the body cavity and ends up unchanged throughout the body, including at the ends of arms and legs (hollow bag model); solids and liquids take separate pathways through the body.	Food goes to the stomach (poor understanding of the fate of food beyond the stomach); the body breaks food down into smaller pieces to help extract nourishment; solids and liquids take separate pathways through the body.	Food goes to the stomach (poor understanding of the fate of food beyond the stomach); the body breaks food down into smaller pieces to help extract nourishment; solids and liquids take separate pathways through the body. Starts to think about the digestive system as a differentiated tube of different organs.

Figure 2.2 How learning progresses: Animals including humans

	Typically 5–7 years	Typically 8–9 years	Typically 10–11 years
Egestion of food	All ingested food leaves the body through the bottom, or faeces not related to digestion at all.	Some food leaves the body through the bottom; the rest is kept inside the body.	Some food leaves the body through the bottom; the rest is kept inside, being sent around the body in the blood.
Skeleton	Bones are often dumbbell-shaped.	Bones are often dumbbell-shaped; they support the rest of the body; they are not living tissue.	Bones are often dumbbell-shaped; they support the rest of the body; they *are* living tissue because they grow and can repair themselves.
Muscular system	Muscles are located exclusively in the arms and legs.	Muscles are located exclusively in the arms and legs.	Muscles are located exclusively in the arms and legs. Starts to link muscles with movement.
Location of the heart	Drawn as a 'valentine' shape in the abdomen.	Drawn as a 'valentine' shape in the left side of the chest.	Drawn as a 'valentine' shape in the left side of the chest.
Blood circulation	The heart beats; blood is a red liquid that keeps you alive; blood splashes around freely inside the body and is not contained by blood vessels; poor understanding of the double circulation.	The heart beats; it pumps blood around the body; blood is a red liquid that keeps you alive; blood is found in veins; poor understanding of the double circulation.	The heart beats; it pumps blood around the body; blood is a red liquid that keeps you alive; blood is found in veins; poor understanding of the double circulation. Starts to appreciate that the blood is a transport system that carries different substances around the body.
Respiratory system	Lungs are not known; the stomach or abdomen is responsible for breathing, or air is breathed in, circulates freely inside the head (or inside an empty body), and then breathed out.	There are two lungs that are connected to the mouth by a tube; actual position of the lungs is not well known (sometimes placed in the abdomen).	There are two lungs that are connected to the mouth by a tube; actual position of the lungs is not well known (sometimes placed in the abdomen); lungs help give oxygen to the blood, or air enters the lungs and then passes directly to the heart via tubes.
Life cycles	Models of insect metamorphosis: larva → adult; or larva → pupa → adult Many have little awareness of metamorphosis in insects.	Model of insect metamorphosis: egg → larva → adult	Model of insect metamorphosis: egg → larva → adult Starts to understand complete metamorphosis in insects.

Figure 2.2 (continued)

A 6 y/o Brazilian child was asked, *what finally happens to food inside the body?*

Child: … it will not go out from the tummy.
Researcher: No? Will it be in the tummy for the rest of your life?
Child: Yes.
Researcher: Tell me, Where does pooh come from?
Child: It comes from the bottom.
Researcher: But how did it appear inside us?
Child: I don't know.
Researcher: Is the food changed into pooh?
Child: No.
Researcher: Is there any chance of the food being changed into pooh?
Child: No.

Figure 2.3 What children have to say: Animals including humans (Teixeira, 1998: 102–103)

Human biology is inherently engaging for most children because they enjoy learning about how their bodies work. There is a cross-curricular element, since concepts of physiology are also relevant to physical education lessons (e.g. muscles) and to PHSE in the guise of health education (e.g. nutrition). With KS1, a topic can begin with children learning parts of the body with games such as *Simon Says*. These can be extended with learning about how different parts of the body play a role in differentiating the five senses (e.g. eyes for seeing, ears for hearing, skin for touching, etc.). Young children commonly have little knowledge of what is inside the body – in fact, they commonly draw a hollow bag – so knowledge of the variety of organs present is essential before specific body systems such as digestion are introduced. This will also help them gain an early understanding that a human being is a collection of organ systems that work in close unison. When internal organs are introduced to children, the most well known are the heart and the bones, which act as useful starting points. Relating human organs to what is actually inside their own bodies is an effective approach. For instance, children can use a couple of pieces of sugar paper to draw around their bodies on the floor, then cut out coloured shapes to represent their organs using books or the Internet as a source of information. It is a good idea to remind them that some organs overlap one another and so they must *not* try to make a collage of non-overlapping shapes, like a mosaic. Another variant is to ask children to bring in old T-shirts and then cut out coloured fabric shapes of organs to stick on – they can wear the T-shirt afterwards to give an 'X-ray' view of what is inside their bodies. Aspects of animal classification are traditionally taught with sorting exercises where children have pictures of animals and they decide which set they belong to (e.g. fish, amphibian, etc.). Prior to this, establish appropriate concepts of living by discussing the status of artefacts such as cars and robots – they appear to fulfil the MRS GREN criteria but because they are neither plants nor animals, they cannot be classed as living things.

POS Years 3 and 4 – Animals including humans (identify that animals including humans need the right types and amount of nutrition, and that they cannot
make their own food; they get nutrition from what they eat; describe the simple functions of the basic parts of the digestive system in humans; identify the
different types of teeth in humans and their simple functions)

Since it appears at the start of the learning progression, a KS2 topic on the
digestive system should begin with a discussion about the true location of the
stomach (most children mistakenly think it lies in the abdomen at around the level
of the navel). Garcia-Barros et al. (2011) recommend that early on in the teaching
sequence, the digestive system should be presented as children naturally imagine it, a continuous tube where what is put in at one end is different from what
emerges at the other. From this simple model the tube can be further differentiated into specific organs: stomach, small and large intestines, etc. This approach
will help address the 'hollow bag' view where swallowed food is believed to end
up in an empty space inside the body, or at the ends of arms and legs. A well-
known demonstration called *Gums to Bums* involves mixing together in a very
messy way food and bodily fluids until the mixture is converted into 'poo' and
leaves the body (search for the associated video clip, which is available free on
the Internet). McShane (1991) describes a primary school activity where different
toothpastes are tested to see if they cause any beneficial changes to teeth. Discussions about healthy eating are more relevant to PSHE than to science, though
can be prompted by reading books such as *Lunch Boxes* (Althea and O'Neill,
2006). The 'eatwell plate' is a common way to depict to children the recommended
proportions of foods a person needs for a balanced diet. This can be followed by
looking in detail at a variety of food labels to determine whether particular diets
are balanced, or to show that a diet high in fats and/or sugars is generally thought
to contribute to poor health, with many problems only emerging later in adult
life. Croshaw and Willis (2011) have used a puppet of a chef to answer questions
children may have about healthy eating.

POS Year 6 – Animals including humans (identify and name the main parts of
the human circulatory system, and describe the functions of the heart, blood
vessels and blood; describe the ways in which nutrients and water are transported within animals, including humans)

As with all science topics, but especially important with blood circulation because
ideas do change as learning progresses, elicit current ideas from the outset so that
each child can be situated at the correct point on the learning progression. The
circulatory system should be introduced at KS2 with its most well-known component, the heart, since although young children will be aware of this organ, they
may not associate it with the blood system. In fact, all children will know that
their bodies contain blood and so making a conceptual link between heart and

blood will link together these two familiar elements. A traditional KS2 experiment is measuring heart rate before, during and after taking moderate exercise. This can be done outdoors with children running to a fixed point and then back again, or indoors by running on the spot, or borrowing a bench from the PE cupboard and doing step-ups. Children will need to be instructed how to take their pulse and in my experience they find it easier to find their carotid pulse (neck) than their radial pulse (wrist). They should count the number of beats in 6 seconds, then multiply the value by 10 to give beats per minute. They will need to take their pulse before exercising (resting rate), immediately afterwards and then every minute until they more or less regain resting rate again. Graphs can be plotted and linked to why the heart beats more quickly during exercise, and also related to the fact that how quickly resting rate is regained is one measure of the level of a person's physical fitness. Electronic devices are available that automatically measure pulse rate, although they will require practice beforehand as some can be unreliable unless used properly. An important aim is to encourage children at the lower end of the learning progression who think blood splashes freely inside the body cavity to progress to the halfway-house idea of blood being contained in blood vessels. Once this is secure, it can lead to the next step of understanding the double circulation. Davies (2013) describes how a giant diagram of the body laid out in a large room such as the assembly hall allows children to physically move around the circulation as red blood cells, which can be useful for making these conceptual steps. Respiration is linked closely with circulation and a method of teaching about the respiratory system is summarized in the final section of this chapter.

> POS Year 5 – Living things and their habitats (explain the differences in the life cycle of a mammal, an amphibian, an insect and a bird)

Studying the life cycles of captive frogs and butterflies is engaging for children when they are presented with living specimens in the classroom, whose life cycles are closely followed by the class from birth to adulthood, at which time they can be released. Hachey and Butler (2012) promote the encouragement of wild insects into school gardens, especially butterflies and moths, so life cycles can be studied.

Research exemplar: Constructing a working model of the human lung

Hmelo et al. (2000) conducted a study to test whether children who built physical models of human lungs understood better the anatomy and physiology of the respiratory system. The researchers were interested in finding effective ways for children to learn about complex systems that comprise many interacting elements, such as the weather, a car or animal organ systems. They note that the more traditional classroom approaches such as drawing posters of complex systems, memorizing definitions and answering written questions are not always successful ways to optimize learning for all children. The particular approach they used was 'learning by design', or LBD (Hmelo et al., 2000: 248). The rationale was that if children were able to build a physical working model of the components of a complex system in a hands-on way, then this may be a better approach than presenting static, two-dimensional representations as found in books and posters. In contrast to traditional methods, with LBD, learners are actively creating something that they have ownership of, rather than passively receiving information. It is well known that when children carry out science practical work, they often focus preferentially on outcomes related to task completion such as producing a good set of results, rather than learning science concepts (e.g. Schauble et al., 1991). Learning by design aims to address this problem in three ways: by mixing doing with reflection; integrating real-world knowledge but in a controlled way, so that children do not go off at a tangent; and emphasizing science understanding over task completion.

The sample consisted of three classes of 11–12 y/o from the same middle school in Atlanta, Georgia. Forty-two children from two classes formed the intervention group, while the remainder from another class acted as the control group. The same teacher taught both intervention classes over 2½ weeks. The control group were taught the human respiratory system by a different member of staff (who I presumed was their usual class teacher) over a 2-week period by means of traditional methods that included completing work from textbooks and participating in teacher-led discussions. Although the research was carried out with children just beyond the primary school age range, this approach is relevant to Year 6 children in the UK because aspects of the respiratory system would be taught in conjunction with blood circulation. The intervention lessons involved four stages; Figure 2.4 gives full details.

Learning before and after the lessons was assessed by interview and a written test. Analysis revealed that after the intervention, the children understood more about the anatomy than the physiology of the respiratory system than the control class, with the difference between the two groups being statistically significant. One limitation of the research is that it was quasi-experimental, meaning that the sample used groups that were not randomized. Results from quasi-experiments are not as robust as those from randomized studies but are very common approaches that still produce valuable findings.

Research exemplar: Constructing a working model of the human lung

Main learning outcome (for ages 10–11 years)
Over the course of several lessons come to understand the basic anatomy and physiology of the human lung.

Setting the scene
- Pose the following scenario: *Imagine that you are an inventor who has just watched a TV documentary about the high incidence of respiratory disease in the UK, and the long waiting lists for lung transplants. Your task is to invent a mechanical lung that would help ease this situation.*
- To further orient the children, provide suitably child-friendly articles sourced from news websites, newspapers or magazines to groups of 3–4 children to look through, e.g. people with spinal cord injuries who are unable to breathe without mechanical assistance, the prevalence of asthma in the UK population and its possible link to air pollution, etc.
- Bring the whole class back together to discuss what they have learned.

Planning for design
- In the same groups of 3–4 children, next think about the design process while still having the scientific concepts of respiration firmly in mind. Get them to think about and then write down the potential problems they might encounter. These could include: *How will we get our lung to move? How does the human body do this? How will our lung simulate absorbing oxygen and excreting carbon dioxide? What is the volume of a human lung? Do we need to make protection for our lung, like the ribs?*
- Direct them to suitable information resources such as the Internet, CD ROMs or books that will help them answer these questions and get them thinking about the first steps they will take in drawing out a basic design 'blueprint'. Supplement these with physical resources, such as spirometers and heart beat monitors that can assess oxygen saturation (these are cheaply available).
- Try to make their learning as self-directed as possible.
- Bring the whole class back together to discuss their early design thoughts. This will help them piece together their fragments of knowledge into something more meaningful.

Designing and building the lung
- Groups draw up a blueprint of the model lung, preferably using a computer program such as Microsoft Word, PowerPoint or Publisher. Present possible resources to use as building materials, including plasticine, elastic bands, large plastic bottles, balloons, and straws. If possible, provide motors such as found in Lego Technic sets, as some children may have quite sophisticated plans.
- When groups have a feasible plan, they can start to construct their working model of a human lung.

Group presentations
- Each group presents their model lung to the rest of the class. They explain the functions of each different component, comparing it with its counterpart in the human respiratory system.
- They must still play the role of inventors and try to 'sell' and market their lung as being the best alternative. Other groups can ask questions and offer comments or constructive criticism.

Figure 2.4 Lesson outline for Animals including humans (adapted from Hmelo et al. 2000)

3

Plants

As will be explained in the following sections of this chapter, laypeople have differences of opinion about what a plant actually is. Scientifically, a plant is *a living organism with fully differentiated organs that is able to photosynthesize*. All living things require energy in order to remain alive and carry out daily tasks. As discussed in Chapter 2, animals acquire this energy by eating food and digesting it down to simple chemicals that cells can use as energy sources (especially glucose). In contrast, plants are unable to eat food or even absorb it through their roots; instead, in order to sustain cells they must manufacture their own food from raw materials. They do this by absorbing water and carbon dioxide gas, and then by utilizing energy from sunlight, convert these two substances into the useful chemicals glucose and oxygen. This takes place in areas of the plant that contain the green pigment chlorophyll, in the leaves mainly, and the whole process is termed *photosynthesis* ('making by light'). Note that algae such as seaweeds also photosynthesize but are not part of the Plant Kingdom because they do not have fully differentiated organs – they instead belong to the Protoctista Kingdom. The Plant Kingdom is itself divided into four groups, or phyla: lichens; mosses and liverworts; ferns, horsetails and clubmosses; and flowering plants and conifers. At primary science level, we look almost exclusively at flowering plants.

Flowering plants include species you might expect such as daffodils and roses but also include all trees that are not conifers such as the oak, sycamore and beech, and all grasses including wheat and barley. All of these species have four basic anatomical features: flowers, a stem, roots and leaves. The flower contains a plant's reproductive organs and all flowering plants reproduce in much the same way, enabling male sex cells (inside pollen) to meet up with female cells (ova) of a different plant to eventually produce seeds. Seeds are then dispersed from the parent and sprout, becoming new individual plants. Of course, because a plant has no means of locomotion it cannot, like an animal can, meet together with a different plant so that transfer of sex cells can take place through an act of copulation. A plant needs vectors to carry its male sex cells, which reside inside pollen, to other plants. These vectors are mainly insects or the wind and this movement of pollen from one plant to another is called *pollination*. Plants are adapted differently depending on the vector of pollination, for instance, insect-pollinated flowers are often brightly coloured, scented and contain nectar, all of which attract insects to land on the flower and pick up pollen. After pollination, the pollen settles on a female part of a flower called the stigma and grows a tube down to the ovary, which contains ova, the female sex cells. The tube allows the male and female sex cells to meet in the ovary and fertilization takes place to produce a zygote, which then develops into a seed. This whole process is an example of sexual reproduction.

Once the seed has been formed, the tissues surrounding it become thicker to form a fruit. This fruit is then dispersed from the parent plant usually via the wind or by animals that eat the fruit and then settles on the ground away from the parent. This is important because if the new plant grows too close, it will compete with its parent for resources such as light, water and minerals from the soil and may die. Once in its new 'home' and if the conditions are right, the seed will sprout – or *germinate* – becoming a seedling, eventually growing into an adult plant that is capable of reproduction itself. Before a seed can germinate, it requires water, warmth and air. The following sections will summarize research on how children learn these ideas, although it should be noted that compared with animals, less work has been carried out on plant classification, structure and function (Andersonet al., 2014), which is why this chapter is comparatively brief.

Children's ideas about plants

What exactly is a plant?

Young children have difficulties believing that some types of plant are actually living things. In Villarroel and Infante's (2014) sample of Spanish 4–7 y/o, nearly all the children recognized a typical flowering plant (e.g. a rose) as a living thing yet only half considered a tree to be alive. Only around 10% thought fruits and roots were living and less than 5% imagined that a seed was alive. Older children can also be susceptible to these beliefs; Stavy and Wax (1989) found that a quarter of a small Israeli sample of 8–11 y/o thought that plants in general were not living things. As discussed in Chapter 2, Nurettin et al. (2009) argue that there is a developmental progression from thinking that humans are the only living things, to then including animals and finally plants in the category, which may go some way to explaining these views. In addition, Patrick and Tunnicliffe (2011) explain that as children become older, they develop more of an interest in animals than plants and tend not to notice the latter and reject them as living entities (plant-blindness). Alternatively, children may decide plants are non-living because of the apparent absence of life processes (see Chapter 2); for instance, children often believe plants are incapable of self-initiated movement and so cannot be alive (Opfer and Siegler, 2004). At a practical level, Kinchin (1999) noted that teachers sometimes find it more difficult to teach plants than animals because children have preferential interests about the latter.

As well as having difficulties deciding whether plants are alive, people also are quite restrictive with regard to the kinds of species they call 'a plant'. When asked to draw a plant, both children and adults usually depict exclusively the archetypal flowering plants (McNair and Stein, 2001). Barman et al. (2006) explored US elementary children's ideas about the kinds of things they thought were plants by asking them to respond to a series of pictures of plants and non-plants. Most children aged 4–11 years believed that flowers, grass, trees, bushes and ferns were plants. However, around a half incorrectly thought that a mushroom was also a plant and that a seed was *not* a plant. Anderson et al. (2014) reported similar frequencies among American 4–7 y/o for grass, bush, tree, flower and mushroom. In contrast, in Bell's (1981) study, New Zealand 10 y/o similarly thought flowering plants were archetypal though trees were less commonly named, while considering carrots and cabbages to be vegetables, not plants. Gatt et al. (2007) found that Maltese 4–5 y/o thought plants had to be small, green and have straight stalks.

What does a plant need to survive and grow?

Like the work summarized in Chapter 2 about what children think animals require for continued survival, similar studies have been carried out regarding plants' requirements. It is perhaps easier for some children to think about plant rather than animal needs because they can relate this to experience with caring for plants at home, knowing that unless plants are given certain things they can easily wilt or die. When asked what a broad bean plant needed in order to help it grow, nearly all of the English primary children in Russell and Watt's (1990) study correctly thought water was an important requirement. As well as recognizing the importance of water, the 10–11 y/o commonly named soil, warmth and air as being vital; in comparison, fewer of the 5–9 y/o mentioned soil and very few listed any other requirements. However, most of Barman and colleagues' (2006) large American sample of 4–11 y/o said that in order to grow, a plant needs sunlight, water, soil and air. Most 8–11 y/o correctly knew that carbon dioxide and oxygen were necessary, compared with fewer 5–7 y/o. That said, most of the whole 5–11 y/o sample incorrectly stated that soil, bees, worms and plant food were important for growth. Few children understood that artificial light could take the place of sunlight. When asked to draw a place where plants might grow best, nearly all English 10–11 y/o drew an indoor location, while the 5–9 y/o drew both indoor and outdoor locations. This may have been due to the older children recognizing the commonality of ornamental plants inside the house (Russell and Watt, 1990). Similarly, Osborne and Freyberg (1985) found that children took an anthropocentric view, believing that plants need humans to survive in order to give them water, and that they need us to place them in soil and put them in a well-lit area. In response to the question 'when do you think the [broad bean] plant grows?', half of 10–11 y/o thought correctly that continuous growth occurs during both day and night, compared with fewer 5–9 y/o (Russell and Watt, 1990: 50).

Plant nutrition

An erroneous view common among learners of all ages is that the mass of an adult plant is completely derived from the soil instead of from photosynthesis. Primary-aged children have a strong notion that, like animals, nourishment for a plant must come from an external source (Cañal, 1999). Stavy and Wax (1989) found that three-quarters of Israeli 8–11 y/o thought that plants eat food. When Russell and Watt (1990) asked primary children where the leaf material in a broad bean plant had come from, a quarter of 5–7 y/o and around a half of 8–11 y/o believed that it came from inside the bean seed. Only one student (10–11 y/o) in the small sample alluded to any aspect of photosynthesis or growth and mentioned that the leaves had originated from water or air outside the seed. Growth of the leaves was viewed as an unfolding of material already present in the seed: '[The seeds came from] out of the bean – they were inside the broad bean. We didn't see them [because] they were curled inside' (11 y/o child Russell and Watt, 1990: 44).

These ideas are often due to children using an everyday definition of 'food' as nourishment that any organism takes in from the outside. There is sometimes confusion when teachers refer to a plant making its own food, as children sometimes misinterpret this as food that the plant later ingests in the same way that an animal eats (Smith and Anderson, 1984). Most of Barman and colleagues' (2006: 77) 4–11 y/o sample thought commercial 'plant food' was essential for growth, not understanding that it is fertilizer providing nutrients such as minerals and *not* a source of food. Very few 4–7 y/o recognized roots as common features of plants (Barman et al., 2006) and Stavy and Wax (1989) found that 13% of 8–9 y/o and 69% of 10–11 y/o mistakenly thought that plants breathe (although there were only eight children per year category in their study). It is important to note, however, that in an indirect way the soil does act as a source for some of the mass of a plant. Water absorbed from the roots eventually becomes transformed into sugar, while sap forms a good percentage of the mass of an adult plant. But soil matter itself does not become part of plant bulk, apart from trace elements such as minerals whose contributory mass is very small. In fact, Alonzo et al. (2009) place the understanding that plants require non-food materials such as minerals at the very top of their learning progression continuum.

Plant reproduction

Topics of plant reproduction are often introduced at primary level as 'the life cycle of plants'. The fact that flowering plants reproduce in the same way as animals by undertaking sexual reproduction is not well understood by primary children, and it can come as a surprise to younger age groups that plants are capable of reproduction *per se*. Stavy and Wax (1989) found that only 44% of Israeli 8–9 y/o were aware that plants reproduce, although this rose to 90% at age 10–11 years. Assessing the drawings of American 9–10 y/o that illustrated the steps involved in a plant's life cycle, Schussler and Winslow (2007) concluded that less than two-thirds could associate a seed as originating from a flower. Despite knowing that fruits come from plants, less than 5% knew that a fruit came from a flower; over a quarter drew a fruit growing on a plant, but distinctly away from the flower. Some children drew a seed being produced directly from a flower, missing out the step of fruit formation. Only a third of children showed seeds dispersing away from the parent plant. Smith (2004) interviewed 8–9 y/o who were confused about aspects of pollination, believing that insects are attracted to flowers to drink honey, or that pollen is merely the insects' food.

Although little work has been done with primary children regarding their concepts of plant reproduction, we can look tentatively to research with secondary and older students that may give clues about the ideas of younger learners. For instance, Lewis and Wood-Robinson (2000) found that only 7% of 14–16 y/o knew about pollination, and that very few of them linked it with sexual reproduction in plants. Students often confuse the processes of pollination and fertilization (Hershey, 2004), stating that the transfer of pollen between flowers is fertilization (instead of pollination).

The best ways to teach plants

POS Year 1 – Plants (identify and name a variety of common plants, including garden plants, wild plants and trees, and those classified as deciduous and evergreen; identify and describe the basic structure of a variety of common flowering plants, including trees)
POS Year 2 – Living things and their habitats (identify and name a variety of plants and animals in their habitats, including microhabitats)

Plant topics are prominent in the science National Curriculum at KS1 and KS2, reflecting a long tradition in English primary schools of children learning about their immediate outdoor environment. In fact, prior to the introduction of the National Curriculum in 1988, primary science lessons often focused on the study

	Typically 5–7 years	Typically 8–9 years	Typically 10–11 years
Plant classification	Plants are non-living (especially trees, seeds, roots, fruits). Flowering plants are typical plants. A seed is not a plant. A mushroom *is* a plant.	Flowering plants are typical plants. A seed is not a plant. A mushroom *is* a plant.	Flowering plants are typical plants. A mushroom *is* a plant. Trees and seeds are not plants. Carrots and cabbages are not plants, they are vegetables. Starts to consider non-typical species as plants.
Requirements for growth	Water, sun, air/oxygen, soil, bees, plant food, worms.	Water, sun, air/oxygen, soil, bees, plant food, worms, carbon dioxide.	Water, sun, air/oxygen, soil, bees, plant food, worms, carbon dioxide, warmth. Plants grow best indoors.
Plant nutrition	The mass of an adult plant comes completely from the soil (i.e. a plant gets its food from the soil). A plant's nourishment needs to come from an external source. Commercial 'plant food' is essential for growth Not all plants have roots.	The mass of an adult plant comes completely from the soil (i.e. a plant gets its food from the soil). A plant's nourishment needs to come from an external source. Commercial 'plant food' is essential for growth. Plants 'eat food'.	The mass of an adult plant comes completely from the soil (i.e. a plant gets its food from the soil). A plant's nourishment needs to come from an external source. Commercial 'plant food' is essential for growth. Plants 'eat food'. Starts to think about nutrients such as minerals. (Plants breathe.)
Plant reproduction		Plants do not reproduce. Fruits and seeds do not originate from a flower. Fruit formation is poorly understood. Plants grow from seeds. Seed dispersal not acknowledged.	Plants reproduce. Fruits and seeds do not originate from a flower. Fruit formation is poorly understood. Plants grow from seeds. Seed dispersal not acknowledged. Pollen is from plants.

Figure 3.1 How learning progresses: Plants

Comments made by a 4–5 y/o Maltese child. She lists archetypal 'flowers' together with the less commonly named trees.

Researcher: What plants can you name?
Child: Flower, sunflower, a rose, bluebell … I don't know any more. Trees (after looking around).
Researcher: Who showed them to you?
Child: We did a show of Alice in Wonderland on stage.
Researcher: Here at school?
Child: No, my sister and I and some of my friends go to drama lessons. We put on a show of Alice in Wonderland, and I was the rose, and my other friends were sunflowers and bluebells.
Researcher: Is that where you saw them?
Child: Yes.

Figure 3.2 What children have to say: Plants (Gatt et al., 2007: 118)

of local flora and fauna, involving activities such as nature walks, flower collecting and pond dipping. Educating children about nature while outside of the classroom is still very much in vogue in English primary schools (e.g. Bianchi and Feasey, 2011). Obvious advantages include children being able to link ideas learned in the classroom with authentic versions of the natural world that can be interacted with first-hand.

Plant topics are best taught in the summer term when species are plentiful and many are in flower. A starting point with year 1 is identifying basic flowering plant anatomy – flower, stem, leaves and roots – which is especially important for younger children who may not appreciate that the roots make up a substantial part of the body of a plant. Abundant species such as the dandelion can be picked from the school grounds or nearby, stuck onto paper and the different anatomical parts labelled. The specimens can be pressed by placing a heavy book on top and then dried out to become a permanent record that will last for many years. You can stretch the children's thinking by providing plant species with different anatomical forms, which they have to label similarly. For children at the higher ends of the learning progression, these can be used as a trigger for thinking about exactly where the mass of their plant has come from. Contrasting areas of the school grounds could be explored to determine the different plant species that grow there, linking a particular species with specific requirements; for example, some plants are able to grow in quite dry soils, others prefer a very sunny aspect, while hardy species can flourish in paved areas. Emphasize to the children that most wild plants must not be picked and even abundant species should only be picked in small numbers. With younger children, explain that living plant specimens are often fragile and should be handled only very gently. You could introduce a plant topic by reading from a book, such as *Fran's Flower* (Bruce,

2000) or *Apple Pigs* (Orbach, 2015). Zangori and Forbes (2014) warn that during a hands-on practical session that involved American primary children examining and drawing different seeds and fruits, the written work they produced did not indicate any scientific reasoning. This emphasizes the need for careful teacher-direction during practical experiments in order to focus thinking along desired progressions.

At the lower reaches of the learning progression, the belief that plants are non-living is prevalent. It can be a straightforward process to persuade children that common plants such as daffodils and oak trees are alive once they understand that they are capable of growth. The most important factor governing children's living/non-living decisions is the capability to move in a self-regulated way (Margett and Witherington, 2011), although plants move only very slowly and so pass unnoticed by children. Many digital cameras have the capability to produce a time-lapse film of an indoor plant such as the sunflower slowly moving its leaves as it follows the course of the sun across the sky (heliotropism), or unfurling its petals in the morning. These demonstrations also show that plants are capable of sensing their environment, so must therefore be alive. Alternatively, use the Internet to source an appropriate video clip. Other species that move very quickly can be bought as classroom plants, including *Mimosa pudica*, which closes its leaves when touched, or Venus flytraps. Children usually only think archetypal flowering species such as the daffodil are classified as plants. Giving them access to a variety of other species will help them to widen the boundaries of their plant set.

POS Years 2 and 3 – Plants (observe and describe how seeds and bulbs grow into mature plants; describe how plants need water, light and a suitable temperature to grow and stay healthy; explore the requirements of plants for life and growth [air, light, water, nutrients from soil and room to grow, and how they vary from plant to plant]; investigate the way in which water is transported within plants)

At KS2, plant growth can be studied over an extended period by germinating broad bean seeds in the classroom, which is helpful in dealing with concepts related to successful growth, especially incorrect ideas that exist throughout the learning progression, such as plants need soil, worms, bees, and so on. Line the inside of a glass jam jar with a paper towel, wedge a broad bean seed about half-way down the jar, and then leave to grow close to a light source, such as next to a window. Encourage children to look after their seeds as they grow from seedlings to adult plants, which will reinforce the fact that like animals, plants have their own physiological needs such as water and light. Eventually the adult broad bean plants can be potted in soil and nurtured further by the addition of fertilizer (plant 'food'), which illustrates the requirement for nutrients such as minerals that the plant is unable to make itself. Digital photographs can be taken every week to make a permanent record. Other, quicker-growing plants such as cress can be planted in different conditions to test for the optimal combination of factors for healthy growth (plenty of water, no water, sugar water, dark cupboard, in a refrigerator, on a radiator, etc.). Cid and Fialho (2013) describe a successful intervention that required children to grow seedlings and concluded that even with 6 y/o, meaningful links could be made with respect to plant physiology, such as that light is always required for healthy growth.

The erroneous idea that a plant absorbs its food from the soil is found throughout the learning progression, is very common even in adults, and can be difficult to address successfully. One exercise involves weighing a sample of watered soil in a pot, planting a seed in the soil, and then letting it grow for a few weeks. The adult plant is then removed from the soil and the soil reweighed. If the plant has been kept fully watered, the mass of the should be approximately the same as before. Finally, you should weigh the plant and pose the question, *where has all this extra mass appeared from?* Barman et al. (2006) recommend making it clear that soil is definitely not required for plant growth and suggest using aquarium plants as exemplars. Children need to understand how water is transported within plants and a quite effective demonstration is to use a stick of celery with the leaves still attached. Cut the bottom 1 cm of the stem and place the celery in a jar containing a small amount of blue ink. After a few hours the ink rises in the stem and turns the leaves blue, while cutting open the stem will reveal that the water vessels (xylem) have likewise turned blue. A similar exercise can be done with carnation flower stems left in different food colourings, with the petals changing colour as a result. In all leafy plants, water is constantly being transported from the roots, up the stem to the leaves where it evaporates into the air – this is *transpiration*, and is the way that certain materials are moved through the plant – it is the plant's version of a circulatory system.

POS Year 3 – Plants (explore the part that flowers play in the life cycle of flowering plants, including pollination, seed formation and seed dispersal)
POS Year 5 – Living things and their habitats (describe the life process of reproduction in some plants and animals)

Comparatively little is known about primary children's ideas of plant reproduction, though at KS2 the topic is taught in the context of a plant's life cycle from germinating seed → seedling → adult plant → pollination → seed formation → seed dispersal and back to germinating seed again. You can emphasize the importance of the flower as the organ of reproduction by having the children learn the different parts of the flower and the role of each part in the reproductive process. Children can dissect the flowers of species with large colourful petals such as the daffodil, separating parts such as the anther, stigma and ovules, sticking them down onto card and labelling them. They can make plasticine models of flowers that show these same parts. Pollination can be acted out as a role-play, with children becoming bees or flowers and carrying 'pollen' tennis balls from flower to flower. Seed dispersal can be introduced, perhaps as part of a food technology lesson, with a display of the more unfamiliar exotic fruits such as kumquats, kiwi fruits and lychees. Children can learn their names and how they have evolved to use animals to spread the seeds away from the parent plant. Reading books such as *Katie and the Sunflowers* (Mayhew, 2001) can help engagement, especially at KS1; however, Schussler (2008) warns that some children's trade books (i.e. books aimed at a general audience, not school textbooks) contain errors about plant reproduction that may lead children to construct scientifically inappropriate ideas. Tolman and Hardy (2000) recommend using *Amarylis* to teach plant life cycles in part due to its fast growth rate.

Research exemplar: Forest in a jar

Powell and Wells (2002) carried out a study to explore the effectiveness of a hands-on, practical approach to teaching plant growth and adaptations. The teaching sequence was informed by *learning cycle theory* (Kolb, 1984), an educational approach that has risen in popularity since the early 2000s (Figure 3.3). Kolb believes that ideally teaching should encourage a cyclical process that overtly links together the learner with the learning experiences, and consists of four distinct parts (as summarized by Powell and Wells, 2002). The first part, the *concrete experiential stage*, elicits the learner's past experiences that are relevant to the material being taught so that memories can more easily connect with the taught concepts. Second, during the *reflective observation stage*, new concepts are introduced and considered from a variety of perspectives. The *abstract conceptualization phase* involves the learner using the new concepts in different ways in order to make generalizing statements that can be used to solve problems. The fourth *active experimentation stage* uses the new concepts to solve novel problems, being a period of trial-and-error testing where the limits of the concepts are tested and deep learning takes place. The concepts then become part of the learner's cognitive repertoire and feed into the first concrete experiential stage of a new cycle. Therefore, learning is seen as a profoundly personal experience where the learner takes full responsibility for the construction of their own concepts, with the teacher acting as facilitator or mediator to help them move through each phase of the cycle.

The sample was four fifth-grade classes (10–11 y/o) recruited from the school district of Poudre, Colorado; no numbers are given but assuming 30 children per class suggests approximately 120 took part. Children were given a pre-test and post-test in order to establish the learning that took place as a result of the intervention, which took the form of a written test that focused on concepts of plant growth and how plants can tolerate different amounts of water in the environment. Children also were required to complete an open-ended questionnaire that

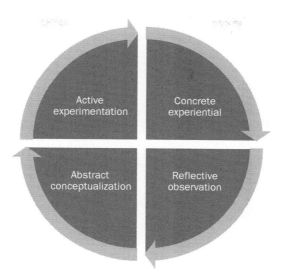

Figure 3.3 Kolb's learning cycle (adapted from Powell and Wells, 2002)

similarly tested understanding. The intervention itself was sourced from *Project WILD* (Wildlife Investigations through Learning Designs), a curriculum written by two regional bodies in the Western United States that taught science from environmental and wildlife perspectives (WREEC/WAFWA, 1992). The lesson Powell and Wells chose was *Forest in a jar*, which involved creating a changing environment and observing the different plant species that grew over a period of several weeks. They modified the lesson so that it better represented Kolb's learning cycle theory (Figure 3.4).

After analysing the pre- and post-tests, Powell and Wells found that the children had made statistically significant advances in conceptual understanding. The researchers in fact tested three different approaches to teaching plant growth with four different classes of fifth-graders undergoing each treatment; just one of these approaches is described here. It would, however, have been informative if a control group had been included in the research design that reflected 'typical' teaching methods, so as to allow a comparison with 'typical' learning advances.

46

Research exemplar: Forest in a jar

Main learning outcome (for ages 10–11 years)
Understand how plant adaptations govern the type of environment in which successful growth can take place.

Preliminary lesson (concrete experiential stage)
Teach aspects of plant growth focusing on how different plants are adapted to grow in different environments, and if an environment changes, some plant species will die out while others will begin to appear (this is *succession*). The process will allow children to elicit past, relevant experiences so they can link them to the new learning that will take place.

Forest in a jar (reflective observation stage)
Children make a model of a pond that will gradually (over a period of a few weeks) change into a model of a forest due to the succession of plant species. Children keep a journal of observations to allow continuous reflection upon new learning.

- Place 4 cm of garden soil and 5 cm of water in a jar and leave overnight to settle (without a lid). This is 'the pond'.
- To reflect the appearance of a new species at the pond, plant a small aquatic plant in the soil, placing the jar near a light source such as a window or lamp.
- Leave the aquatic plant to grow, allowing water to gradually evaporate from the jar. This simulates the onset of a drought.
- Twice a week add three birdseeds to the jar. While there is still a good level of water, the seeds should germinate but die, because they are not adapted to living in a pond.
- When the water level sinks to below the soil surface, the aquatic plant will die since its adaptations only suit a watery habitat. Keep adding the birdseeds, which should now begin to grow and flourish. The environment is now in a state of transition from pond to forest.
- Keep adding birdseeds but also add sunflower seeds, which will grow tall and represent trees in the forest. Once these establish themselves, the succession is complete and 'a forest' has been created.

Debrief (abstract conceptualization phase; active experimentation stage)
This takes the form of a question-and-answer session where children more sharply define the concepts they have learned. Encourage them to challenge any erroneous concepts about growth, adaptations or succession that may arise during the discussions.

Figure 3.4 Lesson outline for Plants (adapted from Powell and Wells, 2002 and WREEC/WAFWA, 1992)

4

Ecology, evolution and inheritance

Plants and animals living in the same area depend upon each other in several ways, usually as part of feeding relationships where one organism acts as a food source for another. This *interdependence* of living things can also be non-food-related, such as the beetle that lives in the bark of an elm tree and depends on it for shelter. Terminology is important because some words in ecology have slightly different meanings in everyday life. A *habitat* is a place or area where an organism lives and where its needs are provided for (e.g. food, water, space and shelter). A *microhabitat* is a small habitat; for instance, a red admiral caterpillar lives on a single nettle plant. An *ecosystem* is a collection of habitats that covers quite a large area and types include woodland, desert, ocean, polar and rainforest. Ecosystems can sometimes be represented by smaller, discrete places such as a pond or a rotting log. In ecology, the word *environment* means all of the factors that affect an organism during its lifetime. These factors can be physical (e.g. temperature, humidity, weather and sunlight) or biological (e.g. other organisms that live in the same area). The word can also have a broader, more global meaning, as in 'recycling is good for the environment'. A *community* of organisms means all the different living things that co-exist in the same ecosystem, and *population* just refers to a group of the same species within that ecosystem.

Ecological concepts are taught during years 2 and 4 as part of the *Living things and their habitats* topics and are centred on how living things have become adapted to their habitats and the interdependence of organisms within an ecosystem, particularly feeding relationships in the form of food chains. A food chain is a linear diagram that shows how organisms depend on each other for food: a classic example is grass → rabbit → fox, denoting that rabbits feed on grass, and in turn foxes feed on rabbits. Although not explicitly stated in the programme of study (POS), children usually learn that changes in the numbers of one organism affect other organisms in the same food chain. If rabbits start to die out due to disease, then there will be less food for foxes, whose numbers will also begin to diminish through starvation. At the same time, the fact that there are less rabbits means that less grass will be eaten and so grass plants will flourish and increase in number. These basic ideas are a simplification and may not always be reflected in a real-life food chain. If there are fewer rabbits, for example, then the foxes may switch to another food source and their numbers will remain constant. Also, another animal that had previously been in competition with the rabbit might eat the grass instead, thus not allowing the grass to proliferate. In more abstract terms, a food chain shows the transfer of matter and energy through a succession of living things, which is why the arrows point in the direction they do.

As part of ecology, children learn about the diversity of living things and the reasons why different species vary to such an extent. Within the same species, offspring are always slightly different to their parents due to cellular events that occur during the process of sexual reproduction. Occasionally, as a result of random but significant genetic mutations, these differences are so great that a population of plants or animals diversifies markedly, giving rise to biological variation. All early humans originally had dark hair. However, at some point in history a completely random genetic mutation of just a single letter of DNA code produced a baby with fair hair. The baby grew up and had children of its own, passing the mutation on to successive generations with the outcome that fair hair is now a very common human characteristic.

If there is a wide variety of organisms of the same species living in an area, then this is advantageous because that species is better equipped to survive catastrophic environmental change. The polar bear and the American brown bear had the same bear ancestor that lived about 5 million years ago. At that time, most of the bear ancestors resembled the modern brown bear, although due to random mutations, some possessed characteristics such as white fur and a thick layer of fat under the skin. A sudden cooling, glaciation event in the place we now call the Arctic meant that white and fat bears now possessed an advantage over the other bears that would have died due to being out-competed, or migrated south to a warmer, more hospitable climate. This is an example of *natural selection*, which is part of Charles Darwin's theory of evolution, where one species has competed with a second species with a favourable outcome and the population of the second species gradually declines or even disappears completely.

It may seem at first glance that a polar bear is perfectly suited to its environment and that its adaptations have been acquired as a result of exposure to environmental change. It might have been the case that as the weather became colder, the bear ancestor developed thicker skin, white fur, smaller ears, and so on in order to adapt. The polar bear seems so well adapted to the Arctic that one might even conclude that its attributes were pre-designed by a creator. The theory of natural selection asserts that the opposite is true, that adaptations arise as random mutations that are passed down to offspring. It is like going on a trip into town to meet a friend and go to the cinema. After watching the film your friend suggests that you go shopping together. You reach into your pocket and find you have unknowingly brought a shopping bag with you – as luck would have it, you are now equipped for this unplanned event. In contrast, the idea that an organism can change to become more adapted in response to its changing environment is scientifically incorrect, and called *Lamarckian*. Using the same analogy, this would mean that you decide to buy a shopping bag in town after watching the film in response to the unplanned event. At primary level, children learn about adaptations during years 2, 4 and 6, and in year 6 these adaptations are linked to Darwin's theory of evolution.

Children's ideas about ecology, evolution and inheritance

The interdependence of living things

Within Leach and colleagues' (1992) small sample of English primary children, those aged 5–7 years tended not to think of interdependent relationships between organisms living in the same area. Instead of understanding that species live as members of populations in a community that are constantly competing for scarce resources in a struggle for survival, they thought of plants and animals as individual, isolated entities. Younger primary children in particular tend to adopt anthropocentric reasoning, finding it difficult to imagine that wild plants and animals could exist without human involvement, for instance, ducks survive because people feed them bread (Demetriou et al., 2009). The ideas of Leach and colleagues' (1992) 5–7 y/o were similarly anthropocentric, with some of these younger children believing that in a similar way to domesticated animals, all wild animals are cared for and fed by humans, or that a food chain exists purely to provide food for humans. The 8–11 y/o did think more about interdependent relationships, understanding that in an ecosystem there are more plants than animals. However, many used teleological (end-point driven) reasons to explain why, such as there are more plants because animals will die if there are not enough plants to eat, and birds need trees to live in. As was the case with the younger children, there were also anthropocentric reasons such as there are more plants because humans have planted them and care for them. In contrast, most 5–7 y/o thought that there would be more animals and fewer plants and again their reasons tended to be teleological, such as there are more owls because they only come out at night and so have fewer enemies.

Primary children typically talk about single predator/prey relationships where one animal hunts another and not in terms of populations affecting each other (Leach et al., 1992; Strommen, 1995). When Leach and colleagues' 5–11 y/o were asked to describe relationships between organisms that lived in the same area, although some mentioned feeding relationships, these were usually described as pairs of organisms and not food chains (which have three or more links). Some 5–7 y/o thought that animals of different species were able to communicate and help each other.

Feeding relationships, food chains and food webs

An incomplete understanding of interdependence will not allow one to fully appreciate the far-reaching impacts of changes to a single population. For instance, one might trivialize a media report about an endangered species, believing that species alone is under threat when the likelihood is that many members of an ecosystem will be adversely affected due to ripple effects. Showing the intimate links between organisms in a graphic way using food chains and webs has been a pedagogical method of illustrating interdependency to learners. This is particularly the case when demonstrating the ways that human intervention can cause wide-reaching ripples through food webs in unintended ways; for example, the use of highly toxic pesticides such as DDT and the human introduction of the cane toad in Australia.

Learners, however, typically make common errors when working with food chains and webs that limit or prevent them understanding interdependency, the most well-known perhaps being the tendency to reverse the arrows in a food chain (Schollum, 1983). Demetriou et al. (2009) found that 9–10 y/o in Cyprus tended to only focus on a limited section of the food chain or web and did not appreciate that changes in that section can affect other sections, sometimes the entire food web. Gotwalls and Songer (2010) report similar beliefs with their 11–12 y/o in the USA. One reason for the lack of a wider understanding could be the fact food chains are presented to children as simple, static linear equations to be memorized and not as complex dynamic systems that are subject to change (Hogan, 2000). A related problem is thinking that changes in food chains only affect organisms that are adjacent to one another (Leach et al., 1992), something that has also been reported in studies sampling students beyond the primary years, including Griffiths and Grant's (1985) high school students. All of these findings reflect the fact learners find it more difficult to reason about indirect actions than direct actions. However, when asked openly what foods animals eat outside the context of food chains, most 8–11 y/o took an erroneous view along the lines of: 'organisms can eat a wide range of foods, and change their diet easily should the availability of one food source decrease' (Leach et al., 1992: 47). All these beliefs can impact on an appropriate understanding of situations where one population is reduced in numbers.

Within a food chain there are usually a greater number of herbivores than carnivores. A single carnivore needs to eat many herbivores during its lifetime, thus only a sufficient supply of herbivores can sustain a particular number of carnivores. If for some reason the carnivore numbers equal or exceed the herbivore numbers, the equilibrium shifts and carnivores will begin to die due to overcompetition. Some learners reason teleologically that there are more herbivores than carnivores because otherwise the carnivores will get hungry (Leach et al., 1992) or because humans purposely breed more herbivores than carnivores. In a more general sense, learners tend to think that food is always plentiful for wild animals rather than there being life-and-death competition between them for scarce resources (Leach et al., 1992). This idea of infinite resources within an ecosystem is problematic, as it prevents a correct understanding of sustainability. More recently, some studies have focused upon how students' deficiencies in causal reasoning have limited their understanding of food webs, and suggest that improving students' general reasoning powers would help comprehension in ecology (e.g. Hogan, 2000; Bravo-Torija and Jiménez-Aleixandre, 2012).

Children can more easily understand the effects of changing populations up the trophic levels than down them – that is, in the direction producer → herbivore → carnivore (Leach et al., 1992; Demetriou et al., 2009) – in part because children can more readily understand how a population can starve due to a declining food source, rather than thrive owing to there being fewer animals that would normally eat them. For example, many 5–11 y/o in Leach and colleagues' sample were able to successfully predict that removing deer from a food web will affect the number of lions (though others thought that it would have no effect on the lions). On the other hand, all 5–7 y/o thought that if the top predator was killed, no other organism would be affected (half of 8–11 y/o also thought this). Similarly, it was rare for the primary children in the sample to think that removing deer would affect the numbers of plants. Interestingly in contrast to the findings of these studies, Hogan (2000) interviewed 11 y/o in a US middle school and found the opposite trend: that children better understood that a lack of predator meant the prey population would thrive. When Leach et al. asked what would happen when the plants were removed, most 5–7 y/o thought no other organism would be affected (compared with a quarter of 8–11 y/o); this 'plant blindness' correlated with the research of Hogan (2000) and Hogan and Fisherkeller (1996). Munson (1994) reports that learners sometimes think that the removal of one species from an ecosystem will be inconsequential because its place will be easily taken by a different species. Leach et al. found that few 5–7 y/o were able to imagine population changes to affect more than one trophic level (i.e. changes in the numbers of one species only affects species directly adjacent in the food chain).

How organisms are adapted to live in a habitat

In year 2, children first learn about the habitats of different living things, which is timely because, according to Strommen (1995), by 6 years of age children begin to understand that animals have their own particular place where they live, or habitat. The ability to predict the habitat of an organism based on its adaptations may not appear until 11 years, however (Leach et al., 1992). Leach et al. also report that 5–7 y/o were not knowledgeable about the specific habitats where animals lived, for instance, some placed rabbits and deer as living in a tree. Furthermore, children across the primary range tended not to think that organisms have a constant habitat and are instead highly mobile, choosing freely where they live, which may affect the way they view population changes in food chains and webs. When asked the reasons why organisms live in certain habitats, children aged 5–7 could generally not provide an answer, while those that did gave simple responses such as birds live in trees because they like it. The 8–11 y/o offered more responses though tended not to cite interdependence or adaptation reasons (Leach et al., 1992). An organism's habitat comprises components that may affect it during its lifetime. Endreny (2006) found that 8–9 y/o in the USA could readily name and discuss the living components of a habitat that may have an impact on an organism (usually other animals) but rarely the non-living ones, such as air, soil or the sun.

Ideas about how living things are suited to their environment can be used as a lead-in to the teaching of evolution. However, the idea that animals can readily change their bodily structure in response to their habitat is a very common view held by secondary pupils (Engel-Clough and Wood-Robinson, 1985a) and leads to an incorrect understanding of evolutionary theory. Children aged 8–9 years have also expressed these same ideas, including a dolphin that moved to the North Pole could survive if it grew fur; these views were very resistant to teaching (Endreny, 2006). Kampourakis (2013) states that secondary pupils in the USA often cite teleological reasons for why an animal has adaptations and that they reflect Lamarckian viewpoints of evolution (see later). For example, a giraffe has a long neck so it can reach the leaves on high trees, an attribute that evolved due to ancestor giraffes constantly stretching their necks upwards. Kampourakis notes that a child's religious background has a significant influence on their understanding of organisms' adaptations, since creationist beliefs oppose a scientific view of how adaptations arise through gradual evolution.

Inheritance of characteristics

As has already been stated, any natural population of living things consists of a variety of individuals that have different characteristics. This is termed *variation* and occurs mainly due to random cellular factors inherent in sexual reproduction and genetic mutations. Once a characteristic appears in an individual, such as purple flowers in a pea plant, there is the possibility of it being passed down to (inherited by) offspring via the parents' genes. By the time they start school at age 4 or 5 years, children are already aware of simple aspects of inheritance and parenthood, such as offspring usually resemble their parents in some way (Schroeder et al., 2007) and babies come from their mother's tummy (Springer, 1995).

Although true of learners of all ages, primary children can become particularly confused about which characteristics are acquired during an organism's lifetime and which are inherited from parents, usually before they have been exposed to formal teaching about inheritance (Engel Clough and Wood-Robinson, 1985b; Wood-Robinson, 1994). A study of 7–11 y/o Canadian children found they had gender-oriented ideas about inherited human characteristics, such that a child inherits most of its characteristics from the mother (perhaps due to the intimacy of pregnancy) or alternatively a baby boy inherent traits mainly from its father, or vice versa (Kargbo et al., 1980). Singaporean 10–11 y/o knew that traits can be passed down from grandparents to parents and then to themselves, believing that their own appearance was due to a combination of their parents' genes, though some gave gender-oriented responses (Chin and Teou, 2010). In a different twist on the same theme, Weissman and Kalish (1999) found that 4–5 y/o in the USA thought that a mother could determine the eye colour of her baby should she wish to. As will become clear from the next section, an appropriate understanding of inheritance is a prerequisite for the study of evolution in later primary years.

Evolution of species

Dennis et al. (2015) explain that the basic premise of evolution is difficult for many primary children because they do not have a notion of geological time and so cannot appreciate the long timescales over which species evolve. There has, however, been a substantial amount of research activity concerning the place of evolution in schools, particularly in the USA where there is intense debate in some states concerning whether or not evolutionary theory should be included in the school curriculum. Fundamentalist Christian groups are opposed to the teaching of Darwinian evolution because it refutes the biblical creationist view of how the world and its living inhabitants first appeared. Creationism takes the position that God designed all living things when he first made the Earth around 6000 years ago and organisms have not changed their form since that time. That debate aside, there is a smaller body of work that has examined primary children's own ideas about how living things have evolved. A rather disheartening view (for science education at least) is taken by Evans (2008), who concludes that many learners of a variety of ages do not naturally hold a Darwinian view of evolution, instead thinking that all species have been created and so organisms' adaptations have been purposely designed by a creator. In Evans' earlier (2001) study, these ideas appeared to be especially prevalent among 8–10 y/o in the USA; similar results were obtained from a sample of 7–10 y/o in the UK (Kelemen, 2003).

There is evidence to suggest that learning about evolution can be emotionally stressful for learners as well as intellectually challenging, despite the ideas underpinning it not being that difficult conceptually compared with other science concepts children have to learn (Sundberg and Dini, 1993). This is probably due to the ideas being so counter-intuitive to what children nat-urally believe, for instance, that one living thing can transform (albeit over long periods of time) into a different living thing (Smith, 2010b). When asked explicitly, American 5–7 y/o did not believe that one kind of animal can be descended from a completely different animal, a view that may have been associated with them also expressing creationist views, such that animals had been made by God (Gelman, 2003) and that animals have always existed on the Earth (Evans, 2001). They see living things as unchanging and eter-nal (Evans, 2008). In contrast, both Gelman and Evans found that American 8–9 y/o are more consistently creationist in their opinions than their younger counterparts, firmly rejecting a common descent line that links humans with other animals, probably because at that age children are starting to consider questions of their own existence, life and death, and look towards mystical explanations (Evans et al., 2001). However, 10–11 y/o were more accepting than younger children that one kind of animal could be descended from a dif-ferent kind. When American primary children were asked whether four types of animal had evolved (butterflies, frogs, mammals and humans), most 6–9 y/o thought not, while 10–11 y/o thought that butterflies and frogs did evolve but not mammals and humans (Evans et al., 2005). At all ages, the tendency to think these types of animals evolved decreased in the order butterflies → frogs → mammals → humans, which the authors attribute to the fact that but-terflies and frogs undergo metamorphosis and so are susceptible to a radi-cal change in their form. Apart from a disbelief that organisms can change, another difficulty with understanding evolution is that because it takes place gradually over very long periods of time, it cannot be directly observed and so proved to have happened (Taber, 2013). Despite the fact that children from creationist families are more likely to reject evolutionary ideas, as teachers, as well as being understanding of the religious sensitivities of our charges we must also ensure that we do not shy away from our responsibility to deliver an education to children that reflects current thinking in science. In any case, it may be that children holding creationist beliefs are able to successfully com-partmentalize the two opposing sets of concepts and save one set for school and the other for church (Smith, 2010a).

Lessons about the fossil record can be taught in two contexts, either during an Earth science topic as common constituents of sedimentary rock and so indi-cators of the passage of geological time, or as evidence of evolution of species. There has been some work done with secondary pupils and university students determining their ideas about fossils (e.g. Oversby, 1996). However, there has been very little research with primary age groups apart from discussing the fossil record in an indirect way during explorations about children's concepts of geo-logical time (e.g. Trend, 1998). The current lack of material is probably due to the fact evolution is new to the primary curriculum. There is, however, a number of articles about using fossils as learning tools, including going on fossil hunts (e.g. Powell et al., 2007).

	Typically 5-7 years	Typically 8-9 years	Typically 10-11 years
Interdependence of organisms	Feeding relationships only occur between pairs of organisms (predator-prey) and not as food chains of three or more. Wild plants and animals need humans to survive. Species live as isolated individuals and are not interdependent upon each other. Animals of different species are able to communicate and help each other.	Feeding relationships only occur between pairs of organisms (predator-prey) and not as food chains of three or more.	Feeding relationships only occur between pairs of organisms (predator-prey) and not as food chains of three or more. Some start to think about food chains of three or more organisms.
The comparative numbers of organisms in a food chain	There are more animals than plants in a food chain.	There are more plants in a food chain because animals need to be fed plants.	There are more plants in a food chain because animals need to be fed plants.
Food chain diagrams		Arrows are reversed, i.e. (carnivore→ herbivore→plant).	Arrows are reversed, i.e. (carnivore→ herbivore→plant).
Food chains	Changes in a food chain only affect adjacent species in the chain. Changing populations cause changes up the trophic levels (from plant to herbivore to carnivore) but not down. Removing plants will have no effect on other species in a food chain.	Changes in a food chain only affect adjacent species in the chain. Changing populations cause changes up the trophic levels (from plant to herbivore to carnivore) but not down.	Changes in a food chain only affect adjacent species in the chain. Changing populations cause changes up the trophic levels (from plant to herbivore to carnivore) but not down. Some start to appreciate trophic effects in both directions.

Figure 4.1 How learning progresses: Ecology, evolution and inheritance

56

	Typically 5-7 years	Typically 8-9 years	Typically 10-11 years
Food webs		Changes only affect a small area of the food web, e.g. one food chain.	Changes only affect a small area of the food web, e.g. one food chain. Early appreciation of wide ranging ripples throughout the food web.
Habitats and adaptations	An animal can freely move to a different habitat and survive if it so chooses. A species can become adapted in response to that habitat changing. Not particularly knowledgeable about which animals live in which habitat.	An animal can freely move to a different habitat and survive if it so chooses. A species can become adapted in response to that habitat changing.	An animal can freely move to a different habitat and survive if it so chooses. A species can become adapted in response to that habitat changing. Species are adapted because of natural selection.
Inheritance	Characteristics can be passed down from parents to offspring.	Characteristics can be passed down from parents to offspring. Gender-oriented views of inheritance.	Characteristics can be passed down from parents to offspring. Characteristics can be passed down from grandparent to parents to offspring. Gender-oriented views of inheritance.
Evolution	Species evolve by becoming adapted during their lifetimes and pass these adaptations to offspring (Lamarckian). All species were made at a single point in time. Animals cannot evolve from one type to a different type.	Species evolve by becoming adapted during their lifetimes and pass these adaptations to offspring (Lamarckian). All species were made at a single point in time by a creator. Animals cannot evolve from one type to a different type.	Species evolve by becoming adapted during their lifetimes and pass these adaptations to offspring (Lamarckian). Species evolve due to natural selection mechanisms.

Figure 4.1 (continued)

This excerpt relates to a conversation with an 8–9 y/o American child about the food chain, grass → rabbit → fox → wolf. The responses suggest some understanding, although the final comment implies that the child has missed the point that the changing population of rabbits may have an effect on the fox.

Researcher: What does the wolf eat?
Child: Meat.
Researcher: What animal would the wolf eat?
Child: The fox.
Researcher: Do you think it might also eat the rabbit?
Child: Yes. I think it would eat both of them.
Researcher: Suppose the wolf ate up all the rabbits. What would the fox do?
Child: It would run away, because it is probably scared of the … wolf.

Figure 4.2 What children have to say: Ecology, inheritance, and evolution (Smith, 2004: 119)

The best ways to teach ecology, evolution and inheritance

POS Year 2 – Living things and their habitats (identify that most living things live in habitats to which they are suited and describe how different habitats provide for the basic needs of different kinds of animals and plants and how they depend on each other; identify and name a variety of plants and animals in their habitats, including microhabitats)

Looking specifically at concepts at the early phases of learning progressions, children frequently hold a limited view of what plants and animals actually are, so the approaches described in Chapters 2 and 3 are relevant here. Ecological concepts at the primary level have traditionally been taught in practical ways, which usually means going outdoors and observing nature first-hand. This can be done formally, as in visits to woodland centres or zoos, as well as informally by utilizing the outdoor spaces around the school. The summer term is the best time in which to do this because plant and animal species are more plentiful. In year 2, activities can be as basic as scouring the school field in a 'bug-hunt' to find small arthropods, sometimes called 'mini beasts' (insects, spiders, centipedes, etc.), and catching them using 'pooters', shake sheets and sweep nets. Once captive, they can be examined with a magnifying glass, identified and named. Deadfall pits involve digging a small hole in soil and inserting a plastic cup, and covering it with a piece of wood or plastic roof to keep the rain out. If left overnight, wandering creatures fall into the cup and are unable to escape. Identification of species can be aided using a biological key, preferably with pictures, and there are free interactive keys available on the Internet. Larger animals like birds, rodents, fish and even grass snakes can be observed (not caught). Of course, children need to be told to handle all animals with extreme care and return them as soon as possible in the place where they were captured. Photographs can be taken to help later identification in class. You can support these key concepts by reading books, such as *Norman's Ark* (Foreman, 2006).

POS Year 2 – Living things and their habitats (describe how animals obtain their food from plants and other animals using the idea of a simple food chain, and identify and name different sources of food)

Simple observations of local flora and fauna should be a starting point for discussing food chains and webs, with children having to create potential food chains for the animals and plants that they have been observing. Library books and the Internet can be valuable sources of information about species' precise diets (i.e. what eats what). This can be then extended to food chains in other habitats such as tropical rainforest, African savannah, polar areas, etc. Because children throughout the learning progression naturally think of feeding interdependence as involving only two species, an appropriate halfway house is first learning about simple paired relationships of prey/predator (e.g. zebra/lion, or deer/tiger). Once these ideas are secure, start to include plants using the same prey animals (e.g. acacia tree/zebra, or grass/deer). Finally, explain that a food chain is a string of at least three species (e.g. acacia tree → zebra → lion) and that the arrow means 'is eaten by' (watch out for children who reverse arrows). Although beyond the POS, primary schools have frequently taught in year 4 how changing one population in a food chain can affect other populations. Understanding these changes involves a degree of abstract thinking and the ability to conserve number, so may not be suitable for younger children at the lower end of the learning progression. However, this depends on the general attainment of your class and research shows that at least some 5–7 y/o are capable of grasping the basics of population change. Due to the probability of 'plant blindness' at the lower end of the learning progression, early in the topic emphasize that both plant and animal populations play a vital part in food chains. McGough and Nyberg (2013) enabled their 6–7 y/o students to understand the basic concepts of food chains through peer discussions about the things that animals need to survive, utilizing both classroom and outdoor habitats.

Because children more easily understand changes up the trophic levels, this represents a good halfway house concept to initially aim for. Start with herbivore/carnivore relationships rather than plant/herbivore, by asking questions such as *what might happen to the foxes if the rabbits left the wood?* Once children can cope with this level of work, start to introduce plants into the scenarios – *what would happen to the rabbits if all the grass was burned away in a fire?* And last of all test understanding of changes that occur down the trophic levels: *if more foxes appeared in the wood, what would happen to the rabbits?* Highlight the fact that an effect on a population can only occur if species are adjacent on the food chain because there needs to be a direct feeding relationship. That said, ripple effects in the form of chain reactions do occur; for example, if foxes disappear, rabbits will thrive and more grass will be eaten.

> POS Year 4 – Living things and their habitats (recognize that environments can change and that this can sometimes pose dangers to living things)

Linked to the conditions existing in ecosystems are the ways in which species are adapted to those environments. Present children with a picture of a plant or animal and ask them to explain how it is adapted to living in its home ecosystem. Common examples are the polar bear (Arctic), penguin (Antarctic), camel (desert) and cactus (desert). Extend this task by presenting pictures of less familiar species and ask the children to guess which ecosystem it inhabits, or get them to design an imaginary animal that is suited to their chosen ecosystem. Because children often think that animals can freely choose where they live, emphasize the fact that many animals are so especially adapted that they would find it difficult to live in other ecosystems (e.g. a polar bear could not live in the Sahara desert). Rule et al. (2008) provided a box of common household items to American 7–8 y/o and asked them how they were similar to the adaptations of organisms. Examples included how an electrical insulator from a telegraph pole keeps wires off the ground in the same way as the trunk of a tree lifts branches and leaves, and the arms of a pair of glasses hook around the ear while the hooks on a spider's feet hook the tiny irregularities of surfaces to enable it to climb vertical walls. A small sample was used but children made gains in learning that were statistically significant. Ecosystems can also be studied in a wider sense during geography lessons and cross-curricular links made with science.

> POS Year 6 – Evolution and inheritance (recognize that living things have changed over time and that fossils provide information about living things that inhabited the Earth millions of years ago; recognize that living things produce offspring of the same kind, but normally offspring vary and are not identical to their parents; identify how animals and plants are adapted to suit their environment in different ways and that adaptation may lead to evolution)

Evolution and inheritance are new to the year 6 primary curriculum and so there are presently few traditional, tried-and-tested approaches. That said, classwork on adaptations provides a convenient link into discussions on evolution, since adaptations have an impact of natural selection mechanisms. Build upon the simple ideas that children already understand about how offspring can inherit characteristics from parents. Use familiar species such as the domestic dog; for example, two pedigree dogs of the same breed will always produce puppies of that breed, whereas the puppies of two dogs of different breeds will show characteristics of both parents. Aside from variation within the same species, the basic idea that an organism can completely change into something else will be alien to children at the lower and mid-points on the learning progression, as will thinking that all life on Earth has *not* been made by a creator. Also difficult to address are Lamarckian viewpoints of how adaptations can appear during an animal's lifetime and then be passed on to offspring. Dennis et al. (2015) describe a number of drama activities, one of which involves children pretending to be a cockroach that has one of two adaptations (likes sweet things or likes bitter things). They have to act what happens when they are presented with a sweet poison – the sweet-likers die, while the bitter-likers survive – thus illustrating how natural selection works in a visual, hands-on way.

Research exemplar: Teaching food webs as dynamic systems

Demetriou et al. (2009) tested the effectiveness of a particular approach on the understanding of food chains and webs by 9–10 y/o Cypriot children. They wanted to move away from teaching the topic as currently presented by textbooks – as a series of food chains and cycles that have to be memorized – and further towards the real-life nature of feeding relationships as dynamic systems that are subject to change. The only way to do this was to increase the complexity of the material. As well as understanding how changes in populations affect simple linear food chains, they felt that extending these principles to whole food webs was essential.

The used a sample of 46 fourth-grade children from the same elementary school in Nicosia, and divided them into two groups, experimental and control. The authors do not state this explicitly but it appears that the two groups were probably 'intact' classes – that is, the children were kept in their normal, everyday class and there was no creation of new groups through randomization. Thus the methodology was quasi-experimental, and while not as powerful as a true, randomized experiment, nevertheless it does provide the opportunity to compare the effects of different teaching approaches in a valid way. The children in the experimental group were taught five science lessons focusing on integrated concepts of food chains and webs that involved an initial trip to a wetland habitat (see Figure 4.3 for full details). In contrast, the control group followed the official Cypriot textbook curriculum for food chains, which also took up five science lessons and involved learning about the feeding preferences and predators of the bee, ant and snail. This information was then used to construct simple

---

Research exemplar: Teaching food webs as dynamic systems

Main learning outcome (for ages 8–11 years)
Construct 'real-life' food webs and understand the various effects of changing populations.

Introduction
The sequence involved the researchers teaching the material over a period of five 80-minute science lessons. However, there is no reason why teachers cannot adjust this according to the time they have available. The important thing is to keep the essence of the approach by teaching the ideas in the order suggested, trying not to leave out any of the steps. The sequence is best carried out in the summer or early autumn terms when flora and fauna are most abundant.

Preparation period
- Choose a suitable site in the local area – a pond, woods, parkland or even the school grounds. It is preferable that a site be chosen that is nearby,§ as it fosters an appreciation of the local neighbourhood and the biodiversity that exists therein. A risk assessment must be carried out, which is especially important if the site is watery (pond, river, swamp, etc.).
- Before the visit, show pictures of and name the organisms that are likely to be encountered. You might want to include actual examples of material from the site such as a selection of plants, leaf litter or soil.
- Practise capture techniques as 'dry runs' in the classroom. This might include learning how to use apparatus such as plastic cups, pooters, sweep nets, and magnifying glasses, as well as becoming familiar with any picture keys, books, etc. that are to be taken on the trip.

The field trip
- Emphasize that the overall aim is to determine the feeding relationships of organisms that live at the site. Before this can take place, organisms need to be identified, and research carried out in order to determine what they eat in the wild.
- Give children clues of where to look, e.g. under rotting logs, stones, in tree bark, on the under-surface of leaves. Remind them that as well as animals, we are also interested in plants.
- Children work in groups of 3–4 and look for species to capture using the techniques previously learned in the classroom. Once captured, take photographs of the organism or make sketches. Magnifying glasses are useful for these activities.
- Warn children about treating animals and plants with care and to return them to where they were found after identification/photographing.
- Make especial note if you see an animal actually eating anything, such as a caterpillar eating a leaf, or a spider eating prey in its web.

Figure 4.3 Lesson outline for Ecology, evolution, and inheritance (adapted from Demetriou et al., 2009)

Constructing a food web
- Back in the classroom, download and collate the photographs of organisms on a computer or tablet.
- Using previously vetted free interactive website programmes, or hard copies of keys and books, identify the organisms.
- Once identified, again using previously vetted websites, determine what each animal eats in the wild.
- Collate all the information into a class spreadsheet that can be projected onto the interactive whiteboard so the class can see and refer to it.
- Still working in the same groups of 3–4, the children start to construct a food web on a large piece of sugar paper. Print out the photographs that were taken of the organisms to include on the food web, then stick down arrows to link organisms where a feeding relationship is known to exist.
- Compare the food webs of different groups in order to promote discussion where they do not agree.
- Using the food webs, set questions for the children that will encourage them to think about how changing the population of one species would affect another. For instance, *if all the water boatmen died out due to disease, how would this affect the other species in the pond?* Start by asking about effects down the trophic levels, as these ideas appear earlier in the learning progression (i.e. from plant to herbivore to carnivore). Try to ensure they appreciate 'long-range' effects due to ripples of population change – even though one species may not eat another species, changes in its population can easily affect the other species in an indirect way.

Figure 4.3 (continued)

food chains. Perhaps unusually, the same teacher taught the two groups (whom I presumed was a member of staff employed at the school and not one of the researchers).

The children's learning was measured using pre- and post-tests. With both tests children were asked to compile a food web on their own from pictures of organisms. They also were presented with an existing food web and questioned about the effect that changing populations would have on other organisms in that food web. Although both groups made progress with their learning, only the experimental group showed statistically significant gains. This group made fewer errors, provided more sophisticated responses to questions, and were able to understand effects on populations both up and down the trophic levels. This last point is notable because the ability to appreciate these changes is at the top of the learning progression. The authors recommend that instead of being presented with textbook examples, children should be allowed to find out for themselves the feeding relationships within food chains and webs, preferably in conjunction with hands-on fieldwork.

5

Properties of everyday materials

Since the National Curriculum was first introduced in 1988, there has always been an element that reflects the branch of science and engineering called *materials science*. Professional material scientists study how different substances vary in their structure, properties and performance, and conduct experiments in the search for new and improved materials. At primary level, a material is the 'stuff' from which an object is made, for instance, a knife is made from the material steel. Typically, KS1 teachers would start a materials topic by presenting familiar, everyday materials such as wood, plastic and rubber to children and asking them to identify each material. The next step would be to highlight that there is a difference between the name of an object and the materials from which it is made, just as a pencil is made from the materials wood and graphite.

Materials differ from each other in the ways they behave: some are hard and tough while others are soft and fragile, and some are stretchy while others are rigid. These *properties* of materials are used to help children sort objects into different sets. The material that an object is made from influences the job we want it to do, and that job depends on the particular properties of that material. One of the properties of steel is that it is a very hard material that can be sharpened to make an edge, so is ideal for making a pair of scissors. The study of materials, their properties and uses in primary schools tends to focus on human-made objects that have a specific function such as glass windows, paper towels and elastic bands. That said, the concept of a material crops up in other areas of the science curriculum principally when states of matter are taught, in the sense that everything that falls into the categories of solids, liquids and gases is classed as 'materials'.

Children's ideas about properties of everyday materials

Defining key terms

Material is one of those words in science that has a different meaning to that used in everyday situations. People think about a material as something that has a particular use such as writing materials, building materials or clothes being made out of 'material'. Part of this meaning includes the idea that materials are parts of a whole or are ingredients to do a job, as in raw materials. Also, a material has to be something solid and worldly – for example, *the money suddenly materialized out of nowhere*. Children do not usually regard anything outside of these every-day interpretations as being a material (Bouma et al., 1990), particularly liquids and gases, which are regarded as too insubstantial to be materials. However, the scientific definition states that a material is anything made from matter, and mat-ter essentially is anything made from atoms. Since every substance in the uni-verse consists of atoms (or their derivatives such as ions or subatomic particles), every substance is thus a material, including all liquids and gases. Furthermore, in science the distinction is made between matter and energy, with energy being classed as non-material because it is not made from atoms. At a more basic level, Smith et al. (2006) remind us that many primary children may not completely understand what teachers mean by the word *property*.

When teachers discuss the properties of materials with children, they use opposing comparisons such as hard vs. soft, stiff vs. stretchy, strong vs. weak, and magnetic vs. non-magnetic. One might expect that these familiar words have agreed, universal meanings that are more or less the same for both children and adults alike. When Russell et al. (1991) asked 68 English primary children what their understanding was of the word 'hard' in relation to testing the properties of solids, there were age-related differences in the children's interpretations of when a material was 'hard'. When deciding whether one solid was harder than another, 5–7 y/o erroneously thought that harder materials had to be heavy, stiff, have a certain texture, could hurt you, and are more difficult to cut into. The 8–9 y/o gave many of these same responses but also thought harder materials had to be brittle. Some of the 10–11 y/o thought that harder materials could make an impression or dent in another material, which is an approximation of the scien-tific view of hardness – if one material is able to scratch another, then that is one indication of it being harder. Ideas of hardness/softness are influenced when a solid is in powder form. For instance, Varelas et al. (2008) found that some Ameri-can 8–9 y/o thought that powdered salt was 'soft', despite a larger lump of rock salt being a relatively hard material. Therefore, it is worth bearing in mind that children, particularly in younger age groups, could misinterpret words we com-monly use to describe material properties.

Is a gas a material?

It has been known for some time that primary children imagine that a gas such as air is an ethereal, otherworldly entity that cannot be touched (Piaget, 1929), much less has properties that can be described. When Russell et al. (1991) surveyed primary children's ideas about the properties of air, more than half of 5–7 y/o could not think of any properties and those that did only associated air with movement that could be felt (e.g. a cold wind) or said that it was invisible. All of the 8–11 y/o children were able to name at least one property, similarly stating that air is invisible, or is necessary to sustain life/is important for breathing. However, Krnel et al. (2003) note that when Slovene primary children were asked to classify gases, they focused on the container instead of the gas inside, classifying it as a solid, probably because gases are less obvious materials at a perceptual level.

The difference between identity and matter

Krnel et al. (1998) argue that one of the fundamental ideas of chemistry that young children need to understand is that there is a difference between objects and matter, that is to say, what an object is called and the material from which it is made. When primary children are presented with samples of materials, they sometimes confuse the identity of an object with the material that it is made from, such as calling a loose piece of plain glass 'a window' (Jones and Lynch, 1989). Alternatively, they think that different objects made from the same material are actually different substances, such as an iron bar and iron filings are different kinds of iron (Vogelezang, 1987). Krnel et al. (2003) found that only at age 11 years and above could children correctly recognize that wood powder is made from the same material as a larger piece of wood. This kind of thinking indicates the inability to conserve the matter an object is made from, when the object itself is changed, and Liu and Lesniak (2005) state that generally children under 11 years find it difficult to conserve matter in this way.

If teachers ask children to categorize everyday objects according to the materials that they are made from, they sometimes lose the thread of the task and instead place them into sets based on perceptual qualities (what objects look like) or functionality (the jobs objects do) (Russell et al., 1991). Krnel et al. (2003) asked Slovene primary children to place familiar objects such as metal keys, party balloons, Lego bricks and honey into sets of their own choosing based on what they thought might go together. Similar to Russell and colleagues' findings, the younger children aged 5–7 years tended *not* to want to group objects according to material, for example, they did not place all metallic objects together. Instead, they grouped for simple perceptible reasons, generally the colour and shape of objects. From 8 to 10 years colour was still important, although there was an emerging tendency to group objects according to the type of material, collecting all textiles together, then metals, then plastics. At age 11 years, type of material was the most important criterion and colour the least important, and functional reasons started to appear –

how objects can be used (can play with these, can eat these). Galili and Bar (1997) found that when they changed the shape of a ball of plasticine into a disc, over 40% of Israeli 5–7 y/o thought that its weight had also changed, compared with less than 20% of 9–11 y/o. One can conclude therefore that younger primary children focus more on the perceptual properties of an object in preference to the material that it is made from, and that these properties can be easily changed, for instance, by simply changing an object's shape (Wiser and Smith, 2008). Children find it more difficult to make the generalization that some of the properties of a material do not change – they do not conserve matter. We can alter the shape or size of a piece of rubber as much as we like but it will still possess the property of flexibility. The year 1 programme of study (POS) requires children to group materials by simple physical properties, and so it is worth noting that most children aged 5–6 years may find this difficult without support because they will tend not to conserve matter and not be able to generalize a material property as being a constant thing. In addition, for them, perceptual properties such as colour and texture will be simpler to understand and remember, compared with the more abstract properties of materials like strength. Skamp (2011) concludes that children generally understand metal materials better than non-metal materials, so metal objects are best used as a starting point for discussing properties.

	Typically 5–7 years	Typically 8–9 years	Typically 10–11 years
'Hardness' means ...	Heavy, stiff, could hurt you, difficult to cut into.	Heavy, stiff, could hurt you, difficult to cut into, brittle.	Heavy, stiff, could hurt you, difficult to cut into, brittle, makes an impression into a softer material.
Properties considered when sorting materials into sets	Sets are based on perceptible properties (e.g. colour and shape).	Sets are based on perceptible properties (e.g. colour), though also compositional properties (type of material, e.g. metal).	Sets are based on compositional properties (type of material, e.g. metal) and functional properties (e.g. can play with).
Conservation of matter	Properties of materials are those that can easily change (e.g. perceptible properties). Has difficulty conserving the property of weight in some contexts.	Properties of materials are mainly those that can easily change (e.g. perceptible properties). Has difficulty conserving the property of weight in some contexts.	Properties of materials can remain constant even if the object is changed (e.g. flexibility). Able to conserve the property of weight in a variety of contexts.

Figure 5.1 How learning progresses: Properties of everyday materials

Some of the properties used by different Slovene 5 y/o when they grouped objects into sets of their own choice. Types of property are given in frequency order (most frequent was colour, least frequent was action).

This is silvery. (colour)
They are both round. (shape)
They are both thin. (shape)
It is wood. (substance)
It is plastic. (substance)
You can roll the can and the glass. (action)
We can pour the water in. (action)
It is possible to break it. (action)

Figure 5.2   What children have to say: Properties of everyday materials (Krnel et al., 2003: 628–629)

The best ways to teach properties of everyday materials

POS Years 1 and 2 – Everyday materials/Uses of everyday materials (distinguish between an object and the material from which it is made; identify and name a variety of everyday materials, including wood, plastic, glass, metal and water, and rock; describe the simple physical properties of a variety of everyday materials; compare and group together a variety of everyday materials on the basis of their simple physical properties; identify and compare the uses of a variety of everyday materials, e.g. wood, metal, plastic, glass, brick, rock, paper and cardboard for particular uses)

In 2006, Liu and Lesniak argued that it is difficult to characterize a learning progression for the properties of matter because of the lack of research with the primary age group. Despite this, using the limited material available it is possible to make tentative predictions about how children will conceptualize matter when planning lessons. At year 1, a useful starting point is to ask children to list the qualities of everyday materials, concentrating mainly on simple, perceptible features. The aim is to get them into 'describing mode' whereby they think up a variety of adjectives they could apply to a material. Using perceptual properties will help the children, most of whom will be at the lower ends of the learning progression where they naturally have difficulty operating with more abstract categories such as uses of objects. Blowing soap bubbles is an appealing way to grab children's attention and to encourage descriptive thought (e.g. Ling et al., 2006). Using pictures or videos of more exotic substances such as a diamond or volcanic lava will help engage and stretch the more able in the class. This kind of task is analogous to what children are often asked to do during an English lesson when, for instance, a story is read to them and they come up with adjectives that describe how the story had made them feel.

Once children become familiar with simple properties (an acceptable halfway house stage), they can use them to sort materials into sets. Emphasize that set belongingness should depend on properties of the *material* that objects are made from (bendy, hard, see-through) and not properties of the *objects* themselves (green, big, triangular). This will help address ideas found at the lower levels of the learning progression and encourage children to conserve matter by thinking about the fact that some of the properties of the material that an object is made of are constant, even if the object itself is changed. A good example to use is a piece of plasticine in a bar shape. When twisted, bent, cut up, etc., it still retains the properties of flexibility and plasticity. Roy (2012) explains how modelling clay can be used generally in the primary classroom for tasks such as these, although warns that safety precautions need to be adhered to (e.g. dry clay should never be swept up due to the possibility of inhaling clay dust).

POS Year 5 – Properties of everyday materials and reversible change (compare and group together everyday materials on the basis of their properties, including their hardness, solubility, transparency, conductivity (electrical and thermal), and response to magnets; give reasons based on evidence from comparative and fair tests for the particular uses of everyday materials including metals, wood and plastics)

As the children progress into year 5, explain that in science we are mainly interested in only certain properties of materials – those properties that we can test by using scientific enquiry. The focus therefore will be on things like hardness, stretchiness, bendiness, brittleness, transparency, water absorbance, magnetism and electrical conductivity. There are well-established practical tasks that primary teachers have used to compare these properties in materials. Strength can be tested by dangling lengths of various cotton threads over the back of a chair and adding masses one by one until the threads snap. A similar method can be used with elastic bands to test bendiness or stretchabilitly (elasticity) by measuring how long each band will stretch if the same mass is added. The absorbencies of different kitchen paper towels can be tested by spilling water in a tray and counting the number of wipes needed to dry the spill, or weighing the paper towels before and after to measure how much water has been absorbed. All of these practicals can be done as open-ended investigations in which different independent variables are tested. For example, in the cotton thread strength test, in addition to varying the types of thread tested, you could change their lengths, use wet and dry threads, and so on. Alongside these tasks, the results of these tests can be used to justify why certain materials possess properties that make them ideal for doing a specific job.

Materials science is a branch of engineering as well as being a scientific discipline and so there are plenty of cross-curricular opportunities with design and technology. For instance, the primary Design and Technology curriculum requires children to build structures by using materials that have suitable properties. Monson and Besser (2015) explain how science and engineering concepts can be taught in a science lesson by having children design a storage system to help dispose of used milk cartons left over from lunchtime. This incorporates the challenges of finding materials with the right properties so that the cartons can be easily crushed and designing a system that is the most effective and energy-efficient.

Research exemplar: The physical properties of rocks

Sargianis et al. (2012) describe a sequence that can be used to teach about material properties by asking children to consider how different rock samples behave (Figure 5.3). The sequence approaches the problem from an engineering perspective, thinking about the demands a material must meet to fulfil the job required. The sequence of lessons is part of a curriculum called *Engineering is Elementary* (2011), a scheme designed by a team from the Museum of Science in Boston, Massachusetts. It has been taught in elementary schools in at least five US states and is aimed at promoting progress in engineering and science by the presentation of a series of hands-on design challenges. This specific unit is taught to 7–10 y/o, although the authors state that it could be taught to younger age groups with some modifications. Because children are asked to fully apply their knowledge of materials in order to solve the challenges, it is best taught at the end of a materials topic. Also, since rocks are used as the focus, children will have preferably been taught some information about the properties of different rock types.

The unit starts by asking children to think about the 'technologies' that are all around them (Sargianis et al., 2012: 56) – human-made systems such as the telephone network, national grid and the Global Positioning System (GPS). They also include things like buildings and roads, and it is these rock-related technologies that are the focus of the unit. Next, the teacher draws an engineering triangle (Figure 5.4) to reinforce links between the properties of a material and its function. This technique allows children to think about the properties of a material and how the material is used to make something useful (process), an idea that is near the top of the learning progression. The engineering triangle links properties and process by also considering the structure of the useful material.

Adopting the engineering triangle in Figure 5.4, the properties of cotton thread were linked to the structure of a sample of towelling (terry cloth), and from this the process, with the class deducing how the cotton thread was put

---

Research exemplar: The physical properties of rocks

Main learning outcome (for ages for 7–10 years)
Over the course of a series of lessons, be able to use a problem-solving approach that involves testing material properties and linking them to a specific use.

Initial questions:
- How do people use rocks when they create technologies such as buildings, tools, and roads?
- What makes a rock good for one purpose but not another?
- What is the engineering design process used?

Introduction
Take the class on a walk around the school building and grounds, asking them to identify technologies made from rocks, e.g. walls, paved areas, roofs, ceilings, arches, paperweights, granite table surfaces. Ask them about the properties of these rocks (texture, strength, hardness, etc.). What kinds of materials would not be good to do these jobs, and what would be the properties of these unsuitable materials? Back in the classroom, summarize the properties of the rocks that are used in technologies and emphasize this is why these rocks are good materials for the job that they do. Let children handle actual samples of the rocks under discussion.

Children examine samples of thread and bathroom towelling (terry cloth) using magnifying glasses and describe their properties (flexible, soft, fuzzy, etc.). The teacher summarizes responses on an engineering triangle (Figure 5.4). Link properties, structure and process (see main text). Show cotton balls and explain that this is the raw material for thread – some of the cotton's properties are different as a result of spinning the thread (e.g. it becomes stronger), but some remain the same (e.g. colour).

Ask children to think about a towel and a pair of trousers – would both of these articles need materials having exactly the same properties? What properties would be needed for each article? Present different samples of fabric and ask children to carry out brief experiments that test them with respect to the properties required for trousers and a towel. Test absorbency, toughness (e.g. sandpaper), etc.

Main activity – Design a cave carving (petroglyph)
- Show pictures of real cave carvings to stimulate interest. Provide small samples of rocks and other materials that children will be testing as part of the design challenge (the original study used small samples of limestone, granite, pumice, foam, wax, marble and alabaster).
- Ask children to list the properties required of a material onto which a cave carving can be made.
- Draw a results table to summarize these necessary properties. They must include the properties 'hardness' and 'durability'.

Figure 5.3 Lesson outline for Properties of everyday materials (adapted from Sargianis et al., 2012)

- Pass the different materials around and record the properties of each onto the table.
- Test hardness by trying to scratch the material with an iron nail. Test durability by trying to erase this scratch with sandpaper, which simulates the effect of erosion over time. You can test whether the scratch has disappeared by making a wax rubbing – rub a wax crayon over a piece of paper held onto the scratch to see if there is still a faint mark on the rock. Safety glasses must be worn. Encourage fair testing, e.g. pressure applied to the nail, time taken for rubbing with sandpaper.
- When all materials have been considered, children consult their results tables and decide which would be the most suitable for a cave carving.
- If you can get hold of flat samples of material, children would be able to create their own cave carvings on the samples they have chosen to be the best. Once made, test their durability using the sandpaper/wax crayon method described above, and rank each attempt in order of the most enduring carvings.
- An additional task can be introduced where children have to sort the samples by whether they were human-made or natural, and by rock type (igneous, sedimentary, metamorphic).

Figure 5.3 (continued)

together to make towelling. Explicitly linking properties to structure in this way encourages an understanding of why certain materials are good for certain jobs. This technique should also help children at intermediate levels of the learning progression to successfully conserve matter – that is, understand how some of the properties of a material remain unchanged even when the material itself is arranged in different ways.

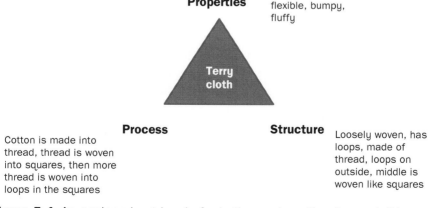

Figure 5.4 An engineering triangle for bathroom towelling (terry cloth) (adapted from Sargianis et al. 2012: 56)

The next step involved a brief experiment where children had to test different fabrics in order to assess their suitability for making either a towel of a pair of trousers. Only after this preliminary work on material properties was the main task of the teaching sequence introduced. Children were told they had to act like materials engineers and were given a challenge – to design a replica of a stone-aged cave carving (petroglyph) to be placed in a museum. The effectiveness of this specific sequence of activities was formally assessed in combination with the rest of the Engineering is Elementary (EiE) curriculum (Lachapelle and Cunningham, 2014). Pre- and post-tests were used to assess the children's understanding of science and engineering concepts. Significantly greater gains were made when the EiE children were compared with a control group.

The unit described here was assessed independently of the other units in the curriculum and again there were significant learning gains. The report specifically cited 'better understanding of materials [and] their properties' as among the science concepts that the intervention improved (Lachapelle and Cunningham, 2014: 6). A limitation of this approach is that it requires children to be able to access the mid- and upper levels of the learning progression, especially the ability to conserve matter. For this reason, it is best recommended for upper KS2.

6

States of matter

We can categorize the things around us in a variety of ways. In a living room we could sort objects into different sets according to their use, such as items of furniture, electrical appliances, lighting, heating, containers, and so on. Science is essentially reductionist in nature, so scientists try to explain how the world works in as simple a way as possible, which includes creating systems of sorting (taxonomies) that have a minimum number of sets for categorizing things. As a result of this, materials are organized into only three sets based on their properties at room temperature: solid, liquid or gas – the three *states of matter*. The expression 'room temperature' in science means exactly 20°C and is an important consideration because materials can change their state if they are heated above or cooled below 20°C. For instance, margarine becomes a liquid if exposed to temperatures in excess of 30°C.

An understanding of properties (Chapter 5) needs to precede any classification of states of matter. Regardless of state, all materials possess the properties of having weight and taking up volume or space, and consist of atoms (or their derivatives). However, when the properties of solids, liquids and gases are compared, they are quite different (Figure 6.1 summarizes these). Although beyond KS2, the three states of matter are a simplification because matter can exist in other ways – *plasma* is often called the fourth state of matter, being a collection of usually very hot gas particles whose electrons have been stripped away or added to. Also beyond the primary curriculum is the idea that matter consists of extremely tiny bits, or particles (mainly atoms and molecules). Even though particle theory has never been a part of primary science, many schools have taught it at a simple level and for that reason children's concepts of particles are included in this chapter.

As mentioned in Chapter 5, when teachers first introduce the solid/liquid/gas system in year 4, the children would not naturally categorize materials in this way; they instead create groups based on perceptual appearance, type of material or functionality. This chapter covers children's concepts of the properties they believe each state of matter possesses and includes criteria children use when deciding whether an object is solid, liquid or gas (Chapter 7 details state changes). An overriding factor is that because children do not naturally think of the solid/liquid/gas taxonomy, they experience problems during categorization tasks.

	Solid	Liquid	Gas
Does it have a fixed shape?	Yes	No	No
Does it have a fixed volume	Yes	Yes	No (it can be compressed)
Can it flow?	No	Yes (it can be spilled)	Yes (it flows very freely)
How are the particles arranged?	Particles are closely packed and fixed in position	Particles are closely packed though not fixed in position	Particles are widely spaced apart and move randomly
What would the particles look like?			

Figure 6.1 Properties of the three states of matter

Children's ideas about states of matter

Solids

When Russell et al. (1991) asked English 5–7 y/o to draw or categorize objects as solids, they tended to gravitate towards everyday things that are heavy such as a wall or a person. The more typical materials that teachers might present as solids during a science lesson such as steel were mentioned much less frequently. At 8–9 years, heaviness remained an important criterion, although children were willing to include more of a variety of objects in their 'solid' set, including those that are hard or rigid like a brick or a book. Heaviness was less important to 10–11 y/o – while they considered hardness and rigidity to be relevant criteria, the scientific idea that a solid has its own shape began to emerge. Primary children's fixation with solids having to be strong, hard or rigid is well established and has resulted in softer or pliable materials such as wax, plasticine, jelly, wire objects and cotton being incorrectly considered as non-solids (Jones and Lynch, 1989; Stavy, 1994; Krnel et al., 2005). However, Stavy and Stachel (1985) found that with some non-rigid materials (e.g. plasticine, sponge, powder, cotton wool and cloth), Israeli children placed these in an intermediate category that is between solid and liquid. As will be discussed in the next section, powders are sometimes thought to be liquids because they appear to behave more like liquids than solids. Galili and Bar (1997) comment on the difficulties experienced by younger primary children when conserving weight, specifically the idea that when an ice cube melts, the water produced is lighter than the original ice cube, noting that only at age 10 do they start to understand in significant numbers that weight is conserved.

More recent studies have confirmed many of these earlier findings. For instance, Varelas et al. (2008) interviewed small numbers of American 7–9 y/o who held beliefs that included all solids must have a fixed shape (a baggie containing salt loses its shape, so must be a liquid or a gas), are hard, and a straw is not a solid because it is hollow. These ideas lead to 'soft' materials such as candle wax, plasticine, footballs and balloons not being categorized as solids.

Liquids

When the 5–7 y/o in Russell and colleagues' (1991) sample were asked to name liquids, their thinking when triggered by the word 'liquid' resulted in them mainly choosing substances with liquid in the name, such as Fairy Liquid or washing-up liquid. Interestingly, none chose to name water as a liquid. At 8–9 years, the word 'liquid' remained a trigger with children making these same choices, though more diverse examples were chosen, including drinks, coloured liquids and non-aqueous liquids (e.g. cooking oil). Water was named as a liquid by only 26% in this age group. In contrast, Krnel and colleagues' (2003) American children used water as the exemplar liquid throughout the primary age range, so appear to have been less influenced by this linguistic link. Russell and colleagues' 10–11 y/o were more inclusive than the two younger age groups, depicting a greater variety of drinks, coloured liquids, non-aqueous liquids and viscous liquids such as treacle. Many more (70%) included water. Any reluctance to portray water as a liquid by children under 10 years is challenging, since in primary science we hold up water as *the* exemplar used to represent the liquid state. Galili and Bar (1997) also note weight conservation issues with liquids, with more than two-thirds of children across the primary age range believing that when water evaporates, the vapour produced becomes lighter (technically, water vapour has the same weight as the liquid water from which it derives, but because it takes up more space its density is less than dry air, and so is able to float). Nearly a half thought that water running from a tap has no weight.

The older children in Russell and colleagues' study were more likely than their younger counterparts to correctly think that a liquid must be runny or can be spilled. In contrast, Stavy (1994) describes how Israeli children were more sci-entifically accurate than English children when defining liquids likely because of linguistic reasons – the Hebrew word for 'liquid' is the same as the word for 'pour', and so even at a young age children associate liquids with the particular property of runniness. Israeli children did, however, tend to make the same error as the English children when believing viscous liquids such as honey were not liquids because they were not runny enough, and this idea similarly diminished with age through the primary years (Stavy and Stachel, 1985). It also appears that once water is recognized as being the archetypal liquid, children can overgeneralize and assume that all liquids are actually water (Stavy, 1994). A related problem is overgeneralizing the knowledge that a liquid is pourable to powders, which are thought to be liquids because they flow, can be spilled, take the shape of their container, etc. Because of this, Stavy (1994) found that children throughout the primary years tended not to classify powders as solids; to counter this view, Opfer and Siegler (2004) recommend emphasizing that every small grain within a powder is a tiny solid.

Gases

Compared with solids and liquids, limited research has been conducted on how primary children conceptualize a gas. Gases are not part of children's conscious, everyday experiences and so they find it difficult to describe their properties. This prevents them categorizing substances into the gas set because the set criteria are not well known (Figure 6.1). It is common for children to think that a gas is not a material at all (Smith et al., 2006), which leads onto thinking that gases have no weight or negative weight and this is why they rise or hang in the air (Sere, 1985). In fact, Brook and Driver (1989) suggested that the idea of all gases rising may come from a familiarity with helium balloons, and children are not aware that gases such as carbon dioxide are more dense than air and tend to sink. Stavy (1991) found that this view persists throughout the primary years, though can be addressed by demonstrating that like all matter, gases have weight and volume. When Russell and colleagues' (1991) primary children were asked to draw gases, in a similar way to the liquid example given in the previous section, if something's name contained the word 'gas', then this acted as a trigger throughout the primary age range to draw gas cookers and gas heaters. Allied to this was a strong association with a gas to danger, heat or smoke that similarly did not diminish with age, for example 'gas is a fire' (Russell et al., 1991: 104). Hardly any of the 5–9 y/o could give the name of any gas. In contrast, over half of 10–11 y/o were able to give the name of at least one gas, air being a frequent choice, and could name simple perceptual properties such as having a smell, you can't hold a gas or that gases can be either visible or invisible. Skamp (2011) confirms that older Australian primary children can name gases such as carbon dioxide and oxygen but cannot expand much further on their properties. As was the case with water not being recognized as the exemplar liquid by children under 10 years, not being aware that air is a gas is problematic since in primary science air is nearly always given as a standard example by teachers.

The particulate model

Particles are not part of the primary curriculum, although many primary teachers have successfully taught particle concepts at a simple level at upper KS2, myself included. Despite this, there has been recent activity in the literature promoting the benefits of teaching a particle model in primary schools (e.g. Lee and Tan, 2004; Skamp, 2009). This has been partly driven by growing evidence that using a particulate model with primary children helps them to better understand areas of chemistry such as chemical and physical changes (e.g. Tytler et al., 2006). For instance, thinking about the fact materials are made from particles (usually atoms and molecules) enables children to think about how solids, liquids and gases are different in the way that their constituent particles are arranged (Figure 6.1), how chemicals link with each other during reactions, and the conservation of matter during physical and chemical changes (see Chapter 7).

Owing to the lack of a requirement for the teaching of the particulate model at primary level, few studies have focused on these concepts in primary children and, importantly, there is nothing that provides clues about a clear learning progression. Skamp (2009) summarizes this limited literature and concludes that in most contexts, it is very difficult for children under 10 years to appreciate the abstract concepts that underlie particle theory because they have a high conceptual demand. They imagine particles not as atoms or molecules, but as tiny 'bits' of material that look like and behave like the material as a whole. Even the oldest primary children are poor at relating particle theory to chemical change (ibid.). That said, there is some evidence that children can remember particle explanations of solids, liquids and gases over a period of two years after instruction (Skamp, 1999).

There has been more research into secondary pupils' ideas about particles, and these may apply in particular to upper KS2 children if particle theory is to be taught in primary school. Misconceptions include: thinking that gas particles do not fill their container, but are bunched together in the top or bottom of the container (Novick and Nussbaum, 1978); particles have macroscopic properties, such that they melt, expand/contract, and get hot (Brook et al., 1984); liquid particles are further apart than solid particles of the same material (Novick and Nussbaum, 1978); and atoms are alive – they grow and divide (Harrison and Treagust, 1996).

POS Year 4 – States of matter (compare and group together materials according to whether they are solids, liquids or gases)

The best ways to teach states of matter

Although the idea that materials can be categorized as solids, liquids or gases first appears in the year 4 POS, children experience earlier topics that are related. In years 1 and 2, they learn about how materials have properties that

	Typically 5–7 years	Typically 8–9 years	Typically 10–11 years
Using states of matter as sets during sorting	Do not spontaneously sort materials into solid, liquid, gas.	Do not spontaneously sort materials into solid, liquid, gas.	Start to spontaneously sort materials into solid, liquid, gas.
Properties of solids	Heavy. Powders are not solids – they are liquids. Hollow objects are not solids.	Heavy, hard, rigid. Powders are not solids – they are liquids. Hollow objects are not solids.	Hard, rigid, has its own shape. Powders are not solids – they are liquids.
Properties of liquids	Water is not recognized as being a typical liquid. Viscous liquids such as treacle are non-liquids.	Water is not recognized as being a typical liquid. Viscous liquids such as treacle are non-liquids. Liquids are runny.	Water is a typical liquid. Liquids are runny.
Properties of gases	Gases are not materials. Air is not recognized as being a gas. They rise, therefore have no weight or negative weight. Gases are associated with heating and cooking, and are dangerous.	Gases are not materials. Air is not recognized as being a gas. They rise, therefore have no weight or negative weight. Gases are associated with heating and cooking, and are dangerous.	Gases are not materials. Air, carbon dioxide and oxygen are examples of gases. They rise, therefore have no weight or negative weight. Gases are associated with heating and cooking, and are dangerous. Have a smell. Are either visible or invisible.
Conservation of weight	Solids are heavier than liquids of the same material. Liquids are heavier than gases of the same material.	Solids are heavier than liquids of the same material. Liquids are heavier than gases of the same material.	Solids have the same weight as liquids of the same material. Liquids are heavier than gases of the same material.

Figure 6.2 How learning progresses: States of matter

can be described and that these properties influence the job that an object made from that material can do. In year 4, when teachers ask children to categorize objects using the solid/liquid/gas system, they must consider the properties of materials in order to make correct choices. Therefore, the KS1/early KS2

This is part of a discussion between two American 8–9 y/o about whether a small plastic 'baggie' of salt is solid, liquid or gas.

Terrance: [Takes the baggie of salt from the gases category.] Hold it. [He has a frown on his face.]
Joe: What you doing?
Terrance: I'm trying to see something! [He jiggles the bag of salt.] It doesn't keep its shape. That's one point for gas. But … but liquid is soft. [He looks at Alla, a research assistant, who is operating the camera.] Is liquid soft?
Terrance: [He holds the baggie over the center of the table to show Joe and then seems to be thinking while pouring the salt from one part of the baggie to another. He puts his finger to his chin and looks closely at the baggie.]
Alla: Is it gas?
Terrance: It is gas because it doesn't keep its shape.

Figure 6.3 What children have to say: States of matter (Varelas et al., 2008: 79)

activities described in Chapter 5 would be relevant for laying down the foundation concepts that are used more fully in year 4; for instance, asking year 1 children to think of describing words they could apply to familiar objects. Royce (2015) notes that getting children to interact with real materials in a hands-on way is important, particularly to show how the properties of a material remain the same even when its shape changes. She suggests asking them to make different shapes out of play dough and pour water into differently shaped containers to illustrate how properties are conserved. These properties are then used to categorize each material into solid, liquid and gas sets.

A common year 4 activity is to have a collection of real objects (i.e. not pictures) on a table with the aim of sorting them into solids, liquids and gases, using plastic hoops to sort and place the objects. Beforehand, do not share with the children the scientific criteria for sorting (Figure 6.1) and let them make their own errors in order to elicit preconceptions so that their current location on the learning progression can be ascertained. Later, teachers can reveal correct categories, justified by the criteria summarized in Figure 6.1. The same can be done with cards or pictures, which although it may remove the tactile and fun element of handling and inspecting real objects, it allows more 'exotic' materials such as water vapour, sea water and smoke to be considered. It needs to be made clear to children that when sorting using the solid/liquid/gas system that they need to think about what a material looks like and how it behaves, and discourage the use of sorting criteria based on functionality (what an object is used for) or origin (the place where an object comes from), such as when grouping together all objects found in the home. Do not forget to include the more challenging examples like toothpaste, treacle, jelly, ice cream, soap bubbles and powders such as sand. Making the material 'Oobleck' (Barcus and Patton, 1996), which is a simple mixture of two-parts cornflour and one-part water, makes for a particularly intriguing classification problem for children at the upper end of the learning progression. Oobleck is a non-Newtonian fluid that has properties of both solids and liquids at the same time and was mentioned in *Bartholomew and the Oobleck* by Dr Seuss (Geisel, 1949).

The issue of powders being considered as liquids appears early in the learning progression, so should be addressed in the initial period when solids are discussed, as should any reluctance to categorize hollow objects as solids. This idea and others, such as viscous liquids like honey not being runny enough to be classed as a liquid, are present throughout the learning progression and so tend to be the more strongly held. They can be tackled by referring to the criteria for inclusion into the liquid set, for example *honey takes the shape of the bottom of its container so is a liquid*. Some children at the top end of the learning progression will know that honey is not a solid because it does not have a fixed shape. Try to avoid miscellaneous sets or mixed state sets, otherwise children will start to think of things they are not sure of as having a mixed or intermediate state (e.g. soft solids such as plasticine). If children cannot decide between two sets, ask them which state does something fit into the most? With colloids such as the foam on washing-up liquid, two or more states are present in the same system. This can cause confusion and I generally advise at primary level that children try to allocate them to one of the three named states rather than introduce a fourth more 'woolly' set called 'mixed phase' or 'colloid'. Washing-up liquid foam, for instance, is made from liquid bubbles filled with gaseous air, but the predominant state of matter present in the foam is gas (by volume anyway), so it should be categorized as such.

With the focus on experiencing real materials, allow children to melt a small ice chip (around 1 cm^3) in their hands while they play with it with their fingers (Purvis, 2006). Ask them to make verbal comments about how they can see or feel the properties of the solid water changing as it melts to become liquid water. If desired, this could also be related to how the particles in solids and liquids are arranged differently, which is why the properties change. Another common approach to teaching the properties of states of matter is to have three syringes, filled with sand, water and air respectively (Oversby, 2004). Children compress each of the syringes in turn to show that solids and liquids are not compressible, whereas gases can be compressed because there are spaces in between the air particles, but not the sand or water particles. Oversby, however, advises us to be careful that the syringe with water is free of air bubbles, because otherwise it will be compressible. Particle theory can also be taught through role-play. Have the class in an open space and ask children to link hands for a solid, unlink and move around close to each other for a liquid, and run around freely in all directions for a gas. Useful analogies of liquid particles include the coloured ball-baths found in indoor play areas. Air is not seen as a typical gas until late on in the learning progression, thus to help children think more about air, use activities that enable it to be perceptible. For example, waft a large piece of card to create a wind, or outside in the playground have pairs of children run races with open umbrellas that catch air like a parachute. Adams (2006) recommends using fizzy drinks as examples of gases that can be seen, although this raises issues of mixed phase categorization, mentioned above. They can also be used to demonstrate that a gas has weight because, for instance, fizzy cola is actually heavier than flat cola.

Research exemplar: Sorting solids, liquids and gases

Varelas et al. (2008) describe a particular approach that helped 7–9 y/o in a Chicago elementary school make sense of a solid/liquid/gas sorting activity. They note that there has been a prevalent attitude in primary science education that older age groups pursue scientific enquiry to use and improve science process skills. Younger children, on the other hand, are deemed not to possess faculties that are well enough developed, their science experiences being limited to simply observing and describing phenomena (Metz, 2004). Contesting this, Varelas et al. argue that the literature supports the view that younger primary children are able to use reasoned explanations and link theory to their observations; children can, especially if given the chance to take part in collaborative talk with peers and the teacher, 'explain the "whys" of what they have noted and described' (Varelas et al., 2008: 66). Essentially, they believe if teachers can deliver lessons in which children take part in scientific enquiry that encourages argumentation, this will promote learning.

The focus activity used by the researchers will be a familiar one to experienced primary teachers (and a typical approach was described in some detail earlier in this chapter). Children were asked to sort a collection of familiar objects into the three sets of solid, liquid and gas. The difference between the researchers' activity and the typical approach is that the sorting task was preceded by having the teacher read out loud to the class a book that was an inherent part of a unit called ISLE (Integrated Science-Literacy Enactments), the aim of which was to encourage open-ended discussions between child/child, child/teacher and teacher/child. Thus, the pedagogy is constructivist in nature (see Chapter 1) and distinct from more traditional, teacher-led approaches. An integral part of this unit was the link with literacy, specifically the reading out loud of story books as primers for practical tasks. These books portray scientific ideas that are accurate and include scientific terminology. The teaching sequence required that a specific book was read out loud and then a task carried out by the children; then a different book was read followed by a new task, and so on. The lesson that was the focus of the research involved the book *What is the World Made of? All about Solids, Liquids, and Gases* (Zoehfeld, 1998), and was followed by the solid/liquid/gas sorting task (see Figure 6.4 for details). The researchers made observations

---

Research exemplar: Sorting solids, liquids and gases

Main learning outcome (for ages 7–9 years)
Understand how to correctly sort a variety of materials into solid, liquid and gas sets.

Introduction
Read out loud to the class the book *What is the World Made of? All about Solids, Liquids, and Gases* (Zoehfeld, 1998: 1–19) [available from Internet book stores in the UK]. This book focuses on the properties of the states of matter.

Hands-on sorting task
- Children work in small groups.
- Prepare a results sheet with three columns, *Solid, Liquid, Gas*, plus a final column where they write the reasons for their choices.
- Use the following objects (or similar): a bottle of liquid soap, a bar of soap, shaving cream in a baggie, a can of soup, a pencil, a drinking straw, a helium balloon, a non-inflated balloon, a piece of clay, a sponge, salt in a baggie, a baggie puffed up with air, a bottle of water, a piece of string, a tube of paint, and a rubber band.
- Carry out the task of sorting materials into the three states of matter. As each object is sorted, place it onto one of three pieces of A3-sized paper labelled *Solid, Liquid*, or *Gas*.

Discussion session
- Record and tally on a large piece of poster paper or the interactive white board the choices that children have made.
- Discuss as a class the reasons why children made these choices.

The success of this pedagogy relies on the teacher 'creating spaces' for collaborative (child/child) and dialogic (teacher/child or child/teacher) discussions. Encourage this by:

- Prompting children to think about having reasons for choices, and not just making random choices.
- Promoting the attitude that children should discuss their ideas with each other during the choosing task and not just do what one person in the group thinks.
- Repeating/summarizing children's answers so that the whole class can hear and understand.
- Challenging them to persuade both the teacher and the class that their choice was the right one, and welcome (polite) rebuttals from other children who wish to challenge this view.
- Finally, refer to the properties of matter table in the book *What is the World Made of? All about Solids, Liquids, and Gases* to show the scientifically appropriate groups.

Figure 6.4 Lesson outline for States of matter (adapted from Varelas et al., 2008)

using a video camera in two classrooms (second- and third-grade) and analysed their data using qualitative methods.

The researchers looked at a wide variety of classroom interactions and commented on how personal relationships can enhance discussion. These discussions revealed differences in how children and scientists interpret concepts, including criteria for belongingness to a solid, liquid or gas set. For instance, with the baggie of air, some children categorized it as solid because they thought the focal part of the object was the plastic baggie itself and not the air inside. Purposely allowing for the creation of spaces for free discourse helped make the teachers aware of what children were thinking, with ambiguous or difficult cases such as shaving cream or a baggie of salt further encouraging debate. This study was ethnographic in the sense that part of the research team spent a year working alongside the teachers and children. In contrast to most of the other 'research exemplars' summarized in this book, such a methodology does not rely on objective, quantitative measures of what children learned as a result of the intervention. Instead, the researchers made the assumption that if an intervention enhances skills such as argumentation, then learning will naturally follow.

7

Reversible and irreversible changes

A material can be changed from its original form into something else. For instance, liquid water can be frozen and become ice, a paper clip bent into a new shape, a spoonful of sugar made to dissolve in a cup of tea, or a piece of bread grilled to make toast. In primary science, changes in materials are of two types: *reversible* and *irreversible*. Reversible changes are non-permanent – we can always revert back to the original material(s) we started with. Therefore, the first three examples given above are all reversible changes, while when we toast bread the change is clearly permanent and so in science terms is irreversible.

The most common examples of reversible change that we present at primary level are state changes, with water being the usual exemplar due to its familiarity to children. As discussed in Chapter 6, materials can exist in one of three states – solid, liquid or gas – and can change from their current state primarily by the addition or subtraction of heat. Water in the liquid state can be cooled in a freezer to change into the solid state, becoming ice. However, if we warm this ice, it changes state once more, returning to the liquid state. This is the reason why all state changes – freezing, melting, boiling, evaporating and condensing – are examples of reversible changes: we can always revert back to what we started with. A different distinction is made between *physical changes* (which include state changes and dissolving) and *chemical changes* (otherwise known as chemical reactions), although this terminology is used more at KS3 than at primary level. A common belief is that all physical changes are reversible, although breaking glass or tearing paper are changes in the physical condition of a material that are clearly not reversible. Another term you may meet is *phase change*, which has the same meaning as state change. Before introducing the idea of state changes to children, their ideas about exactly how materials are categorized into the solid/liquid/gas system need to be confirmed (Chapter 6).

The water cycle illustrates a number of state changes working simultaneously within the same system. The processes can be thought of as a series of events that take place inside a closed 'vessel' that contains the atmosphere and the surface of the Earth. As with all materials, water changes its state principally according to the surrounding temperature. As liquid water on the Earth's surface in the form of rivers, lakes and seas is heated by the Sun, it evaporates, becoming gaseous water vapour. This water vapour rises until it reaches a certain height where it condenses back into liquid water, becoming a cloud. This happens because temperature decreases the further you get away from the Earth's surface, and when a particular cooler temperature is reached (the dew point), water vapour condenses and clouds form. The liquid water in a cloud is different to liquid water found in rivers, lakes and seas because it exists as very fine droplets, even smaller than the droplets of liquid found in, for example, a spray of perfume. Because the liquid water droplets are so tiny, they have very little weight and so are able to be supported by rising air currents, and this is why a cloud does not fall to the ground despite being made of liquid water. The conditions inside a cloud are often very turbulent and the liquid water droplets are constantly colliding with each other. If they stick together (coalesce), they become heavier and can no longer be supported by rising air currents, so fall as precipitation, commonly rain. The rain falls back into rivers, lakes and seas and the water cycle begins again.

Some changes are not reversible in the sense that we can alter a material in a permanent way. For example, if we cook food, we can never get back exactly what we started with and therefore in science terms such a change is irreversible. In primary science, the irreversible changes that we focus on are chemical changes, also known as *chemical reactions*. Cooking food usually involves chemical reactions taking place in order to change it into something more edible. A concept that lies at the core of understanding chemical change is that something new is always created – the starting materials undergo a transformation and change into the end materials. The two most common exemplars of chemical change presented to primary children are combustion (burning) and acid/base reactions (usually vinegar added to bicarbonate of soda). During any chemical reaction there are starting materials, called reactants, which interact with each other to make new materials, called products. During these interactions, atoms swap places. Figure 7.1 summarizes the chemical reaction that takes place when a domestic gas cooker is burning, the reactants being on the left side of the equation and the products on the right. During this combustion process, the gas methane reacts with oxygen in the air to create two new materials – carbon dioxide and water; Figure 7.1 illustrates how the various atoms have swapped places in order that the two new substances are able to form. Combustion and acid/base reactions are usually quite fast, although other reactions occur more slowly. Iron reacts with oxygen in the air over a long period to make the product rust (iron oxide).

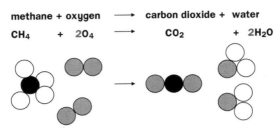

Figure 7.1 The combustion of methane

At primary level, we make the distinction clear to children that all state changes are reversible and all chemical changes are irreversible. But this is a simplification and not always the case, as many chemical reactions, including most of the biochemical reactions that are taking place inside our bodies right now, are actually reversible. As soon as the starting materials begin to react together and products are made, the products themselves start to react together or break down, reverting back to the very same starting materials, which then react together again to form products, creating a continuous 'cycle'. Reversible chemical reactions have always been excluded from primary curricula in England because of their complexity.

Children's ideas about reversible and irreversible changes

The evaporation of water

Science education research has focused mostly on state changes at the liquid/gas interface, that is to say, on children's ideas about evaporation and condensation, and water is used as the typical exemplar because of its familiarity. In particular, the evaporation of water has been a special focus of research and takes a prominent position in primary science curricula. State changes at the solid/liquid interface (i.e. melting and freezing) have received less attention probably because they are readily demonstrable in visual and tactile ways by melting ice or freezing liquid water, and children find it easier to understand such perceptually grounded phenomena. In contrast, evaporation and especially condensation are less familiar to children and require a degree of imagination and abstract thought because they involve the transformations of the invisible gas, water vapour (Löfgren and Helldén, 2008). Children have particular difficulty understanding that liquid water that has condensed on a cold surface, or in a cloud, comes from gaseous water vapour in the air, which impacts on their learning of the water cycle and other scientific models (see later).

Russell and Watt (1990) presented 58 English primary children with a scenario where water had been left in an open container and its level had gone down over a period of time. When asked where the water had gone, all 5–7 y/o who offered a response said that it had either gone into the ground (including a drain) or up to the Sun. Fewer 8–9 y/o gave these reasons, tending instead to focus more on the atmosphere as a destination for the water, specifically the air or the clouds. The most frequent responses of 10–11 y/o were also atmospheric in nature, with nearly 50% citing that the water had ended up in the clouds. Bar and Galili (1994) characterized a similar progression of stages that Israeli children pass through during the primary years. Children aged 5–7 years tended to think that evaporated water has disappeared – it simply ceases to exist. From 6 to 8 years they are more able to understand that in any system, matter must be conserved and so the water has to end up somewhere, with a common explanation being that it is absorbed by the surface of its container. At 9–10 years they began to understand that it rises upwards and its final destination is as water dispersed into the air, with Bar and Galili suggesting that this understanding is prevalent only when children reach 11–13 years. However, Johnson (2005) has argued that for children to fully understand what happens during evaporation, they need to be able to appreciate a simple particle model and visualize the movement of molecules during the process. This viewpoint underlines the approach taken with the research exemplar described at the end of this chapter. When generalizing evaporation to other liquids such as cooking oil, bear in mind that some people (including some teachers) incorrectly believe that only water or water-based liquids can evaporate (Chang, 1999).

Despite the focus on evaporation there is a surprising lack of research in primary science that has looked specifically at boiling as a different way that liquids can become gases. One small-scale study did find that many Korean primary children generally understood that during boiling, water turns into a gas, thus they may find the process of boiling more intuitively comprehensible than evaporation (Paik et al., 2004). Indeed, Stavy and Stachel (1984) note that when Israeli 6–8 y/o were asked what happened when water boiled away, they tended to conserve matter and understand that it became 'vapour', probably because the clouds of mist above boiling water are readily perceptible. This finding concurs with Bar's (1989) claim that an understanding of boiling naturally precedes one of evaporation.

Condensation is the least perceptible of the state changes

Few studies have explored primary children's ideas about condensation. The key to understanding this less familiar phenomenon lies in appreciating that there is a reversible change at work – the process of evaporation can be paired with condensation – and that one is 'the opposite' of the other. Russell and Watt (1990) asked children about whether it would be possible to get back water that had evaporated from a tank. Around a half of 5–8 y/o said it was not possible to get the water back, while many others argued it could come back as rain. Only one child mentioned the term condensation. Southerland et al. (2005) presented 8–9 y/o in the USA with a cold aluminium drinks can that was wet on the outside due to condensation and asked them to explain the source of the wetness. The children suggested causes that the authors characterized as moving from the simple to the more scientific. At the simplest level, the condensation appeared because the can was cold, with no further explanation given. Other children said that the water had seeped through the side of the can from the drink inside to the outside, or had evaporated out of the top of the can before condensing on the outside. The explanation children gave that was closest to the scientific model was that vapour in the room comes into contact with the cold surface of the can, cools and condenses. Similarly, Paik et al. (2004) found that 5–8 y/o were less able than 9–11 y/o to conserve matter when explaining the condensation on a cold glass. Most of the younger children could not say where the wetness had appeared from; however, the older children who could offer an explanation did not realize that a state change was involved and commonly used the water seepage model (Paik et al., 2004). Tytler (2000) examined Australian 6–7 and 11–12 y/o's ideas about condensation and found that the older age group understood to a much greater extent that during condensation, an exchange takes place between the air and the surface of liquid water. Children's ideas about evaporation and condensation have relevance to children's models of the water cycle, discussed in a later section of this chapter.

Melting and freezing

There has been even less research on primary children's ideas of melting and freezing. In one study, Paik et al. (2004) asked Korean children what made ice melt. The 5–8 y/o gave answers based on simple perceptual experience (e.g. 'because the wind is blowing'; Paik et al., 2004: 218), while 9–11 y/o mentioned that heat is required and often knew melting was associated with 0°C. The researchers found a similar age-related pattern when they asked about when liquid water freezes to become ice. Ross (2013) discusses a common idea expressed by English primary children when posed the question *will a block of ice melt more quickly when covered with wool?* Most children answer in the positive, but wrapping wool or any other insulation material around ice prevents the movement of heat from the outside atmosphere towards the ice, so slowing down the rate of melting.

Several studies with secondary pupils have focused on ideas of melting. In one small-scale study, Ross and Law (2003) presented data suggesting that pupils commonly (and erroneously) think that when liquid water freezes, it becomes heavier, and when it melts, it becomes lighter (this links with concepts of conservation of weight discussed in Chapter 6). The 11 y/o in the sample were more likely to have these ideas than the 16 y/o, possibly because they have the notion that when water freezes, the molecules are compressed more closely together, taking up less room, thus ice is more dense than liquid water (Osborne and

Cosgrove, 1983). Anyone who has taken ice cubes from a freezer knows the opposite to be true, that ice expands during freezing and so takes up more room than liquid water, which is why ice cubes are often difficult to remove from their tray. Because ice takes up more room, it is less dense than liquid water, which is the reason why ice floats.

Dissolving

Possibly because a proper understanding of the ideas behind dissolving requires knowledge of particulate theory, limited research has explored detailed ideas of dissolving among samples of primary children. In primary school, dissolving is usually kept at a practical level; for instance, learning how to make solutions of salt and water, then separating those solutions using evaporation techniques. In one study, Stavy (1990) noted weight conservation issues with some Israeli 9–15 y/o who thought that when a substance dissolves in water its weight disappears – that is, the original weight of the water = the final weight of the substance + water. Several studies of secondary and older pupils' ideas of dissolving have reported typical misconceptions, including confusing dissolving and melting, when something dissolves it becomes a liquid, weight decreases on dissolving (all Kingir et al., 2013), and dissolving is an example of a chemical change because it looks like new materials are made (Stavridou and Solomonidou, 1998).

The water cycle

The water cycle can be linked to two themes of the science education literature – state changes and the weather. Children's learning progressions with respect to state changes have been detailed in preceding sections and clearly, if children have not constructed scientifically appropriate ideas about evaporation or condensation, then this can interfere with their learning of the water cycle. In particular, children need to understand that water is a material that undergoes reversible changes of state and because of this can be freely exchanged between surface water and the atmosphere.

Children's changing ideas about the weather

A body of research has explored children's ideas about the weather and I will consider here those studies where the emphasis was on weather events that occur in the water cycle. Five-year-old children's ideas about clouds are usually limited to their possible source, such as clouds are made by God (Piaget, as cited by Bar, 1989). By the time they reach 7 years, they start to think about the composition of clouds, for instance, they are made of cotton wool (Philips, 1991). The idea that clouds are bags of water is prevalent in the early primary years, but decreases with age, while the more scientific view that clouds are water or contain water vapour increases steadily from age 5 to 11 years (Bar, 1989). The idea that the clouds are the source of rain seems to be well understood from 6 years upwards (e.g. Za'Rour, 1976).

It has been reported that 7 y/o have emerging ideas about how clouds are created that approach the scientific model, including empty clouds are refilled by the sea (Philips, 1991), and clouds are produced from vapour from a kettle (Bar, 1989). Alongside these concepts, ideas about precipitation develop. Children aged 7–9 years often believe melting clouds cause rainfall (Dove, 1998), while the idea that rain falls because a cloud becomes too heavy steadily increases in frequency between 6 and 14 years (Bar, 1989). Bar also found that children throughout the primary age range expressed the incorrect idea that rain falls when clouds collide, while Russell and colleagues' (1993) 5–7 y/o sample thought that collisions between clouds create thunder. At 5–7 years, clouds and rain are phenomena that are sometimes thought to occur independently from each other (Bar, 1989).

The water cycle as a whole process

When Israeli 9–10 y/o were questioned about aspects of the water cycle, they tended not to see different areas of surface water such as rivers, lakes and seas as being connected (Ben-Zvi Assaraf and Orion, 2010). They had more of a tendency to focus on the atmospheric parts in preference to the surface parts of the water cycle (ibid.). Children may see the water cycle as something that exists in a textbook, not viewing the process as something that is constantly happening around them (Shepardson et al., 2009). When Tytler (2000) looked at Australian 6–7 and 11–12 y/o's ideas about evaporation and condensation, many used the water cycle as a means to explain evaporation but none of the children used it to explain the less familiar phenomenon of condensation. As discussed in a previous section, part of the problem lies in the fact that most primary-aged children do not appreciate that an invisible gas, water vapour, is an essential component of the water cycle.

Irreversible changes

Many children find the concepts that underlie a scientific understanding of chemical change difficult to assimilate even in the latter years of their secondary education (Stavridou and Solomonidou, 1998). They sometimes have a restricted view of what constitutes a chemical change. Children can believe that chemical changes only occur as dramatic or unusual events, such as an explosion, fizz or colour change (Bouma et al., 1990). For them, these phenomena need to be perceptible – things have to be seen or heard, such as hissing, bubbling or blowing (Ahtee and Varjola, 1998). Given that the examples that teachers typically present to children involve combustion (burning) or acid/base reactions that fizz, such views are perhaps unsurprising. As with other areas of study in primary science, burning is used as an exemplar of a chemical change because of its familiarity: most children aged 8–11 know that burning gives out heat and light (Gabel et al.,

2001). But it must be borne in mind that if phenomena are familiar, then children will have preconceived ideas about them and some of these ideas may not correlate with the science that we ultimately have to teach. For instance, it has been established that children may use their own scientifically inappropriate words to describe burning, including melting and evaporating (Meheut et al., 1985).

Children find it difficult to conserve matter during irreversible change

Using data from the *Third International Mathematics and Science Study* (TIMMS), Liu and Lesniak (2005) looked at how American 8–9 and 12–13 y/o understood chemistry concepts. They found that the younger age group were able to comprehend more informal ideas about materials, including their physical properties, and changes that involved water and air. However, they had difficulty with concepts that involved conserving matter; for instance, some believed the idea that after an animal dies, its atoms vanish. In comparison, the older age group were beginning to understand ideas of the conservation of matter, which suggests that during the upper elementary school years in the USA, children will generally undergo these learning progressions (Liu and Lesniak, 2005). It is common for children of other nationalities to have problems with these areas of chemistry. They may think that instead of being converted into products as a result of chemical change, a burning substance disappears without trace, or is converted directly into heat energy (Watson et al., 1997). Alternatively, they may believe that products of a chemical change appear from nowhere, and are unrelated to the reactants (Pfundt, 1982). Problems with conservation include not appreciating that a chemical change means that something new is produced. Children often believe that burning results in a substance merely changing into a different form of the same thing (Watson et al., 1997; Smothers and Goldston, 2010), that the products were already present within the starting materials (Papageorgiou et al., 2010), or that during a chemical reaction materials simply mix together or separate, and nothing new is made (Nieswandt, 2001).

Evolving ideas about transformations of matter

Löfgren and Helldén (2008) carried out a longitudinal study in which they followed the ideas of the same 25 Swedish children over a period of six years (ages 7–13). The study focused on how materials change in given situations, or transformations of matter. In one of the three scenarios they presented, they asked questions about the disappearance of wax from a burning candle. Although over the years the children gave different responses from one another, there was a general pattern of progression over three stages. In the earliest years of the study, the children's answers were based on simple observations, such as wax runs down a candle and/or melts. In the middle years, children understood that the wax disappeared because it burned in the air and became smoke or gas. In the later years, the children's thinking developed to matter changing from one type to another and sometimes their explanations included the incorporation of a particle model. Between 7 and 9 years of age, one child (Inger) expressed ideas in accordance with the first stage of development, and only referred to the candle wax melting, or going back into the candle. At age 11 years, she understood that wax escaped into the air and became invisible, relating it to evaporation, analogous to stage 2. By the time she was 13 years of age, she appreciated that wax was being transformed, changing into something new, which is the reason why the wax had seemingly become invisible (stage 3). The burning candle is a common exemplar used in primary science to illustrate chemical change, despite many children having misconceptions about the process, including only the wick burns and the wax just melts (8–11 y/o; Gabel et al., 2001).

Physical vs. chemical changes

Although this semantic distinction is only made at secondary level in the programme of study (POS), children generally have difficulty understanding the difference between what makes something a physical change or a chemical change (as detailed by Driver et al., 1994). This is hardly surprising because there are notable grey areas, particularly as many physical changes such as breaking a glass mirror are irreversible. Gabel et al. (1999) provide evidence to suggest that the physical vs. chemical dichotomy cannot successfully be taught before the age of 12 years.

The best ways to teach reversible and irreversible changes

POS Year 2 – Uses of everyday materials/POS Year 4 – States of matter (find out how the shapes of solid objects made from some materials can be changed by squashing, bending, twisting and stretching; observe that some materials change state when they are heated or cooled, and measure or research the temperature at which this happens in degrees Celsius [°C])

It can be useful to introduce reversible changes alongside some simple irreversible changes so the two can be compared and contrasted. A simple way to do this is *not* to begin by talking about state changes, but to bend a metal coat hanger out of shape and ask children, *I have changed the coat hanger, but can I ever get back what I started with?* Bending the coat hanger back into shape shows that you can reverse the process, so the initial change was not permanent – it was reversible. Then, using a pair of pliers, snap the wire of the coat hanger to show that other types of change are irreversible – we can never return to what we had before

	Typically 5–7 years	Typically 8–9 years	Typically 10–11 years
Melting/ freezing	Cold is required to freeze water. Uses perceptual experience to explain melting and freezing, e.g. ice melts when it is placed outside. Wrapping wool around ice speeds up the rate of melting.	Cold is required to freeze water. Uses perceptual experience to explain melting and freezing, e.g. ice melts when it is placed outside. Wrapping wool around ice speeds up the rate of melting.	Cold is required to freeze water, which involves a change in temperature. When liquid water freezes to ice, it becomes heavier. Heat is required to melt ice. Wrapping wool around ice speeds up the rate of melting.
Evaporation	Evaporated water ends up under the ground/ absorbed by the surface of its container/has vanished without any explanation.	Evaporated water ends up as clouds or in the air.	Evaporated water is dispersed into the air (sometimes as gaseous water vapour).
Boiling	Boiling is a better understood process than evaporation. Boiling water becomes a gas, or 'vapour'. The source of 'vapour' is boiling water.	Boiling is a better understood process than evaporation. Boiling water becomes a gas.	Boiling is a better understood process than evaporation. Boiling water becomes a gas.
Condensation	It is impossible to get back water that has evaporated.	Evaporated water can come back as rain (without any further explanation). Condensation on a cold container is due to leakage of liquid water from that container.	Condensation is part of an exchange between the air and the surface of liquid water.
Clouds	Clouds are made of cotton wool/made by God/come from another place above the sky.	Clouds are made of water.	Clouds are made of water/come from evaporated water.
Rain	The source of rain is clouds. The sea is *not* the source of rain. Rain falls when clouds collide. Cloud collisions make thunder.	The source of rain is clouds. The sea is *not* the source of rain. Rain falls when clouds collide.	The source of rain is clouds. Rain falls when clouds collide/become heavy or cold.

Figure 7.2 How learning progresses: Reversible and irreversible changes

	Typically 5–7 years	Typically 8–9 years	Typically 10–11 years
Water cycle		Tendency to focus more on atmospheric aspects, especially evaporation, and less on surface aspects. Different 'areas' of surface water are isolated.	Tendency to focus more on atmospheric aspects, especially evaporation, and less on surface aspects. Different 'areas' of surface water are isolated.
Identity during chemical change	Can make simple observations of chemical changes.	Products disappear into the air/become smoke or gas.	During a chemical change, materials change from one form into another.
Combustion		Gives out heat and light. With a burning candle, only the wick burns, not the wax (which just melts).	Gives out heat and light. With a burning candle, only the wick burns, not the wax (which just melts).
Particle theory			Begins to understand how particles behave during a chemical change.

Figure 7.2 (continued)

and we have made something new. From this simple idea, you can demonstrate water freezing, evaporating, etc., and explain that these processes can similarly be reversed. Show state changes as pairs of opposing processes in a visual representation as melting vs. freezing, evaporation vs. condensation. Lott and Jensen (2012: 57) provide a good flowchart that helps children differentiate between chemical and physical changes (although this terminology is not used in the primary POS).

A 9–10 y/o Israeli girl's thoughts about the possible origin of clouds in the sky.

Researcher: How are clouds formed?
Child: There are fumes in the cloud.
Researcher: Can you imagine where the fumes come from? How did they form?
Child: From the kettle that went out through the window. When we make a barbeque there is smoke, then 'fumes reach the cloud'.
Researcher: Where else?
Child: From hot water that contains fumes.
Researcher: Can fumes be created from natural water resources such as the sea?
Child: In nature there is something that could happen that will make the fumes move into the clouds, a fire can happen.

Figure 7.3 What children have to say: Reversible and irreversible changes (Ben-Zvi Assaraf et al., 2012: 461–462)

I advise that melting be the first state change to be introduced, as children at the lower end of the learning progression find this the easiest to understand because it is straightforward to follow visually. Elicit familiar experiences of melting such as ice cream on a warm day, or chocolate melting in the hand (Ashbrook, 2006). Indeed, melting chocolate in a foil tray over a candle is a common exercise. When the melted chocolate solidifies once more, point out that the proper name for this is *freezing*, even though it takes place at warm temperatures. Ice hands can be made in the freezer by pouring water into disposable latex gloves and tying them off. Pose the children questions such as *will a woollen glove make the ice hand melt more quickly?* – this belief is prevalent throughout the learning progression. Encouraging the children to give simple perceptual reasons for why substances melt (e.g. *because it comes out of the fridge*) can form a secure halfway house before ideas about the addition and subtraction of heat are introduced.

Boiling should be introduced before evaporation, as the change from liquid to gas is more dramatic and easier for children to understand. For a simple demonstration, a test tube of water can be heated over a candle and over a period of several minutes boiling, the level of liquid will be seen to go down. Discussions as to where the liquid water has gone can lead to the idea that the air contains gaseous water in the form of water vapour and boiling causes more water vapour to be added to the air. Then introduce evaporation as a different way that liquid water can become water vapour, though unlike boiling, it is a constant process that can take place at normal temperatures. This is what causes that muggy feeling when it is raining outside and children come in wearing wet clothes – the liquid water from their clothes evaporates and becomes water vapour in the air . Children at the early stages of the learning progression may not have any idea where evaporated water ends up and so these discussions would help support their thinking in particular. Children at the opposite end of the learning progression will already understand these processes, so can be extended by introducing more advanced ideas such as percent humidity. Cross and Board (2015) recommend activities outdoors in the playground where children have the space to role-play the particles in solids, liquids and gases and how they change their behaviour in the respective states. One game involves drawing three large chalk circles and labelling them *solid*, *liquid* and *gas*. Start the whole class in *liquid*, then shout out 'boiling' – the children have to move as quickly as possible to the correct new circle (gas), and so on.

POS Year 4 – States of matter/POS Year 5 – Properties of everyday materials and reversible change (demonstrate that dissolving, mixing and change of state are reversible changes; know that some materials will dissolve in liquid to form a solution and describe how to recover a substance from a solution; use knowledge of solids, liquids and gases to decide how mixtures might be separated, including through filtering, sieving and evaporating; identify the part played by evaporation and condensation in the water cycle and associate the rate of evaporation with temperature)

Demonstrate types of reversible change other than state changes. Ask children to mix certain substances and then think about how the mixtures can be separated so that they can get back to the starting materials. Try mixing soil and water (separated by filtering), sand and water (decanting), iron filings and sand (magnet), and salt and pepper (rub a party balloon on your head to so that it acquires a static electrical charge, and it will pick up the tiny grains of pepper, leaving the salt). Dissolving is a reversible change that can be difficult to completely undo in a convincing way for children. It is a simple matter to dissolve a little salt in water and then leave the mixture on a radiator in a saucer so that the water evaporates, so returning the solid salt. However, the liquid water will be lost to the atmosphere. One way to overcome this is for the teacher to carefully heat the salt/water mixture in a foil cake tray over a candle, with a mirror held over the surface. A small amount of the original water can be collected as it drips off the mirror. Referring to the previous analogy, remind them that in a muggy classroom full of wet children, the windows quickly become misty when water vapour in the air touches the cold glass and condenses to become liquid water once more. Teaching the water cycle can be supported using the aforementioned activities, which are designed to help understanding about the state changes of evaporation and condensation. Parker (2015) describes how when teaching the water cycle to a year 5 class, she encouraged them to write a story from the point of view of a raindrop. The children then used the story as a basis for drawing flowcharts of the water cycle, writing a short play, etc.

POS Year 5 – Properties of everyday materials and reversible change (explain that some changes result in the formation of new materials, and that this kind of change is not usually reversible, including changes associated with burning and the action of acid on bicarbonate of soda)

Examples of simple irreversible change such as the breaking of an egg show in a visual, indisputable way that that we cannot go back to the starting point and we make something new – a broken egg. In comparison, with a reversible change such as melting an ice cube, we have not made anything new because we start with water in the solid state and end with water in the liquid state – the material itself (water) has not changed its identity. Some children will have difficulty appreciating that ice and liquid water are made from the same 'stuff' because perceptually the two forms have very different properties. One analogy is to explain that people can change their appearance (e.g. clothes, hair, makeup) or the way they behave, but they are still the same person, and this is also the case with materials during state changes. Typical practical activities at year 5 focus on the phenomenological events of a chemical change and how change can produce new substances that are different from the starting materials. Lott and Jensen (2012) suggest teachers cook simple foods such as pancakes in the classroom on a portable electric hob to give first-hand evidence of irreversible changes that can be used to fuel discussions. A common activity is for children to carefully burn everyday materials (candles, wood, paper, etc.) in a foil or sand tray, record what happens, and then compare the products with the reactants. Another long-established practical task involves mixing vinegar with bicarbonate of soda to produce copious amounts of fizzing as carbon dioxide gas is released. This reaction can be used to show how sometimes the product of a chemical change can be gaseous even when the reactants were not. Burning a candle is useful for demonstrating both chemical changes and state changes because solid wax burns to produce gaseous products, and all three states of matter, solid, liquid and gas, are present simultaneously. Children find many of the ideas inherent in understanding chemical reactions challenging because it requires them to conserve matter during transformations. Those at early points on the learning progression can be helped to progress by first reaching the halfway house concept that during burning, the fuel once burnt does not disappear but becomes something else – ash and smoke. Further progression would involve an appreciation that materials are totally conserved during a chemical change – that is, the weight of the starting reactants exactly equals the weight of the end products.

Research exemplar: Teaching state changes using multiple contexts

Tytler et al. (2006) describe a teaching approach that they carried out with a sample of Australian 11 y/o. In Australia, the concept of evaporation is introduced as part of the teaching of the water cycle. Despite the fact that this gives a good representation of how water is cycled through the atmosphere on a grand scale, it misses local effects such 'as drops drying in a closed room, condensation on cold surfaces, or how we smell liquids' (Tytler et al., 2006: 12). Instead of using the water cycle as a starting point, the authors designed a sequence of lessons to teach concepts of the evaporation of water using a particle model. Teaching children that matter is made up of atoms, molecules and ions (known collectively as 'particles') has never been a part of the English primary National Curriculum. Despite particulate theory being absent from the POS, it has nevertheless been taught at primary level and children have been able to understand, for instance, how particles are arranged in solids, liquids and gases. Skamp (2009) reminds us that a few overseas primary curricula refer to atoms, molecules and the particulate model, as do many primary science textbooks and websites in the English language, so there is an argument for inclusion despite the absence of statutory requirement.

Tytler et al. approached the problem from an atypical pedagogical standpoint. Instead of simply thinking about learning from a conceptual perspective, they emphasized the importance of 'scientific literacies', arguing that children construct different mental representations of a scientific idea depending on the ways it is presented to them.

> ... science is a mix of languages entailing multimodal forms of representation, where linguistic, numerical, and graphic and tabular modes are integrated to represent scientific explanations ... learning science effectively involves understanding different representations of science concepts and processes, being able to translate these into one another, and understanding their co-ordinated use in representing scientific knowledge. (Tytler et al., 2006: 12)

Thus, understanding a single scientific idea requires children to interpret and draw together information from a variety of very different kinds of sources, including literacies such as tables, graphs, text and diagrams (Norris and Phillips, 2003). Teachers need to bear in mind that children use this multi-modal approach when they learn science, so considering how each mode can be presented should be at the forefront when planning activities.

During their study, Tytler et al. worked with teachers to plan a sequence of lessons aimed to encourage children to construct scientifically appropriate models of how water evaporates. They used visual representations of water particles to help explain how invisible water vapour can exist in air, an idea that lies at the heart of understanding the evaporation of a liquid. The research was conducted and analysed using a qualitative methodology and involved classroom observations of three year 5 classes and post-lesson interviews with nine children. The classes took part in a series of practical tasks involving evaporation and condensation. After completing the tasks, children were asked to represent their ideas about evaporation in a multi-modal way that involved drawing pictures, physical hand gestures, verbal explanations and writing text. As part of this, a molecular model was introduced (for details, see lesson outline, Figure 7.4).

During the sequence of lessons, the researchers took notes about the ideas the children expressed and many were similar to the erroneous ideas reported in previous studies that have explored children's ideas of evaporation and condensation, as discussed in previous sections of this chapter. For instance, with the handprint activity, the water had disappeared because it had soaked into the paper towel, or the cold drink can became wet due to water from the inside seeping outwards through the metal. After the sequence of lessons, the researchers interviewed nine children in an attempt to determine their concepts of evaporation post-teaching. The simplest explanations children gave had the evaporated water ending up as a cloud in the sky, which suggests that they had integrated their knowledge with their previous learning of the water cycle. These children did not refer to a particle model in their explanations. However, the researchers found that several other children were able to confidently explain evaporation in a scientifically acceptable way using a particle model. These models included having particles of water distributed within the air, an idea which lies at the top of Bar and Galili's (1994) hierarchy of concepts of evaporation.

Research exemplar: Teaching state changes using multiple contexts

Main learning outcome (for ages 10–11 years)
Use simple ideas of the behaviour of particles to explain state changes.

Elicitation
In order to elicit ideas so children's current state of progression can be determined, at the start of the sequence ask them to write down or draw their ideas explaining why:

- A fish tank level goes down over time
- A puddle dries up
- Sugar dissolves in water
- An aluminium drinks can straight from the refrigerator becomes wet

Tasks for discussion
Plan a sequence of several lessons that includes the following tasks as presented in the order shown:

- Watch the teacher boil a frying pan of water.
- Show a tray of plastic beads and ask children to think about them as molecules of water breaking free of the liquid surface and entering the air. Discuss children's ideas as a class, aided by the teacher producing a scientifically accurate drawing on the whiteboard. The diagram should show molecules of liquid water becoming molecules of gaseous water inside the bubbles that are made during boiling. These bubbles burst and the gaseous water molecules escape into the air and spread out. This sequence links together multi-modal types of representation (diagram, verbal, physical model).
- Working in groups, children carry out further tasks where they attempt to explain what is happening by means of the particle model presented earlier, for example:

  1. Using an aluminium drink can containing ice water and with its top sealed with tape, discuss why the can becomes wet.
  2. With a wet hand, impress a handprint onto a dry paper towel. Draw around the hand and discuss what happened to the water.
  3. As a class activity, place a bottle of eucalyptus oil at the front of the class and ask the children to raise their hand when they are able to smell it. Explain what the particles are doing.
  4. Place a drop of acetone (nail varnish remover) onto a table surface and watch it evaporate.
  5. Create a puddle in the playground and observe how its level changes over a period of time. Ask the children to imagine they had a very powerful microscope, and to draw what the water particles are doing at the edge of the puddle.
  6. Similarly, keep an open jug of water in the classroom over a couple of weeks and record its level daily.
  7. Investigate how wet cloths dry in different conditions (outside, near the radiator, near the window, in a cupboard, on the teacher's desk, etc.).

Figure 7.4 Lesson outline for Reversible and irreversible changes (adapted from Tytler et al., 2006)

Although this sequence was successful in enabling children to construct scientifically appropriate models of evaporation, it was done in a limited setting using three classes in the same school, and the learning of only nine children was assessed in detail. Therefore, this qualitative sample cannot be confidently said to have been representative of the Australian year 5 population and generalizations should in this sense be tentative. There have been studies that claim that the particle model is very difficult for some children to grasp. For instance, Papageorgiou and Johnson (2005) suggest that particle behaviour with respect to chemical change should be reserved for only the most able in the upper primary phase. All this said, the apparent effectiveness of Tytler and colleagues' approach remains convincing.

8
Rocks

What exactly are rocks and where did they come from? To understand their origin, it must first be appreciated that the Earth has not always existed. Scientists believe that our planet was formed together with the rest of the Solar System about 4.5 billion years ago, when a huge swirling mass of dust and gas in space slowly came together due to gravitational attraction. Some of the mass became more compacted to form a spherical object – the early Earth. As this sphere continued to compact together, it became very hot, and materials liquefied, which made the Earth entirely molten. Volcanic activity was intense on the early Earth but it eventually began to subside as the Earth cooled down, making a solid crust appear on the surface, similar to how hot custard develops a solid skin as it cools. The crust developed cracks and became a jigsaw of huge plates that were, and still are, constantly moving. Oceans eventually appeared partly because water vapour in the atmosphere cooled and condensed, and partly from collisions with comets, which are made largely from water-ice and dust. All of these early processes are responsible for the present geology of the Earth, helping to provide a background to explain why there is an assortment of different kinds of rock.

Rocks can be divided into three broad types: *igneous*, *sedimentary* and *metamorphic*. Igneous rocks are made from either volcanic lava (e.g. pumice) or liquid rock called magma that has cooled beneath the Earth (e.g. granite). Sedimentary rock is usually formed when rivers that carry bits of rock reach the sea, stop moving and drop their load. These bits of rock become layers or *sediments* over time and as the bottom layers are squeezed by the weight above, they are compacted, dry out and become harder, eventually turning into sedimentary rock (e.g. sandstone, limestone). Metamorphic rock is formed when igneous, sedimentary or other kinds of metamorphic rock are heated beneath the ground or experience great pressure, which causes them to morph (hence the name) into something different. For example, if the sedimentary rock limestone is heated, it turns into a metamorphic rock (marble). On the early Earth there was no water, therefore rivers did not exist and so all rocks were either igneous or metamorphic.

Although the Earth itself is made from rock, this rock is not always visible on the surface. Over time, the surface rock erodes and weathers down to very small fragments which we call soil (although soil has other constituents as well). At primary level, children compare the properties of different kinds of soil such as 'clayey' and 'sandy', looking at, for instance, the particle size of the rock it is made from and how well a sample of soil holds water. Earth science in the form of rocks and soils is taught during KS2 within the year 3 topic *Rocks*, although rocks also appear in KS1 when properties of materials are linked to their uses (see Chapter 5). Fossils, which are found mainly in sedimentary rock, are also taught to year 6 as part of evolution and inheritance. There are opportunities for cross-curricular work with KS2 physical geography, such as when discussing earthquakes and volcanoes.

Children's ideas about rocks

What is a rock?

Children in KS2 are expected to identify examples of rocks that are found in the local environment, describe their properties and try to use those properties to classify them into igneous, sedimentary and metamorphic sets. Once different rocks have been classified into these sets, links can be made as to how they first originated. Before a rock can be sorted, a decision must be made as to whether an object is a rock to begin with (Happs, 1982). However, children's understanding of what the word 'rock' actually means can be at odds with the definition conveyed in the curriculum. Russell et al. (1993) asked English 5–11 y/o which objects they considered to be rocks. There was a tendency for 8–11 y/o to think that rocks are not smooth but need to be rough or jagged, with smooth samples instead being called pebbles. A few of these children thought nothing small could be rocks, and instead were called stones, possibly because a colloquial understanding of 'stone' is something that is small and that can be thrown. Geologically, irrespective of shape or size, objects are samples of rock because 'rock' describes the material that the object is made from and not properties such as mass or functionality. These ideas echo other research with secondary-aged children who believed that rocks had to be rough/heavy/dull (Happs, 1982), or hard/oddly shaped (Ford, 2003). As discussed in detail in Chapter 5, these responses are another example of children not understanding what 'a property' is, by not considering the difference between an object and the properties of the material it is made from (Ford, 2005).

How old are rocks?

When asked about how long rocks have existed, 5–7 y/o tended to think that they have been on the Earth for a very long time, though not forever, while some of the older children had the (incorrect) understanding that rocks have been present since the world began (Russell et al., 1993). Similarly, Blake (2004) found that many English 9–11 y/o thought that rocks are very ancient, perhaps millions of years old. Since the Earth is made from rock, then some rocks have clearly existed since the Earth's formation, though new rocks are being formed all the time as part of the rock cycle (see below). Trend (1998) explains that upper primary children can have difficulties grasping the vast stretches of geological time and that this can act as a barrier to understanding long-term geological effects. Regarding the ages of actual rock specimens, Ault (1982) found that some primary children thought that older rocks crumble more easily, or that colour indicates age.

Describing the properties of rocks

As stated, an important skill that children need to develop as part of a rocks topic is to observe samples and describe their properties, so that geologically appropriate sets can be created. Evidence suggests that primary children, particularly younger age groups, have difficulty when observing and describing relevant rock properties. Upper primary children usually explain rocks in unscientific ways. For example, Blake (2004) found that 9–11 y/o tended to use non-scientific, perceptual criteria when describing rocks, such as dirty/clean, heavy/light and big/small. Ford (2005) describes how 8–9 y/o in the USA made observations of rock samples. Despite a poster being on display in the classroom that told children to write about scientific properties of rocks, the majority (82%) wrote down simple descriptive words that recorded perceptual features, including colour, how dirty the rock was, texture and shape. The key property of hardness was hardly mentioned, despite the children spending the previous two weeks carrying out hardness tests on rock samples. Ford also found that some children used the word 'texture' in an everyday sense, meaning a surface was rough, sharp or smooth, instead of applying the geological definition of how firmly the constituent grains are stuck together (e.g. how crumbly a rock might be), which in turn affects how rough or smooth a rock feels. Because of this closeness in definition, it could be argued that the distinction might be less relevant; indeed, Trundle et al. (2013) note that in primary schools it has been common to incorrectly view 'texture' simply as how rough or smooth the surface of a rock might be. Ford concludes that children need their attention directing very specifically to relevant geological properties of rocks such as hardness and shininess, and away from size, shape, the fact it has holes, and so on. Only when relevant properties are considered can tentative links be made that explain how particular rocks were formed through igneous, sedimentary and metamorphic processes.

The origin and constituents of soil

Learning about soil can be linked to other topics in the programme of study (POS), such as living things and their habitats (Smith, 2010) and plant growth (Piotrowski et al., 2007). The main constituent of any soil is rock that has been broken down into tiny pieces by the effects of weathering and erosion, which is why soils have a gritty feel. Soil also contains humus, which is mainly dead and rotted plant material, as well as water and air spaces. Russell and colleagues' (1993) primary children were asked to list what they thought were the constituents of soil; their responses included mud, small creatures, plants, rocks, sand and stones. There was hardly any mention of water or air. More of the older children (10–11 y/o) stated that plant material was a constituent of soil. Only a few children knew that soil contains different-sized particles of the same rock ingredient, a factor that is important when assessing the properties of soils. However, when Brass and Jobling explored Australian 9–10 y/o's ideas of soil, some children gave more scientific responses. Examples of the constituents listed by different children were: 'nutrients, dirt, worms and stones' or 'sand, dirt, bark' (Brass and Jobling, 1994: 112–113). Other children mentioned rotting leaves and compost as constituents. That said, a different Australian study (Brass and Duke, 1994) uncovered that 6–9 y/o did not consider that air occupies a significant volume of soil, thinking that soil is a solid mass with no air spaces inside, and so soil-living animals need to breathe by coming to the surface.

When Russell et al. (1993) questioned children about where soil comes from, the most common response was that it has been moved here from another place, mostly from fields or garden centres. More 5–7 y/o gave this explanation than older children, something that might be connected with an anthropocentric view that the purpose of soil is so that people can grow plants. Conversely, none of the 5–7 y/o thought that soil had been transformed from something else, while some of the 8–11 y/o did express this belief, for instance, it had been eroded from cliffs. Geologically, it is appropriate to state that soil has been made from something else *and* been moved from another place (though not garden centres!). When the same children were asked whether rock could turn into soil, most 5–7 y/o thought that this was impossible because, for instance, rock is hard and soil is soft. An understanding of weathering is needed to appreciate how soil is made from larger pieces of rock that have been broken up. A common understanding of primary children is that weathering is due to human action and not slow, natural processes (e.g. a path has worn away because lots of people have walked over it). However, some 8–11 y/o understood that geological change involves rocks breaking up into smaller fragments due to weathering by water and sunlight (Russell et al., 1993). Different types of soils can vary in appearance, colour, size of particles, etc. When children were asked whether different types were actually soil, typical garden soil and peat were most commonly recognized as being soils. The least recognized were sandy and pebbly soils, especially by the 5–7 y/o. There are a number of studies of children's attitudes and knowledge relating to soil erosion in a conservation or environmental context (e.g. Gulay et al., 2010), although these belong more in the geography genre than in science education.

Earthquakes and volcanoes

Although not explicitly mentioned in the science POS, earthquakes and volcanoes are included in the KS2 geography POS and primary teachers have taught about them as part of a rocks topic because they are dramatic, engaging natural phenomena (Ramirez, 2006). Probably because of the non-statutory status of these geological events in the science POS, there is a relative lack of reference in the literature to primary children's ideas about them. One small-scale study by Ross and Shuell (1993) sampled American 5–11 y/o and found most were aware that an earthquake involved shaking and trembling. When asked what causes an earthquake, most children did not know, as was the case when questioned about what might happen beneath the ground during an earthquake. Children expressed a number of misconceptions about earthquakes, including earthquakes are volcanoes erupting, earthquakes cause volcanoes, and earthquakes occur as a result of high winds or tornadoes. Simsek (2007) uncovered a variety of non-scientific reasons given by Turkish 6–8 y/o, such as earthquakes are caused by boiling water underground, a flash of lightning, heavy rains, or due to God's intervention. Schoon (1989) found that many 10–11 y/o from Illinois believed that earthquakes were unlikely to cause severe damage in the near future in nearby Chicago, despite the fact that America's biggest earthquake to date had just occurred locally in the Midwest. This has echoes with the unexpected findings of a study of US university students' ideas about earthquakes, where those who had personally experienced an earthquake were generally less knowledgeable than others who had obtained information about earthquakes from the media, likely due to familiarity blindness (Barrow and Haskins, 1996). In contrast, Ross and Shuell (1993) found that 10–11 y/o who had experienced a major earthquake in their area two weeks before they were interviewed knew more about the causes of earthquakes than other children of the same age who had not.

When Dal (2006) analysed French 10–11 y/o's drawings of volcanoes, their ideas were simplistic and only partially scientific. Most understood that a volcano was cone-shaped and had an internal structure that contained lava but did not know the source of the lava other than somewhere vaguely underground. They thought that volcano formation took place very quickly (several years or less). Most were not aware that lava has a deep origin beneath the Earth's crust and that volcanoes form over very long periods of time, that lava flows form successive layers, or that volcanic activity is associated with wider geologic processes such as tectonic plate movement. Of course, children's difficulties in judging geologic time can interfere when learning about these aspects of volcano formation. Sharp and colleagues' (1995) English primary sample had different misconceptions, including lava comes from the Earth's core, and lava gets its heat from the Sun. Kalogiannakis and Violintzi (2012) asked Cretan 5–6 y/o their ideas about volcanoes (some

Greek islands have active volcanoes). They found the children had some very basic knowledge about the nature and causes of volcanic eruptions, including volcanoes spit fire and they are made when stones rub together.

The rock cycle

Rocks are classified with respect to how they were first formed during igneous, sedimentary and metamorphic processes, so it is helpful that children understand the rock cycle in order to inform their classification decisions, and also when describing the properties of rocks (Duff and Duff, 1993). Rocks are continuously being made and destroyed. Lava and magma from volcanoes cool and harden to become igneous rock, which over time erodes and weathers. Small pieces are washed into rivers and then into the sea, settling there to eventually become sedimentary rock. If sedimentary rock is heated deep underground, it can become molten and ejected from a volcano, thus starting the cycle all over again. Igneous and sedimentary rock can similarly be heated or undergo great pressure, turning into metamorphic rock.

The rock cycle should be taught after the individual processes of igneous, sedimentary and metamorphic have been introduced. Children find the abstract ideas that underpin these processes are often counterintuitive (Trend, 1998). Upper primary children find it difficult to link information about the properties of rocks to how the rocks were first formed (Trend, 1998; Blake, 2004). Primary children also have specific, non-scientific ideas about individual processes within the rock cycle. These include rivers have been dug by people (Dove, 1998), erosion occurs only during rainfall (Martinez et al., 2012), rivers flow away from the sea, towards land (Dove, 1998), all rocks are made by volcanoes (Ault, 1982), and volcanoes are made by the Sun's heat (Ross and Schuell, 1993). Learners of all ages have difficulty accurately judging geologic time and are prone to underestimates (Trend, 1998; Cheek, 2010), which will impact on understandings of the processes of the rock cycle. For instance, Kusnick (2002) examined the essays of trainee elementary school teachers in the USA and found the misconception that sedimentary rock can be created in a puddle, the process probably taking days or hours.

The best ways to teach rocks

POS Year 3 – Rocks (compare and group together different kinds of rocks on the basis of their appearance and simple physical properties; describe in simple terms how fossils are formed when things that have lived are trapped within rock)

	Typically 5–7 years	Typically 8–9 years	Typically 10–11 years
Defining 'a rock'		Rocks are always rough and jagged. Smooth samples are pebbles, not rocks. Small samples are stones, not rocks.	Rocks are always rough and jagged. Smooth samples are pebbles, not rocks. Small samples are stones, not rocks.
How long have rocks existed?	Rocks have existed a very long time, though not forever.	Some think that rocks have been present since the Earth began.	Some think that rocks have been present since the Earth began.
Describing properties of rocks	Use simple criteria when describing properties.	Use simple criteria when describing properties. Use descriptive words based on simple perceptual properties, e.g. colour.	Can describe a variety of properties.
Constituents of soil	Soils are made up of mud, small creatures, rocks, sand and stones. Garden soil and peat are archetypal soils; clay and sand are not soils.	Soils are made up of mud, dirt, small creatures, rocks, sand, nutrients, bark and stones. Garden soil and peat are archetypal soils; clay and sand are not soils.	Soils are made up of mud, dirt, small creatures, rocks, sand, nutrients, bark, compost, rotting leaves and stones. Garden soil and peat are archetypal soils; clay and sand are not soils.
Where has soil come from?	Soil has been moved here by humans from another place.	Some believe that soil has been transformed from something else.	Some believe that soil has been transformed from something else.
Weathering	Occurs due to human action, e.g. people walking over the ground produces a path.	Occurs due to human action, e.g. people walking over the ground produces a path. Some understand that water and the sun over time break rocks into smaller fragments.	Occurs due to human action, e.g. people walking over the ground produces a path. Some understand that water and the sun over time break rocks into smaller fragments.

Figure 8.1 How learning progresses: Rocks

	Typically 5–7 years	Typically 8–9 years	Typically 10–11 years
Rock cycle		Difficulties in linking properties of rocks to the way that they were formed.	Difficulties in linking properties of rocks to the way that they were formed.
Earthquakes	Earthquakes involve shaking and trembling. Non-scientific causes (e.g. a flash of lightning, heavy rains, God's intervention).	Earthquakes involve shaking and trembling. Non-scientific causes (e.g. a flash of lightning, heavy rains, God's intervention).	Earthquakes involve shaking and trembling. Earthquakes are unlikely to cause severe damage in the place where I live.
Volcanoes	Some very basic knowledge, e.g. volcanoes spit fire.		Volcanoes are cone-shaped and contain lava.

Figure 8.1 (continued)

An English 6–7 y/o explains how rocks were formed.

Child: God might have made stones.
Researcher: Have they been here a long time then?
Child: I think so, yeah.
Researcher: How long? Forever, or …
Child: … uh not forever … when God was born, he made the world and when he made the world, he thought, 'There must be people to make things'. He might have made the rocks because … he needed help.
Researcher: He made the rocks did he, or did people make the rocks?
Child: The people made the rocks and he made the rocks because they needed help, because, if they didn't have help it would take millions of years to do it.

Figure 8.2 What children have to say: Rocks (Russell et al. 1993: 47)

Because primary children tend to hold only a limited definition, establishing what 'rock' actually means should be done at the start of the topic by presenting a variety of samples that are smooth, jagged, large, small, etc. Passing around samples of pumice and iron pyrites (fool's gold), a very light and a very heavy rock respectively, can further stimulate interest. Trundle et al. (2013) recommend that links with the familiar are vital during the early stages of a rocks topic. Any children with a rock collection at home should be encouraged to bring it into school for the day. Attention should be drawn to rocks that have been used in the local environment (e.g. for buildings, walls, railway track ballast and patio floors). The reading book *If You Find a Rock* (Christian, 2008) is suitable for young children and discusses rocks they may come across in everyday life. A next step would involve using observation skills to describe rocks and compare their properties. A rock scavenger hunt can be a good introductory task, in which children walk around the school site and collect rocks of various size, colour and shape, and then describe their properties when they return to the classroom. Children's attention should be drawn towards the properties of the material (e.g. hardness, texture) and away from simple properties of the object itself (e.g. weight, size) in order to stimulate progress towards the top of the learning progression. Questions that have a focus on geological properties can be worded using simple language, for instance, 'does it have layers like some cakes? When you rub your rock, is it crumbly and do pieces flake off or is it not crumbly?' (Trundle et al., 2013: 47). Encouraging this type of thinking will help children move away from the mid-point of the learning progression and access the more abstract concepts.

Teachers sometimes ask children to draw and label their rock samples to help them focus on the size of the 'bits' of mineral that the rock is made up from, which helps identification. Once rocks are identified, properties can then be tested in practical ways in order that samples can be compared. A common activity is the hardness test, whereby samples are scratched successively with a fingernail, a coin and then an iron nail, and used to compare how well different rocks resist erosion and weathering in the environment (Whitburn, 2007). [Although technically, hardness is a property of minerals and not rocks (Trundle et al., 2013).] Another is adding vinegar: if fizzing occurs, then this shows that the rock (usually) contains calcium carbonate, examples of which are limestone and chalk. This can be related to chemical weathering of rock such as found with limestone gravestones and gargoyles. These become smooth over time, partly due to air pollution that creates acid rain, which dissolves the rock.

Although part of the geography curriculum, during a science rocks topic children can learn that the formation of pebbles in rivers takes place when rocks carried by water continually collide until they become smooth. This can be demonstrated by shaking sugar cubes in a glass jam jar with the lid tightly shut; after a minute or so of vigorous shaking, the cubes become rounded due to collisions with each other and the glass wall of the jar. Volcanoes and earthquakes likewise are more geography than science but are dramatic events, and videos of eruptions and tremors are engaging and can be linked to rock formation by relating them to the rock cycle. There is a well-known activity called *the choc cycle* where children bring in different kinds of chocolate bar which the teacher then heats up, etc. to simulate the rock cycle (search on the Internet for more details). Chapter 4 gives some hands-on suggestions about teaching fossils.

POS Year 3 – Rocks (recognize that soils are made from rocks and organic matter)

First teach the fact that the soil in a typical garden has not always been there – it was once something else. Establishing this important halfway house concept will allow further progression when children learn about the geologic processes involved in soil formation. Russell et al. (1993) suggest that in the early stages of the topic, children bring to school soil samples from their gardens at home for closer examination. At the same time, focus on what a soil is actually made from, since even children at advanced stages of the learning progression tend to give only partially scientific answers. Summarize that *soil = bits of rock + humus (rotting plant material) + water + air*. There are different types of soils and similarly to rocks, these types have different properties. Children can compare the permeability of samples by filtering water through them and determining which soils hold water the best. The property of permeability depends on the particle size of the constituents of each soil, with very sandy soils (large particle size, lots of air spaces) allowing water to pass through quickly, and very clayey soils (small particle size, few air spaces) providing a slower passage. This leads to discussion about farmers preferring an intermediate soil that can hold some water but still have air spaces. Be wary of the fact that even upper KS2 children may not believe that the more sandy or gravelly soils are indeed soils. Piotrowski et al. (2007) describe an activity in which children grow radishes in three types of soil in order to see the effect on plant growth: sand only, potting soil only, and sand with fertilizer (plant food). This activity makes clear links with concepts about plant growth, structure and physiology (see Chapter 3).

Research exemplar: Teaching rocks through multiple analogies

Blake (2004) looked at how upper primary children's ideas about the rock cycle can be supported by using an appropriate analogy that is easy for them to grasp. He was interested to what extent children described and classified rocks according to their origin, that is to say, whether they were formed by igneous, sedimentary or metamorphic processes. As discussed, the rock cycle comprises all of these three processes and connects them together. Primary children find it difficult to link information about the properties of rocks to how the rocks were first formed. Blake argues that in order to address this problem, we must consider the knowledge children have learned concerning rocks, as well as the ways in which they mentally organize this knowledge. He achieved this by giving practical tasks, questionnaires and interviews to 9–11 y/o from the North East of England before and after an intervention lesson. During the intervention, children were presented with an analogy of the rock cycle that was devised to help them better understand it – specifically, the processes involved when aluminium cans are recycled (Figure 8.3).

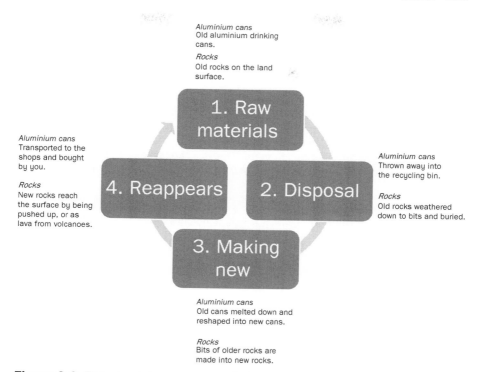

Aluminium cans
Old aluminium drinking cans.

Rocks
Old rocks on the land surface.

Aluminium cans
Transported to the shops and bought by you.

Rocks
New rocks reach the surface by being pushed up, or as lava from volcanoes.

Aluminium cans
Thrown away into the recycling bin.

Rocks
Old rocks weathered down to bits and buried.

1. Raw materials

4. Reappears

2. Disposal

3. Making new

Aluminium cans
Old cans melted down and reshaped into new cans.

Rocks
Bits of older rocks are made into new rocks.

Figure 8.3 The aluminium can story (adapted from Blake 2004: 1861)

Blake chose a sample of sixty 9–11 y/o from the same school and randomly divided them into two groups, experimental and control. He generated two groups of equivalent ability by matching them to intelligence test scores. Both the experimental and control groups were given the same introductory lesson, which focused on how different rocks have different textures and compositions (see Figure 8.4 for full details). The second lesson was different for each group. The control group received a lesson on the rock cycle without the use of analogies, and were given igneous, sedimentary and metamorphic rock samples which they had to match to the correct part of the rock cycle. The experimental group experienced a lesson that was the same as that of the control group, but in addition it was supported by the analogy of aluminium can recycling. Also, before the second lesson, the experimental group only were given an additional lesson about analogies.

Children's ideas were tested before and after the lessons in three ways. Blake first examined children's knowledge about rocks by using a practical rock task in which they were asked to describe rock specimens before placing them into groups of their own choosing. Next, the ways in which their knowledge was structured was explored by having them draw concept maps, and then undergo a word association test. Finally, semi-structured interviews were carried out with 18 of the children, nine from each group. After the lessons, the experimental

---

Research exemplar: Teaching rocks using a recycling analogy

Main learning outcome (for ages 8–11 years)
Be able to categorize rocks and explain the rock cycle in scientifically acceptable ways.

Introductory lesson
Compare different rock samples and make notes of their properties such as texture (including how 'crumbly' they are), the size of the bits that make up the rock (i.e. mineral grains) and others. This is a typical lesson that might be delivered during a primary rocks topic and would be familiar to experienced teachers.

Analogy lesson
This familiarizes children with how and why analogies are useful during learning. It does not have to focus entirely or even partly on rocks concepts.

- Address the question, 'what is an analogy?'
- Give examples, for instance: the shape of the Solar System is like a CD; cells in the human body are like the bricks in a building; atoms are like tiny solar systems.
- Ask children to make up their own analogies, and share them with the rest of the class.
- Inform children that analogies can sometimes cause inappropriate learning if people who use them take them too literally, e.g. with the analogy of an electrical circuit being like a bicycle chain, learners may believe that the particles (electrons) in the circuit move in single file only.

Rock cycle lesson
Earlier in the topic children will need to have learned about igneous, sedimentary and metamorphic formation as individual processes.

- Introduce the rock cycle by presenting children with a diagrammatic representation of the cycle, and then explain each process in turn. The rock cycle links together igneous, sedimentary and metamorphic formation to give an overall appreciation of geologic process.
- Explain how aluminium cans are recycled as a four-step process (see Figure 8.3).
- Tell the children that the aluminium can recycling is an analogy of the rock cycle and that you will be going to link them together.
- Connect aluminium can recycling with the rock cycle, one step at a time.
- Explain the analogy's limitations, e.g. the timescales for the two processes are very different.

Figure 8.4 Lesson outline for Rocks (adapted from Blake 2004)

group (analogy lessons) were able to describe rocks in more scientific ways than the control group and also classify rocks with respect to their origin as having been formed by igneous, sedimentary or metamorphic processes. The concept maps and word association tests showed that post-intervention, the experimental group had organized their knowledge in more scientific ways than the control. All of these differences were statistically significant and show that the experimental group had more knowledge of the origin of rocks, correctly relating samples of rock to the rock cycle, and had mentally organized this knowledge in ways analogous to how Earth scientists think about rocks. One limitation of the study is that it involved only two classes in the same primary school and information about the representativeness of the sample to the general population was sparse, which limits generalizability. Despite this, findings were convincing in the sense that the intervention did help these children learn about the rock cycle more effectively than might have been the case had they experienced a more traditional lesson.

9
Electricity

Electricity is the name that we give to phenomena associated with *electrical charges*, which can be either positive (+) or negative (−) and usually exist due to tiny, negatively charged particles called *electrons*. If electrons are added to an object, the object takes on an overall negative charge; if electrons are taken away from an object, it becomes positively charged. If the electrons are stationary, it is termed static electricity, whereas if they are moving around, it is called current electricity. Electrical charges can pass through some materials very easily (e.g. copper), but others not so easily (e.g. rubber) – these are called electrical conductors and electrical insulators, respectively (not to be confused with heat conductors/insulators).

One of the first people to write about electricity was the Ancient Greek scientist Thales of Miletus in the 7th century BC. He found that if he rubbed a piece of amber vigorously with animal fur, a static electrical charge would build up and, like a magnet, the amber would attract light objects such as feathers and straw (although this is an electrostatic effect and not true magnetism). In fact, the English word *electricity* is derived from *electron*, the Ancient Greek word for amber. More recently, scientists such as the American, Benjamin Franklin, discovered other qualities of electricity, including how it can be 'captured' and stored, and how lightning is a form of electricity. Eventually, electrical circuits were built and thereafter electricity was put to good use in the first electrical appliances, including the electric light. In the late 1800s, large and reliable electrical generators were developed, which enabled electricity to be routinely supplied from power stations for industrial and home use.

In the primary science programme of study (POS), electricity appears in years 4 and 6, with the focus mainly on building simple circuits and learning fundamental electrical principles by performing experiments. This usually is done using specialist kits that are made specially for schools and include components such as cells ('batteries'), wires, small bulbs, switches, motors and buzzers. Together with the practical skills required to build circuits, the basic concepts that children need to grasp are: components need to be connected to a cell at two different ends using wire; a circuit is a continuous loop or series of loops and if there is a break in a loop, electricity can no longer flow; and the 'amount' of electricity in a circuit depends on the number of cells and the voltage of those cells.

Children's ideas about electricity

The nature of electricity: Where does it come from and what does it do?

Even young children are quite familiar with many of the uses of electricity in domestic settings. Because of this, a frequent starting point for introducing an electricity topic in primary school is to elicit this relevant experience and ask, *where and how is electricity used in everyday life?* Perhaps unsurprisingly, Osborne et al. (1991) found that most of the responses English primary children gave to this question referred only to appliances found in the home and they did not mention non-domestic contexts such as street lighting, trains, and factories. With all ages (5–11 y/o), the most common responses were lights and cookers. Children aged 5–9 years also suggested televisions, telephones and irons, while the 10–11 y/o gave a wider range of examples, including radios, video players, washing machines and refrigerators.

Electrical appliances aside, Azaiza et al. (2012) surveyed the electrical ideas of 60 children in Israel (of Islamic faith) focusing on whether they thought electricity was associated with certain natural phenomena. The study was longitudinal and they sampled at two age points, first, when the children were 9–10 y/o and again when the same children had reached 11–12 y/o. The authors found that comparatively few of the children at 9–10 years of age attributed an electrical cause to thunder and lightning, or when taking off a sweater that produces sparks. However, this age group could correctly name electricity as the cause of rubbing a comb to attract small bits of paper, but tended to think that bioluminescent fish were associated with an electrical phenomenon (bioluminescence is actually caused by chemicals in cells that radiate light, similar to those found in 'glow sticks'). By the time the same children were 11–12 y/o, most held scientific views except with the knee-jerk reflex, correctly attributing an electrical cause to all of these phenomena apart from bioluminescent fish.

When Osborne et al. (1991: 50) asked children what 'qualities' electricity has, the most frequent responses were that electricity is dangerous, or is needed for energy/warmth. About half of their 5–7 y/o thought that electricity was linked to gas. When questioned about where domestic electricity comes from, very few of the younger children (5–9 y/o) gave an appropriate response; for example, some mistakenly thought that household electricity came from lightning or arrived by satellite (see Figure 9.3). About a third of the 10–11 y/o's answers were scientifically acceptable and referred to electricity originating from a power station. Similarly, many more of the 10–11 y/o gave scientifically correct answers as to how electricity travels (i.e. through wires).

Electrical conductors and insulators

Ideas about how some materials can conduct electricity better than others have been a long-established part of the primary National Curriculum, because electrical conductivity can easily be tested experimentally by building a simple circuit (see later). Osborne et al. (1991) looked at whether children were aware of whether materials were electrical conductors or insulators. The 10–11 y/o tended to correctly categorize metallic objects such as scissors, paper clips and cooking foil as being able to conduct electricity, and wax and cork as non-conductors. Although the 8–9 y/o gave similar responses, far fewer were able to provide an answer to the questions. Most 5–7 y/o were unable to provide any answer and many of those that did erroneously thought the scissors, foil and paper clips were insulators and cork was a conductor. However, after an intervention, Aydeniz and colleagues' (2012) small sample of American 9–12 y/o with learning disabilities made significant progress with their ideas of which materials were conductors and insulators that was still apparent 6 weeks later. This may suggest that these concepts are among the easiest for teachers to address during an electricity topic.

Fundamental electrical circuit concepts

In England, children build circuits in school in order to provide hands-on experience that will help them understand certain basic electrical concepts. However, children will come into contact with everyday electrical appliances at home and so have their own ideas about what electricity is and how circuits might work, and some of these ideas are at odds with those that teachers are trying to convey in the classroom.

Two fundamental concepts that need to be established are that for an electrical component to work, it must be joined to a cell ('battery') using two connections, and that there must not be a break in those connections. This idea might seem second nature to adults, but Tiberghien and Delacote (1976) were some of the first researchers to recognize that many children erroneously believe that a component connected to a cell by only a single wire will function adequately. Shipstone (1985: 36) called this 'the unipolar model' (Figure 9.1) and can be elicited by asking children to try to make a small bulb light by using just a cell and two wires; note that the bulb must be unmounted and not screwed into a plastic bulb holder. Children who hold this model may believe that electricity is delivered to components in the same way in which water is delivered down a hosepipe, along a single

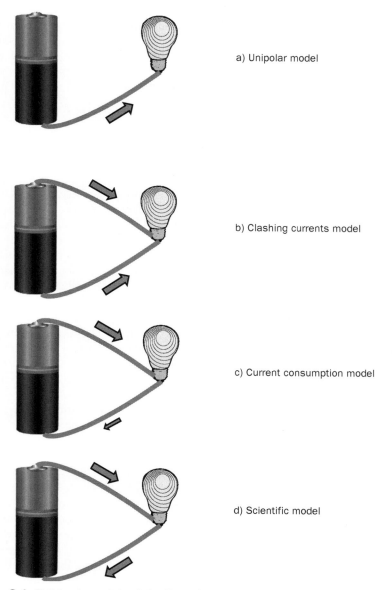

a) Unipolar model

b) Clashing currents model

c) Current consumption model

d) Scientific model

Figure 9.1 Children's models of the flow of electricity

connection and in one direction, and once it reaches the component it is consumed and lost forever (Shipstone, 1985). Osborne et al. (1991) found that around a third of 5–11 y/o thought a single wire that joined a cell to a bulb was sufficient to create a working circuit. Similarly, although just over a third of Glauert's (2009) sample of 4–5 y/o correctly predicted that a cell had to be connected to a bulb in some way for the bulb to light, they did not appreciate the requirement for two connections and a complete circuit. Clearly, children who hold the unipolar model have not yet understood the principle that for a circuit to work, it must be part of a complete unbroken loop. Its origins may lie in the fact that everyday appliances plug into a wall socket via what appears to be a single lead. Of course, this lead contains two discrete wires that connect the appliance with the electrical supply to form a complete circuit loop. The unipolar model is an example of what has been termed a *sink model*, where learners believe entities at an end point just disappear such as electricity, indicating a lack of conservation of elements within a system. Other sink models in science include part of the water cycle when learners think that water entering the ground after rainfall is lost forever.

An extension of the unipolar model is the 'clashing currents' model (Shipstone, 1985: 36) shown in Figure 9.1. Although children may connect a simple circuit correctly with two wires at opposite ends of the cell, they think that electricity is delivered down the two wires simultaneously to a component that then 'uses it up'. With this double hosepipe model, some children posit that electricity flowing through both wires meets at the component and then this clash of currents creates friction, which causes the component to work (Lee, 2007). As children learn more about circuits, many are able to provide sophisticated versions of this sink model, for example, offering a current consumption model where electricity is used up as it travels around a circuit (Figure 9.1). This view has been shown to be extremely common in upper primary children (Mant and Wilson, 2007), secondary pupils and adults, and even trainee secondary physics teachers (Shipstone, 1985). In contrast, Shepardson and Moje (1994) found that after instruction, a minority of a small sample of American 9–10 y/o were capable of understanding scientific ideas of current flow, although most had made no progress and still held one of the three erroneous models described above.

A third fundamental concept is that the amount of electricity within a circuit depends on the number of cells connected to the circuit and the voltage of those cells. Osborne et al. (1991) asked children what would happen if a second cell was added to a circuit. Many 8–11 y/o predicted that the bulb would be brighter as a result, which indicates they correctly appreciate that a cell gives something to a circuit to make it 'more powerful', a concept that is analogous to cell voltage. Hardly any of the 5–7 y/o, however, predicted this. Work with secondary students has consistently found that voltage is a difficult concept to teach. The term is used interchangeably with other electrical terms such as resistance, energy or power (Shipstone, 1985), and is often believed to be a force (Rhoneck, 1981) or part of the current (Osborne, 1983). For this reason, voltage is only usually taught in primary school at a very basic level linked merely to the voltage of cells, with cells of a higher voltage lighting up bulbs more brightly. However, observations such as adding more bulbs to a series circuit shows the bulbs becoming progressively dimmer, helps children construct the concept of a limited resource that is 'shared' by circuit components, which essentially is one way of thinking about voltage.

	Typically 5–7 years	Typically 8–9 years	Typically 10–11 years
Uses of electricity	Domestic use only (lights, cookers).	Domestic use only (lights, cookers, televisions, telephones, irons).	Domestic use only (lights, cookers, televisions, telephones, irons, radios, washing machines refrigerators). Starts to think about non-domestic settings (e.g. street lights, railways).
Electricity and natural phenomena		Electricity is responsible for rubbing a comb to attract bits of paper, and bioluminescent fish.	Electricity is responsible for rubbing a comb to attract bits of paper, thunder and lightning, and taking off a sweater that produces sparks.
Qualities of electricity	Electricity is dangerous; it is needed for energy/warmth; linked to gas.	Electricity is dangerous; it is needed for energy/warmth.	Electricity is dangerous; it is needed for energy/warmth; it originates from a power station; it travels through wires.
Electrical conductors and insulators	Poorly understood.	Metallic objects are conductors, non-metallic objects are insulators.	Metallic objects are conductors, non-metallic objects are insulators.
Models of electrical flow	Unipolar model common.	Unipolar model common.	Unipolar model, clashing current model, current consumption model common. Correct models of scientific flow begin to be understood.
Emerging concepts of voltage	Poorly understood.	Adding more cells to a circuit makes bulbs brighter.	Adding more cells to a circuit makes bulbs brighter.

Figure 9.2 How learning progresses: Electricity

Some English children's answers to the question, *where does electricity come from?*

Kelly Ann (9 years): I think electricity gets here by satellite.
Sonia (8 years): Electricity comes from God.
Alex (6 years): You buy it [from] shops [and] take it home.
Farrukh (8 years): Electricity is like lightning that comes from space – it hits the wires that are in the street and goes to the top of your house and makes the telephone work.

Figure 9.3 What children have to say: Electricity (Osborne et al., 1991: 26–27)

The best ways to teach electricity

POS Year 4 – Electricity (identify common appliances that run on electricity; construct a simple series electrical circuit, identifying and naming its basic parts, including cells, wires, bulbs, switches and buzzers; identify whether or not a lamp will light in a simple series circuit based on whether or not the lamp is part of a complete loop with a battery; recognize that a switch opens and closes a circuit and associate this with whether or not a lamp lights in a simple series circuit)

As discussed, an electricity topic in year 4 typically starts with the contexts that children are most familiar with, and limiting discussions to domestic uses can provide a halfway house for wider contexts. The teacher may bring a variety of household appliances into the classroom to create a table display and ask children to name them and describe what they are used for. Children can then sort the appliances into two sets, mains-driven and cell (battery)-driven, which leads on to discussions about these two distinct types of electrical supply. Children can then start to build circuits using the kits/components previously described. Teachers can begin by trying to elicit, and if necessary, reconstruct the unipolar misconception by the method described in a previous section using an unmounted bulb, two wires and a cell. Next, ask children to build the 'basic circuit', which is a cell with one bulb connected by two wires. This is the simplest series circuit and can be extended into more complex circuits by adding more components and wires. As discussed, different circuits are used as learning tools to help children understand fundamental electrical concepts. The unipolar model is fairly easily addressed during the course of circuit building when it becomes clear that two connections are required to the cell for a component to work. The clashing currents and current consumption models are found at the upper reaches of the learning progression and are more difficult to deal with. One approach is to use a household multimeter, which shows the direction of current in a circuit by giving either a positive or negative readout (Allen, 2014). Once direction can be established, this can lead to an understanding of the precise path that the current actually takes around the circuit. Measuring the current at different points in a series circuit shows that current is the same, and not 'consumed'.

POS Year 6 – Electricity (associate the brightness of a lamp or the volume of a buzzer with the number and voltage of cells used in the circuit; compare and give reasons for variations in how components function, including the brightness of bulbs, loudness of buzzers and on/off position of switches; use recognized symbols when representing a simple circuit in a diagram)

Adding more cells to a circuit increases the overall voltage, which makes bulbs brighter, motors run faster and buzzers louder. These phenomena illustrate the idea that voltage is an indicator of the 'amount' of electricity in the circuit. Scientifically, this 'amount' is current, although at KS2 children do not need to know this term, but teachers can introduce it if they wish because children will realize anyway that there is something travelling around a circuit 'making it go'. The idea of voltage is problematic at all stages of education (Shipstone, 1985) because of its abstractness – it is not something that can be visualized by learners because it is a quantitative measure of differences in potential; it is a number that we give to a circuit or part of a circuit in order to show how much current is able to flow. At its simplest level, voltage can be described at KS2 as a driving force for electricity, with the bigger the voltage (add more cells), the harder the electricity is driven around (bulbs are brighter). It could be argued that learners will have a more complete understanding of the interplay between current and voltage if they understand how energy is transferred within a circuit. However, Shen and Linn (2010) among others have found that teaching the idea of electricity as energy is beyond the understanding of most primary-aged children, as well as a significant number of secondary-aged children. There are some useful and free interactive 'circuit builder' websites available where children can drag and drop components to see the effect on bulb brightness, speed of circuit flow, and so on. These can be used as an introduction to drawing formal circuit diagrams because children will start to learn the meaning of circuit symbols.

There are opportunities for cross-curricular work when teaching an electricity topic, especially with Design and Technology (D&T), and English. *The Lighthouse Keeper's Lunch* (Armitage, 2007) can be used as a basis for designing and building a working lighthouse with bulbs and wiring. Other D&T topics, such as making flashing badges, controllable vehicles and security for a model island (including pressure pad burglar alarms), all require the building of mini electrical circuits. Interestingly, KS2 children have been expected to build parallel circuits in D&T lessons, but never in science. The fact that they need to know about parallel circuits anyway is one reason for introducing them in science alongside series circuits. American researchers Peppler and Glosson (2013) found that when they used a commercial innovation (*Lilypad*) based on sewing tiny electrical components into pieces of textile (called e-textiles), this helped primary children construct correct scientific ideas. They concluded that when children linked components by sewing in special thread that conducted electricity, this enabled them to visualize how current might be behaving (e.g. the direction of flow). Similar materials can be readily sourced in the UK from D&T education suppliers. Sandifer (2009) describes how a shoe box can be used to build a model of a house with multiple rooms, together with a working lighting system made from switches, bulbs and wires. There are several analogies that can be used to model how electricity flows around a circuit – Chapman (2014) describes a few of these in detail. One analogy is that the flow of electricity is similar to the flow of water in a domestic central heating system, with the water pump being analogous to the cell, water pipes to electrical wires, and radiators to bulbs. Of course, children are only able to make the link between the two models if they are capable of understanding how a central heating system works in the first place. Analogies have been found to be very effective tools in the teaching of electrical circuits, as will be discussed in the final section of the chapter.

POS Year 4 – Electricity (recognize some common conductors and insulators and associate metals with being good conductors)

Once children become confident with building circuits, they will understand that only complete circuits work; that is, if there is a physical gap in a circuit, then it will not work, because both terminals of the cell are not connected to the circuit. A variation of the basic circuit (see above) is used to test whether materials are electrical conductors or insulators. A gap is left in the basic circuit and a material is placed in the gap across two wires, physically completing the circuit. If the bulb lights up, then the material is a conductor because it has electrically completed the circuit; if the bulb remains unlit, then the material is an insulator. Davies (2014) has devised several 'magic tricks' that are fun and help engage children with such ideas as a circuit needs to be complete for it to work. For instance, using a commercially available, cheap toy called a 'ghost ball', a large group of children can stand in a circle and make an electrical connection by holding hands to make the ghost ball light up.

Research exemplar: Teaching circuits through multiple analogies

Chiu and Lin (2005) describe a study in which 9–10 y/o children from Taipei, China, were taught electrical concepts by means of activities that used analogies that helped link these concepts with everyday life experiences. As well as assessing whether any learning resulted from experiencing the activities, the researchers examined in detail how children's mental models changed during teaching. For some time, a consensus has existed about how analogies are good at enabling learners to connect 'a familiar domain to an unfamiliar domain'; for instance, the familiar domain of water flow to the unfamiliar domain of electrical flow (Chiu and Lin, 2005: 430). If children understand the principles of one concept, then these can be applied to a new concept, which can be especially useful when the new concept is challenging. The difficult nature of many electrical concepts that we present to children in primary school makes analogies especially useful tools. Chiu and Lin (2005) were particularly interested in using two analogies simultaneously to represent the same concept. Because every analogy is not an exact replica of the new

---

Research exemplar: Teaching circuits through multiple analogies

Main learning outcome (for ages 9–10 years)
Understand concepts relating to electrical circuits by means of two different analogies.

Before the lesson
The lesson is best taught near the end of an electricity topic when children have some familiarity with the concepts and with the practical skills of circuit building. The activities could take place over one or two lessons.

Activity 1: Predict. observe, explain
As revision, give children a variety of circuits to build and ask them to predict the brightness of bulbs, and/or the loudness of buzzers, speed of motors, etc. Typical tasks would involve asking how bulb brightness would be affected by:

- Increasing the number of cells (i.e. increasing the voltage)
- Increasing the number of bulbs
- Changing the rating of the bulbs
- Building the same circuit in parallel
- Adding larger components such as a motor or buzzer
- Adding a variable resistor (dimmer switch)
- Whether the brightness of one bulb is different to another bulb in the same circuit

The idea is to create cognitive conflict by introducing situations where children's predictions are not the same as the observed outcome during the experiment. When this is the case, ask children to try to provide an explanation as to why their prediction might have been incorrect.

Activity 2: Learning the analogies
Two analogies of electrical flow are presented to children – an obstacle race and a water system (Figure 9.5). The researchers ask children to read by themselves

---

Figure 9.4 Lesson outline for Electricity (adapted from Chiu and Lin, 2005)

some material that explains the analogies and then work on their own to answer written questions at the end. Essentially, this is a learning comprehension activity. Teachers might choose to adapt this approach to something that they think might be more accessible to their children, particularly if there are less able readers or there are significant numbers of EAL children in the class.

Similar activities could take the form of group tasks where children have to sequence a series of picture cards that are relevant to each analogy. The important thing is that children are given the opportunity to comprehend both (not just one) of the analogies and relate them to electrical flow. Figure 9.5 provides a description of the detailed elements of each analogy alongside the electrical concepts that they represent.

Figure 9.4 (continued)

Obstacle race analogy
Runners race around a track in one direction. The runners begin when they hear a starting pistol. There is a pit in the track where runners have to cross over a very narrow bridge, which slows the runners down. As each passes the start line, the starting pistol sounds again.

Water system analogy
A water pump at the bottom of the system pushes water up against gravity. The water is pushed via pipes through two water wheels, making them turn, and which slows the water down. Water re-enters the water pump, which pushes the water around again.

Electrical concept	Obstacle race	Water system
Current	Runners moving around a track	Water flowing through pipes
Wire	The track	Water pipes
Cell (battery)	Starting pistol encourages the runners	Water pump moves the water through pipes
Bulbs	Single plank bridge over a pit	Water wheels
Brightness of bulbs	Speed of all the runners	Speed that the water wheels spin
Resistance	Single plank bridge slows the runners down	Water wheels slow the water flow
Voltage	How energetic the runners are feeling (influences speed of the runners)	Speed of the water pump
Cell (battery) connects to the wire	The starting pistol connects to the track	The water pump connects to the water pipe
Wire connects to the bulb	The track connects to the single plank bridge	The water pump connects to the water wheels

Figure 9.5 Circuit analogies (adapted from Chiu and Lin, 2005: 438)

concept under consideration, it has limitations. For example, with the analogy of water flow representing electrical flow, gravity plays a part in water systems but does not influence simple electrical circuits. These limitations can inhibit learning, although if multiple analogies are presented, learners have a better opportunity to make several, different bridges between old and new, and limitations become less of an inhibiting factor.

A sample of 107 children aged 9–10 years from the same elementary school participated in the study. The children were assigned to one of four teaching groups, matched by ability so that the four groups comprised children of equivalent average ability; that is, any subsequent changes in learning could not be the result of one group being more able than another. In order to assess changes in their knowledge and understanding as a result of the intervention, the children underwent tests before and after the lessons; in addition, 32 children (eight per group) were interviewed individually. Each of the four groups experienced their own lesson, each presenting analogies in a different way, as follows: as a single analogy; as two analogies (one simple, one complex); as two analogies (both complex – *complementary analogies*); and no analogy. The sequence of activities that was carried out in the complementary analogies group is described in Figure 9.4, and the metaphors are outlined in Figure 9.5. The lesson began with a practical session in which children had to predict what was going to happen with, for example, changing bulb brightness in series circuits. Next, children were asked to read materials that conveyed the details of each analogy and answer written questions. The results of the post-test indicated that the complementary analogies group outperformed the other groups in the sample to a statistically significant degree.

10

Earth and space

The planet Earth is just one of many heavenly bodies that exist in the area of space we call the *Solar System*. At the centre of the Solar System lies the Sun, the largest object by far. The next largest objects are the eight planets, which all lie at different distances from the Sun, Mercury being the closest, and Neptune the furthest away. Beyond Neptune are regions called the *Kuiper Belt* and *Scattered Disc*, which contain the dwarf planets, including Pluto, Eris and Sedna. Beyond the *Scattered Disc* is a mysterious zone that astronomers cannot yet observe called the *Oort Cloud,*which is thought to comprise millions of comets and extends far off into space, nearly a quarter of the way next to our nearest star neighbour, Proxima Centauri. The outer edge of the Oort Cloud marks the boundary of our solar system.

Planets, dwarf planets and comets are not stationary in space, but move around the Sun in oval-shaped paths called *orbits*. The time it takes a planet to complete a single orbit is that planet's *year*, and the further away that planets are from the Sun, the longer their year. For instance, a year for Mercury is 88 Earth days, while for Neptune it is 165 Earth years. In addition to orbiting the Sun, the planets are also spinning, with the time taken for one complete spin being termed one *day*. Some planets spin very quickly and others very slowly; for example, a day on Jupiter is only 9 hours 56 minutes, while on Venus it is 243 Earth days (a Venusian day is actually longer than its *year*).

As the Earth spins, the Sun remains stationary, which gives the effect of the Sun moving slowly across the sky during the course of the day. This observation intuitively implies that the Sun is orbiting the Earth; indeed, for centuries scientists thought this to be the case, a view supported by religious dogma that maintained that the Earth lies at the centre of the universe. Only relatively recently (about 500 years ago) did scientists such as Galileo and Copernicus persuade others that the Sun was at the centre of the Solar System and the Earth was merely one of many lesser-bodies that orbited around it. Most of the planets have other heavenly bodies that orbit them – these are *moons*. Our own planet has one moon that takes approximately 28 days to complete an orbit around the Earth. Because the Moon is so close to the Earth, it exerts a significant gravitational pull on our planet, which creates the phenomenon of coastal regions experiencing two tides per day. Likewise, Earth's tremendous gravitational pull on the Moon means that we constantly see the same face of the Moon, which is locked into the same rotation period as its orbit around the Earth. In comparison, Jupiter has more than 65 moons but only four of them are large objects approximating in size to Earth's moon. The comparative sizes of heavenly bodies can differ to a large degree. If the Sun was the size of a basketball, then the Earth would be a peppercorn. If the Earth was football-sized, then the Moon would be a tennis ball. The Sun, Earth and Moon are approximately spherical, although the Earth is flattened at its poles thus making it very slightly egg-shaped.

Children's ideas about Earth and space

The planet Earth

Osborne et al. (1994) argue that the impression gained from everyday perceptions is so strong that young children's beliefs about the Earth being flat are overwhelmingly intuitive and so difficult for teachers to address. Piaget (1929) describes how one 9–10 y/o thought that to reach America (on the other side of the world) a train must travel underground through a tunnel that came out at the roof of America. Similar statements from children of various nationalities have been reported. Nussbaum and Sharoni Dagan (1983) found that most Israeli 7–8 y/o thought that the Earth is flat with space situated above the sky, or that the Earth is a hollow sphere where we all live inside on a flat plane. Children holding these views think that 'down' is in a single direction only, and have problems understanding that objects are attracted to the centre of a spherical Earth – they cannot explain, for instance, why Australians do not fall off into space. Some of Vosniadou and Brewer's (1990) American 5–7 y/o were aware that the Earth is a sphere but stated that there are two planet Earths – we live on the flat Earth, and there is a different spherical Earth out in space. Sneider and Ohadi (1998) similarly concluded that most of the 7–9 y/o in their US sample were essentially flat-Earthers. Some of Jones and colleagues' (1987) Australian primary children thought that the Earth, Sun and Moon are two-dimensional, possibly due to the fact that this is way they are depicted in book illustrations, though equally could be due to them being perception-driven flat-Earthers. However, when presented with 3D models, the majority of primary children in their sample chose a sphere rather than a flat disc to represent the Earth, though a quarter of 5–7 y/o preferred the disc. Vosniadou and Brewer (1992) suggested that children's concepts of the Earth's shape and gravity change only very slowly and gradually over time. In contrast, Sharp (1999) discovered that among a small sample of English 7 y/o who had previously been taught about the Earth in space, there were no flat-Earthers.

Children may also have difficulties recognizing heavenly bodies from pictures, and appreciating their relative sizes. Vosniadou and Brewer's (1990) American 5–7 y/o found it very difficult to identify the Earth and Sun in a picture of the Solar System, although three-quarters of 10–11 y/o could. Osborne et al. (1994) found that less than 40% of English primary children were able to place the Earth, Sun and Moon in correct order of size. Their 5–7 y/o commonly had all three bodies of equal size, while nearly a half of 10–11 y/o correctly thought the Sun was the largest object. The vast majority of Sharp and Kuerbis' (2006) English 9–11 y/o could draw scientifically acceptable depictions of the Earth and Sun, but only a third could do the same for the Moon. Only half of the sample drew the comparative sizes of the Earth, Sun and Moon correctly.

Day and night

Understanding the motion of the heavenly bodies can be problematic for children, as it involves mentally visualizing how each of them moves relative to each other. They frequently become muddled about which body orbits which and the durations of their orbits. Baxter (1989) found that nearly half of English 9–10 y/o incorrectly believed that the Earth goes around the Sun once a day to cause daytime and nighttime. Sharp (1996) obtained similar findings with his English 10–11 y/o. Further reasons given by these children to explain day and night include that the Sun and Moon swap places, and during the day the Moon hides behind clouds out of sight, while at night it is the Sun that hides behind clouds (Sharp, 1996). Related to this is the idea that the Moon only appears at night (Sharp, 1996; Plummer and Krajcik, 2010). Sharp's more recent work produced similar data, with less than half of English 9–11 y/o knowing that the Earth completes one rotation every 24 hours (Sharp and Sharp, 2007), while only a third of Sharp and Kuerbis' (2006) English 9–11 y/o drew correct diagrams depicting day and night. Osborne et al. found that the most common response of English primary children as to why day and night occur was that the Sun moved: '[the Sun] goes to America, then goes round the world' (John, 10 years; Osborne et al., 1994: 38). Over two-thirds of 5–7 y/o gave teleological explanations to explain why night occurs, including because people need to rest or go to sleep, which is linked to the anthropocentric nature of many younger children's thinking. However, more 10–11 y/o than the younger age groups correctly thought that day and night were caused by the Earth moving, with most attributing it to the rotation of the Earth on its axis (Osborne et al., 1994). Plummer and Krajcik (2010) explored US primary children's ideas about the Sun's apparent motion and found that although most 6–9 y/o understood that the Sun rises and sets every day, only a third of 6–7 y/o knew that it rises and sets on opposite sides of the sky, compared with two-thirds of 8–9 y/o. None of the children were aware that the Sun did *not* pass directly over-head. At a more basic level, and perhaps surprisingly, less than a third of English 5–7 y/o knew that a day comprised 24 hours when asked in a non-astronomical context (Osborne et al., 1994), which would clearly impact on understandings of an astronomical day (though the majority of 8–11 y/o answered this question correctly).

Despite being an everyday occurrence that one might expect children to be familiar with, Osborne et al. (1994) found that very few primary children could correctly draw the path taken by the Sun across the sky during the course of a day. The most common alternative model had the Sun remaining at the same height in the sky but moving horizontally in a straight line during the course of a day (usually from east to west), although some drew the Sun moving upwards in a vertical line from behind the horizon, then gradually climbing higher in the sky to a fixed point. When asked to draw the shadow of a tree at midday, 80% of 5–9 y/o and 50% of 10–11 y/o depicted scientifically incorrect shadows having inappropriate position and/or relative size, which corresponds with the problems that children generally have judging the orientation of shadows (see Chapter 12). Very few children could give a valid explanation of how a sundial worked.

The Earth's orbit

Geocentrism, the erroneous belief that the Earth lies at the centre of the Solar System, appears to be rife in a variety of cultures and age groups. For instance, Durant et al. (1989) found that two-thirds of English and American adults mistakenly thought that the Sun orbits the Earth. Jones et al. (1987) interviewed 8–9 y/o Australian children whose ideas were mainly geocentric, placing the Earth at the centre of their models of the solar system; in comparison, most 11–12 y/o were heliocentric, correctly placing the Sun at the centre. Osborne et al. (1994) similarly found that more than three-quarters of 5–9 y/o were geocentric, compared with only half of 10–11 y/o. Those children who were heliocentric also understood that the Earth takes a year to orbit the Sun. In a non-astronomical sense, less than a third of Osborne and colleagues' 5–9 y/o knew that a year was 365 days (actually 365¼ days), while most 10–11 y/o provided correct responses.

Since these earlier studies, time does not appear to have changed primary children's reluctance to accept heliocentrism. A recent study of Cypriot 9–11 y/o determined that 70% held geocentric models while only 18% were heliocentrists (Chiras, 2008). Similarly, only about a third of Sharp and Kuerbis' (2006) English 9–11 y/o held heliocentric beliefs; however, none were truly geocentric. Further examples of geocentric and heliocentric modelling were discussed in the previous section concerning children's understanding of day and night.

The Moon

Information about the orbital motion of the Moon is less well known than the corresponding facts about the Earth. Even though Jones and colleagues' (1987)

Australian 11–12 y/o tended to be heliocentric, some did not think that the Moon orbited the Earth, instead believing the Moon orbited the Sun like a planet (sometimes the Moon was drawn in the same orbit as the Earth). Plummer and Krajcik (2010) report that less than half of 6–7 y/o knew that the Moon rises and sets like the Sun, although nearly all 8–9 y/o were aware of this. As mentioned, the Moon is only a sixth the size of the Earth but the two are often drawn as being of similar size (e.g. Osborne et al., 1994).

Another common area of difficulty is the reasons behind why the Moon shows different phases over the course of a lunar month. Baxter (1989) found a large majority of English 9–10 y/o erroneously thought that the phases of the Moon were caused by the Earth's shadow (as did a similar proportion of 16 y/o) – this has been called the *eclipse model* (Trundle et al., 2010). Sharp's (1996) 10–11 y/o thought similarly, with other reasons for the Moon's phases including the idea that passing clouds cover part of the Moon. Some thought that all of the phases of the Moon appear during the period of one night, and every night, because the Earth turns on its axis during the night and we look at the Moon from slightly different viewpoints as the night progresses (Sharp, 1996). Similarly, none of Sharp and Kuerbis' (2006) English 9–11 y/o could explain the Moon's phases in a scientifically correct way.

Although most of Plummer and Krajcik's (2010) 6–9 y/o knew that the Moon appears as different shapes in the sky, hardly any 6–7 y/o were aware that these changes occur slowly, a little with each passing day, or that to progress through the complete cycle of shapes takes 28 days. In comparison, a half of 8–9 y/o could describe these phenomena. Children also have problems naming the different phases: most of Osborne and colleagues' (1994) English primary sample could recognize a full Moon shape but only around 50% could identify a half Moon. Before an intervention that involved recording the phases of the Moon over a period of time, Trundle et al. (2007) asked American 9–10 y/o to draw the phases that they expected to see. The most commonly drawn were full Moon and crescent Moon, with fewer half-Moon or gibbous phases being depicted. Only a third of the sample drew the Moon's phases in the correct sequence. Of course, this lack of knowledge would provide an unsteady foundation on which to interpret explanations of the reasons behind the phases.

Seasons

We experience different seasons in the UK (and elsewhere) because the Earth is tilted in space at an angle of 23.5°. This means that over the course of a year, the northern hemisphere of the Earth is either tilted towards or away from the Sun (or exactly in between, at the equinoxes). During a UK summer, the northern hemisphere is tilted towards the Sun, with the Sun appearing higher in the sky, and so there is a greater concentration of sunlight at the Earth's surface. This means the Earth is heated more intensely and because days are longer is also heated for more hours during the day. In winter the opposite happens, resulting in colder, shorter days. Baxter (1989) found that three-quarters of English 9–10 y/o thought the seasons were a result of the Sun moving closer to or further away from the Earth. Half of Osborne and colleagues' (1994) 8–11 y/o had the same view; in fact, this is a very common model that people of all ages use to explain seasonal change. Many of Sharp's (1996) and Baxter's (1989) 9–11 y/o also gave different, erroneous views of why seasons occur, including that in summer the Sun burns hotter or spends less time behind clouds, or that the longer days in summer are due to the Sun moving more slowly across the sky. Most English primary children were not aware that the Sun is much higher in the sky in the middle of the day in summer compared with winter, with many having the belief that the Sun is at the same height in the sky regardless of the season (Osborne et al., 1994). When asked to explain why day length varies throughout the year, no 8–9 y/o and only a fifth of 10–11 y/o were able to give an explanation that was at least partially correct (Osborne et al., 1994). Likewise, none of Sharp and Kuerbis' (2006) English 9–11 y/o described seasonal change correctly, while none of Plummer and Krajcik's (2010) American 6–9 y/o understood that the Sun's altitude in the sky changes with the seasons.

Planets and stars

There has been limited research on primary children's ideas about planets other than Earth, and stars other than the Sun, although the few studies that have been conducted reveal a number of non-scientific conceptions of planets and stars. About three-quarters of Sharp and Sharp's (2007) 9–11 y/o correctly knew that the Earth was a planet. However, when Osborne et al. (1994) asked primary children to place the Earth, Mars, Jupiter and Saturn in order of size, hardly any 5–8 y/o could do so, compared with a third of 10–11 y/o. Half of Sharp's (1996) English 10–11 y/o produced reasonably accurate diagrams of the Solar System that contained the Sun and all the planets, while all of the diagrams of the 6–7 y/o were incomplete and randomly arranged. Although they were successful at describing what kinds of objects the Solar System contained, very few of Sharp and Kuerbis' (2006) English 9–11 y/o could name all the planets, recognize pictures of planets, or knew how the planets moved in relation to each other (see Figure 10.1).

Osborne et al. (1994) tested English primary children to determine whether they knew the difference between a star and a planet. Children of all ages did poorly, although around a third of 8–11 y/o knew that the Sun was a star. Some of Sharp's (1996) 10–11 y/o did not think that the Sun was a star, but a planet on fire. They also considered stars to be smaller than the Earth because of their small size when directly observed in the sky. Among Plummer and Krajcik's (2010) 6–9 y/o, the idea that the stars appeared to move across the sky during the course of the night and rose and set like the Sun was poorly understood. Hardly any of the 6–7 y/o were aware that the stars are still present during the daytime but the sky is too bright to see them, compared with about a half of 8–9 y/o.

Figure 10.1 Relative sizes of the Sun and the eight planets (distances between heavenly bodies are not to scale)

The best ways to teach Earth and space

<u>POS Year 5 – Earth and space</u> (describe the Sun, Earth and Moon as approximately spherical bodies)

Because it lies at the lower and mid-points of the learning progression, and is a fundamental precursor to understanding other concepts, the starting point for a space topic needs to be establishing the correct shape of the Earth as a sphere and that we inhabit the surface of that sphere. Three-dimensional plasticine shapes can be put into a 'feely bag' and children have to guess which shape best resembles the Earth (Osborne et al., 1994). For elicitation of other concepts, Kibble (2002a) has produced some excellent cards that can be photocopied and used to elicit children's ideas about the Earth and space. The Solar System is an important reference point for children when they learn about space that will be constantly referred to throughout the topic, during discussions about planets, their orbits, day/year length, comets, and practically anything in the wider universe, including other star systems and even simple ideas surrounding big bang theory. It is therefore vital to ensure children construct an appropriate mental model of the Solar System. Commercially available 3D physical models are very good for illustrating the structure of the Solar System (e.g. orreries); these can be supplemented by videos of journeys through space that can be sourced online. Alternatively, children can build their own with modelling clay that reflect the

	Typically 5–7 years	Typically 8–9 years	Typically 10–11 years
Shape of the Earth	The Earth is considered flat, a two-dimensional disc, or a hollow sphere containing a flat area where we live.	The Earth is considered flat, a two-dimensional disc, or a hollow sphere containing a flat area where we live.	The Earth is spherical.
Relative sizes of heavenly bodies	The Earth, Sun and Moon are the same size.	Difficulties placing the Earth, Sun and Moon in the correct order of size.	Difficulties placing the Earth, Sun and Moon in the correct order of size (though the Sun is larger than the Earth or the Moon).
The reasons why day and night occur	The Sun rises and sets every day. Night occurs because people need to go to sleep. The Sun moves horizontally in a straight line across the sky during the course of a day. Difficulties in drawing shadows relative to the Sun's position in the sky.	The Sun rises and sets every day. The Sun moves horizontally in a straight line across the sky during the course of a day. The Sun moves across the sky because the Sun orbits the Earth. Difficulties in drawing shadows relative to the Sun's position in the sky. The Earth orbits the Sun every 24 hours.	The Sun moves horizontally in a straight line across the sky during the course of a day. The Sun moves across the sky because the Sun orbits the Earth. The Earth orbits the Sun every 24 hours. The Earth spins on its axis (although the fact the Earth spins once every 24 hours is not well known).
Earth's orbit	Models are usually geocentric (Sun orbits the Earth).	Models are usually geocentric (Sun orbits the Earth).	Models are usually heliocentric (Earth orbits the Sun), but can be geocentric.
Moon's orbit		Moon rises and sets like the Sun. That the Moon orbits the Earth is not well known.	Moon rises and sets like the Sun. That the Moon orbits the Earth is not well known.
Moon's phases	The Moon can take on different shapes.	The Moon can take on different shapes. Caused by the Earth's shadow (eclipse model).	Caused by the Earth's shadow (eclipse model). Starts to understand the cycle of phases.

Figure 10.2 How learning progresses: Earth and space

	Typically 5–7 years	Typically 8–9 years	Typically 10–11 years
Earth's seasons	That day length and the Sun's altitude in the sky vary with the seasons is not well known.	That day length and the Sun's altitude in the sky vary with the seasons is not well known. Seasons are caused by the Sun moving closer to or further from the Earth over the course of a year.	That day length and the Sun's altitude in the sky vary with the seasons is not well known. Seasons are caused by the Sun moving closer to or further from the Earth over the course of a year.
Planets	Draws pictures of the Solar System with the planets and Sun randomly arranged.	Earth is a planet. Problems with naming all the planets, placing them in size order and recognizing pictures of planets.	Earth is a planet. Able to draw the Solar System reasonably accurately, but problems with naming all the planets, placing them in size order and recognizing pictures of planets.
Stars	Unable to differentiate between a planet and a star. That the stars are still present in the daytime sky is not well known.	Unable to differentiate between a planet and a star.	Unable to differentiate between a planet and a star. Stars are smaller than the Earth.

Figure 10.2 (continued)

correct sizes of the planets, and to scale (it is more difficult to build a model of the Sun that is to scale because of its massive comparative size). Davies (2002) advises using photographs or video animations taken from the perspective of space instead of more familiar Earth-bound views. Even children at upper KS2 level can hold geocentric models, incorrectly believing that the Sun orbits the Earth, and these activities will help instil scientifically appropriate heliocentric models. Upper KS2 children can produce reasonably accurate drawings of the Solar System, which is a good halfway house for further work on naming the order of the planets and knowing their relative sizes.

Excellent videos are available free online that help illustrate in an effective way the difficult concepts that involve spatial reasoning skills that children will need to access in order to construct an appropriate mental model of the solar system. Lievesley (2009) reminds us that there is a wealth of science fiction films, TV and literature that children are already hooked into that can form a basis for engaging them with formal science ideas. Plummer (2009) describes how visits to a planetarium can help children's thinking make

A 7–8 y/o American boy's ideas about the motion of the stars. His responses suggest a lack of awareness of the fact that stars move constantly in the sky during the course of a night around a central point (the Pole Star), and that stars remain in the sky unseen during the daytime.

Interviewer: Do the stars move in the sky at night?
Child: Well, someone told me that the stars were little planets but they're like, like things that they can't land on.
Interviewer: Let's pretend that the flashlight's a bright star ... Let's say you see it there just after sunset when it gets dark out. Where will that star be at midnight?
Child: I think it would be just like there.
Interviewer: So would it stay in the same place?
Child: Yes.
Interviewer: Do we see the same stars in the sky all night long?
Child: I don't know'cause I'm still asleep at midnight.
Interviewer: That's a good point. What happens to the stars at the end of the night when the Sun comes up?
Child: I kind of see a little bit in the morning but when it gets towards the afternoon the stars fade away and go down.
Interviewer: Are there still stars up there in the sky during the daytime?
Child: Uhm, I don't know. I don't really see stars ... I don't think there is stars.

Figure 10.3 What children have to say: Earth and space (Plummer, 2009: 202)

significant bounds regarding a variety of astronomical concepts. The wider universe can be introduced by a card activity where children have to sort objects into size order; include *Moon, Mercury, Earth, Jupiter, Sun, Solar System, star cluster, galaxy* and *universe*. There is scope for stretching the more able children, for instance, by introducing advanced ideas like the sidereal day (a 'day' on Earth is actually only 23 hours and 56 minutes) and the barycentre of an orbit (the Earth and Moon are actually orbiting around each other).

POS Year 5 – Earth and space (use the idea of the Earth's rotation to explain day and night and the apparent movement of the Sun across the sky; describe the movement of the Earth, and other planets relative to the Sun in the Solar System)

Key definitions should be introduced early in the topic so that the terms *day, year* and *orbit* are clearly understood; this is especially the case with the first two of these terms because they have everyday meanings that differ from their astronomical meanings. Again, fairly early on children need to memorize the names of the planets and their order in distance away from the Sun, perhaps set as homework. Make it clear that there are eight planets in the Solar System and they can be learned using an appropriate mnemonic such as *My Very Eager Mother Just Served*

Us Nachos. Note that Pluto is no longer classified as a planet, but a dwarf planet – be wary that some textbooks still show the old classification system of nine planets.

Of all the bodies in the Solar System, the Earth, Sun and Moon should be most focused upon. Children are usually poor at estimating how their sizes compare, so teachers can show that if the Sun is the size of a basketball, the Earth is a peppercorn, and if the Earth is the size of a football, the Moon is a tennis ball (children are usually surprised about how small the Moon really is). As well as size, children need to understand how these three bodies move relative to one another. They can take part in a role-play in groups of three where each child plays either the Earth, Moon or Sun, moving around in circles to illustrate the various orbits (Davies, 2002). You can demonstrate rotation by having the children slowly spinning (be wary of dizziness). Children can learn about the historical events surrounding the change in scientific consensus from geocentrism to heliocentrism, examining the ideas of Ptolemy, Copernicus and Galileo.

To start a lesson about day and night, if it is a sunny day find a few shadows inside the classroom and make chalk marks at their edges. It is surprising how quickly the shadow moves away from the chalk marks (usually within a couple of minutes). This demonstrates that the Sun is slowly but continuously moving across the sky from east to west. This can be underlined by planting an upright stick outside in the soil and asking children to make hourly observations of the length and direction of its shadow. Working models of sundials can be easily calibrated to tell key times during the day: lunchtime, break times, home time, etc. (for details, see Kibble, 2002b). Establishing that the Sun is actually stationary and it is the Earth that moves is the next step, which can be explained by means of a globe of the Earth and a strong light source such as 150-W table lamp, or an overhead projector. This is best done in a darkened room. Project the light onto the globe and turn it slowly, emphasizing how the line between darkness and light is constantly moving, representing dawn or dusk taking place at different times around the world. Internet links (e.g. Skype calls) with a school in a different part of the world can help underline the concepts that embody day and night.

The same globe and lamp set-up can be used effectively to demonstrate the seasons by changing the orientation of the globe. In summer when the northern hemisphere on the globe tilts towards the Sun and the globe is spun slowly, point out that the time spent in the sunlight is longer, and also the Sun is higher in the sky from the perspective on an observer in the UK (and vice versa in winter). The set - up can also be used to show how the Moon rises and sets, again because of the Earth's rotation. As an introductory/revision exercise for seasons, use the interactive whiteboard for a drag-and-drop activity where children categorize simple statements that refer to one of the four seasons (e.g. *leaves fall, it is hot during the daytime, it gets dark very early*).

POS Year 5 – Earth and space (describe the movement of the Moon relative to the Earth)

The Moon's phases are notoriously difficult to teach, in part because it involves children imagining themselves placed at different positions within a physical model or diagram. In fact, some writers have argued that the concepts that underlie the Moon's phases are beyond the developmental abilities of primary children and should be left for secondary school (Stahly et al., 1999). First, they must understand that the shadow on the Moon that causes the different phases is *not* the Earth's shadow (the eclipse model, which emerges at an intermediate point in the learning progression). This can be done by having a white hockey ball in a strong beam of light so that one part is in shadow while the rest is in light – the part in shadow is what creates the different phases – this is not the Earth's shadow, but merely the Moon casting its own shadow on itself because it is a sphere. Show children that different phases are seen depending on the angle from which this shadow is viewed from Earth. A tasty alternative to teaching the names of phases (if done hygienically) is to use Oreo biscuits, which have a white crème centre covered with two dark chocolate wafers. Children remove different amounts of one wafer to reveal the white inside and so can make all the phases, placing them in their correct order of appearance. Keeley (2013) found that one successful approach to teaching the Moon's phases was to present a self-made concept cartoon to 5–8 y/o; by considering several competing hypotheses, the children's thinking was stimulated.

Research exemplar: Teaching the Moon's phases

Trundle et al. (2007) describe a study about the effects of an intervention on US primary children's ideas of the Moon's phases that involved directly observing the Moon over a period of nine weeks. They wanted to explore specifically children's knowledge about the names of the Moon's phases, the cycle of phases over 28 days and what causes the phases to appear. They were also interested in whether learning about the Moon's phases was potentially too conceptually demanding for most fourth-grade children.

The sample consisted of 48 fourth-graders (aged 9–10 years) from an elementary school in the American Midwest. The methodological approach was qualitative with children's learning being assessed from their drawings, and also their interview responses. Three tasks were given as pre-test and post-test in order to judge whether learning had occurred as a result of experiencing the intervention. The first task required children to draw all the Moon shapes they would observe over a nine-week period. The second asked children whether the phases had a predictable pattern, again over a nine-week period. The third task was only put to children who had answered positively in the second task. This subset of children was asked to draw the changing, predictable pattern of the Moon's phases. Interviews were then conducted where 3D models were provided so that

---

Research exemplar: Teaching the Moon's phases

Main learning outcome (for ages 10–11 years)
To understand the concepts that underlie the changing phases of the Moon by undertaking a long-term observational project.

Initial familiarization
The project is best started out at the beginning of a space topic, or even just beforehand, prior to any formal teaching about the Moon. Begin the process with a familiarization session. Take children outside to show them how to orient the direction of north, south, east and west by using distant landmarks on the horizon. This is important later when they record which part of the sky the Moon is located in on a particular day. Ensure that children are familiar with the names and appearances of different phases (full, half, crescent, gibbous, new).

Recording the Moon's appearance
Children will try to observe the Moon every day for the next nine weeks. This will only be possible if (a) the Moon has risen at a time that it can be seen in the daytime or evening, and (b) if the sky is clear enough to permit an observation.

- Each child creates a Moon calendar. Each day record onto the calendar:
  - The shape of the Moon (phase). It is important that the orientation of the Moon is correctly recorded (i.e. which side is dark/bright), as this tells whether the Moon is waxing or waning.
  - The part of the sky the Moon appears in (N, S, E or W).
  - Time of observation.
- For more able learners, measure/estimate the angle of the Moon in the sky.
- Once a week bring the class together and summarize the data they have collected, emphasizing how the phase of the Moon has changed a little each day. Show this visually on the board. If different children have data that do not agree, bring this up for class discussion and reach a consensus.

Analysis
After the nine-week period, children collate all of their data and seek patterns in how the phases change. Encourage them to discover these by themselves. For example:

- How shape changes gradually day-by-day. Explain that when the Moon becomes darker day-by-day it is *waning*, and when it becomes brighter it is *waxing*. Apply these terms to phases, e.g. *waxing half-moon* (when the dark side is on the left in the northern hemisphere).
- The time taken for a whole cycle from full moon to full moon.
- Draw a complete sequence of shapes that covers a whole cycle (28 days); cut-out shapes could be used for this exercise.

Ask children to use their findings to try to arrive at an explanation as to what causes the Moon's changing phases. Use the practical activities described in Chapter 10 as reinforcing opportunities.

Figure 10.4 Lesson outline for Earth and space (adapted from Trundle et al., 2007)

children could try to explain the causes that underpinned the Moon's changing phases (although only 10 of the 48 children were interviewed). They were also asked to use the models to show how they thought the Sun, Earth and Moon were arranged in the Solar System.

The intervention was based on material from the book *Physics by Enquiry* (McDermott, 1996) and required children to directly observe and record the Moon's phases on a daily basis over a nine-week period. Figure 10.4 provides further details of the intervention so that it might be tried out, if desired. Analysis involved coding the children's drawings, which were assessed to determine whether the depictions were scientifically accurate or inaccurate. Interview data were sorted into different categories according to the type of reason that children had given for the Moon's changing phases. Results showed that after the intervention children were far more aware of the full range of Moon phases than before and could accurately name the different phases. Similarly, they understood the correct sequence of phases that appear during the course of a lunar cycle to a greater extent after the intervention. In addition, after the intervention eight out of ten students gave scientific explanations of the cause of the phases of the Moon (the remaining two gave fragmented scientific reasons). Like some other studies summarized in this book, Trundle et al. did not include a control group. Thus it could be argued that gains in learning could equally have taken place using more traditional methods of teaching the Moon's phases that the school would have delivered if the research had not been conducted.

11
Forces and magnets

Refresh your subject knowledge: Forces and magnets

Much of what we teach about forces in school is based on Isaac Newton's work during the seventeenth and eighteenth centuries. Indeed, pupils at secondary level are expected to understand his three laws of motion and theory of gravitation. Newton's work on forces remains the bedrock for understanding a variety of physics topics, explaining, for instance, why some objects move and others remain stationary, the planets' orbits, electrical motors and even how light behaves. Forces concepts are therefore important precursors for learning about these other areas of physics. However, 'forces' is a topic where learners of all ages typically experience some difficulties. This is partly due to the fact that we cannot see forces directly and so the concepts that underlie their characteristics are quite abstract. Although forces are invisible, we can readily perceive their effects. We cannot see the Earth exerting its gravitational pull on our bodies but we still feel a constant force drawing us down towards the Earth's surface.

Forces topics are covered in years 3 and 5 and the programme of study (POS) specifically outlines frictional forces (including air and water resistance), gravitational forces, magnetic forces and the newly introduced area of levers, gears and pulleys. In its simplest terms, a force is a push or a pull. In primary school, the type of force that children probably spend the most time learning about is friction, which can be defined as *a force that acts in the opposite direction to another force, resisting its effects*. Children learn that when pulling an object such as a toy car over a surface, it can be harder or easier to pull depending on what the surface is made from. It is difficult to pull objects across sandpaper because its rough surface generates a noticeable frictional force that acts in the opposite direction to the pull. In contrast, adding cooking oil to a smooth surface such as glass reduces friction, being an example of lubrication. During these experiments, children measure frictional forces by using a piece of apparatus called a *Newton meter* (or force meter), resembling a spring balance that anglers use to weigh fish. Force is measured in units called *Newtons*, which are easily converted from kilogrammes by multiplying by 10 (e.g. 1 kg = 10 N).

Gravity applies a force on objects that is directed towards the centre of the Earth and this pulling force is called *weight*. Children can investigate gravitational forces by comparing how quickly different objects fall to the ground. Wide objects like parachutes fall slowly because they 'catch the air', generating more air resistance (a frictional force that acts in the opposite direction to weight). Streamlined objects such as paper darts fall more quickly because they have less of a frontal area and so create less air resistance. Theoretically, how heavy an object is has no effect on its speed of fall, so if an elephant and a mouse jumped simultaneously from the same diving board into a swimming pool they would both hit the water at the same time. Although beyond the primary curriculum, the nature of gravity is more wide-ranging in the sense that every object in the universe attracts every other object because all objects have mass. The Earth attracts us but at the same time we attract the Earth with an equal and opposite force – this is called a *reaction force*.

Magnet experiments are engaging for children and are used to teach the fact that like gravitational forces, magnetic forces can act when surfaces are not touching, unlike most other forces, which can only be applied when there is direct contact between materials. Every magnet has two poles, north (N) and south (S); when two poles are brought close together, unlike poles attract (N-S) and like poles repel (N-N or S-S). Magnets can only attract three materials: the magnetic metals iron (including steel), nickel and cobalt. In addition, a few non-metallic materials such as some iron oxides are also magnetic. Contrary to popular belief, other metals are not magnetic at all, including aluminium, copper, brass, gold, silver, chrome, zinc and bronze. Likewise, tin is non-magnetic, which is confusing because tin cans are – this is because what we call 'tin cans' are actually made from steel that have a thin coating of tin to prevent corrosion.

Levers, gears and pulleys is a new area within the year 5 forces topic. A fundamental concept is that these machines allow us to apply a bigger force by using a smaller effort, and so are 'force magnifiers'. A physically weak person can use a rigid steel rod such as a crowbar to apply a tremendous force to a jammed door using the principle of leverage. Bicycle cogs and gears convert pedal movement into wheel movement, greatly magnifying the distance travelled in the process. Pulleys allow us to lift weights while only applying a smaller force than would normally be required. Regardless of type, forces are often presented to children as pairs that act in opposition. For example, two tug of war teams each exert a force that pulls in opposite directions on a rope. If each team pulls on the rope with exactly the same force, then there is no movement either way – we call these balanced forces. If one team pulls harder, then movement takes place in their direction due to unbalanced forces. Forces being balanced or unbalanced dictates whether objects are stationary or in motion, although as will be discussed later, balanced forces can still mean an object continues to move.

Children's ideas about forces and magnets

Pushes and pulls

Most of the research focus on forces has been on determining secondary and post-16 students' ideas; nevertheless, the following sections summarize the smaller body of work that has utilized primary samples. At the start of a forces topic, children learn a simple definition of a force as either a push or a pull, but there are differences in the ways children interpret these two words. One study suggested that most English primary children understood that a push means movement forwards or away from your body and a pull means movement backwards or towards your body (Russell et al., 1998). This could be problematic in the classroom when, for example, a toy car on a string is pulled away from a child's body. There is evidence to suggest that learners tend to think a throw or a kick are neither pushes nor pulls (Driver et al., 1994); however, Russell et al. (1998) found that a minority of 5–6 y/o have correctly recognized them as pushes.

The topic of levers, gears and pulleys involves understanding a series of pushes and pulls in more complex systems, and since this is a new addition to the POS it is perhaps unsurprising that there is a scarcity of research focused on the primary age range. The original research on learners' concepts of how pulleys work was done by Gunstone and White in 1981 who used a sample of Australian physics undergraduates (see Figure 11.1). There has recently been some research activity in Finland in which primary children's ideas were explored (Hakkarainen and Ahtee, 2005; Ahtee and Hakkarainen, 2012), and many of Gunstone and White's misconceptions were apparent (e.g. 10–11 y/o thought that any mass that was hanging lower in a pulley had to be heavier).

Gravitational forces

Bar et al. (1994) asked Israeli children why some things fall when they are dropped and others such as clouds or aeroplanes stay in the air. Most 5 y/o and 8 y/o thought that an object falls simply because it is no longer being supported. By age 9 years, the dominant idea was that things fall because they are heavy, although some children were starting to think that an object falls because it is being *pushed down* by gravity. Among Reynoso and colleagues' (1993) sample of Mexican 8–10 y/o, explanations that included the idea of gravity as a force only appeared at 10 years. Russell et al. (1998) uncovered only basic

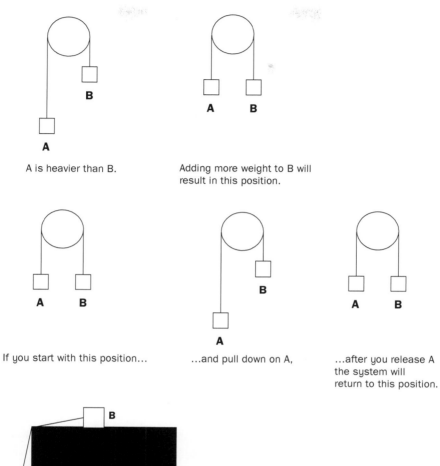

A is heavier than B.

Adding more weight to B will result in this position.

If you start with this position...

...and pull down on A,

...after you release A the system will return to this position.

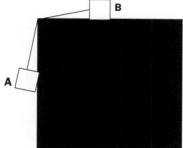

B is being held in position. If B is released, there will be no motion, because A and B are equal.

Figure 11.1 Some pulley misconceptions (see main text; masses A and B are equal; note that all of the examples show static pulley systems)

understandings among 8–9 y/o when asked to explain how gravity works: around two-thirds could not provide an answer, though others gave responses that described the effects rather than the mechanism of gravity (e.g. it keeps things down, or stops them floating away). A few children thought gravity was caused by the push of air, which corresponds with the findings of other studies that gravity cannot act in the absence of air (e.g. Bar et al., 1997). The idea of gravity requiring a medium such as air leads learners to believe that gravity does not exist outside the Earth's atmosphere (Twigger et al., 1994) or there is no gravity in water because there is no air (Stead and Osborne, 1980). Perhaps surprisingly, when asked about the direction of the force due to gravity, only a fifth of 8–11 y/o stated the direction was downwards, towards the ground; the other children in the sample could not suggest a direction of action, with no children mentioning that the force due to gravity acted towards the centre of the Earth (Russell et al., 1998). Many of these ideas can be related to a common-sense view of falling objects as things that do not require a force because falling is a natural phenomenon – it just happens (Halloun and Hestenes, 1985). In contrast, Ioannides and Vosniadou (2002) view the problems that children have understanding gravity as being linked to their concepts of weight as a property of matter (see Chapters 5 and 6). They conclude that younger primary children think that the force due to gravity (weight) is a property that belongs to heavy objects only, though in the later primary years this changes to the idea that a force is an internal property that is given to any object when pushed or pulled. Because of this belief, children cannot understand the difference between force and weight.

Russell et al. (1998) threw a ball vertically up into the air and asked whether gravity was acting (1) as it was travelling upwards and then (2) at the top of its flight. Half of the 8–9 y/o and a third of 10–11 y/o incorrectly believed gravity was *not* acting during the upward journey, seemingly because children found it difficult to associate a downward force with an object moving upwards. Most of the children thought that at the top of its flight, gravity was indeed acting. This corresponds partly with the (incorrect) idea that during its journey, an upwardly thrown object experiences the action of two forces – an upward pushing force and a downward gravity force. When a ball is rising, the pushing force is greater than gravity; once at the top of its travel, both forces are equal; when the same ball is falling, gravity is the dominant force (McCloskey, 1983). There is also a tendency for learners to think that gravity only acts when objects are falling and when they land on the ground, gravity no longer has an effect (Watts, 1982). Similarly, when children were asked whether gravity acts on a seated child, only a sixth of 8–9 y/o and under a half of 10–11 y/o believed gravity was acting (Russell et al., 1998), and some children think that with stationary objects a special kind of force holds them in place that is neither a push nor a pull (Keeley, 2011). An additional problem is misunderstanding what the word 'weight' means. For instance, with a book resting on a table, the book's weight is thought to be the force that it applies to the table, whereas in fact weight is the force that is applied by the Earth on the book (Viennot and Rozier, 1994).

It has long been established that the erroneous idea of heavier objects falling more quickly than lighter objects is very common in learners (from Champagne et al., 1980 to Hast, 2011), even among able students (Allen, 2010). This misconception may be related to the equally common idea that gravity only acts on heavy objects (Palmer, 2001). There is a well-known video clip available on the Internet from the 1972 Apollo 15 mission to the Moon where astronaut David Scott drops a hammer and a feather and both are seen to land on the Moon's surface at the same time. Children were shown the video clip and asked why the objects would not land simultaneously on the Earth. Despite the video clearly showing the objects falling due to gravity, over a quarter of 8–9 y/o and a half of 10–11 y/o stated that the objects land simultaneously on the Moon because there is no gravity on the Moon. Nearly all of the 5–7 y/o were unable to provide an answer (Russell et al., 1998). It is common for primary children to believe that there is no gravity on the Moon or in space generally, sometimes related to the belief that gravity only acts in the presence of air (Reyneso et al., 1993).

Friction forces

Although it could be argued that friction is the easiest type of force to understand because its effects are visually apparent and easily reproduced in the classroom, learners do experience some problems with conceptualizing it. For instance, friction is only thought to be present when objects are moving (Stead and Osborne, 1980), as is the case when an object is dragged across the ground. In fact, friction forces can exist with stationary objects; for example, when a car is parked on a steep hill with the handbrake on, it is friction between the tyres and the road that acts against the car's weight and prevents it from sliding down the hill. As is the case with gravity, friction is sometimes thought to be a generalized resistance to an object's motion with no direction of action (Stead and Osborne, 1980). Some studies show that young children have a limited or no understanding of friction in the form of the retarding effects of a rough surface on motion. For instance, Ravanis et al. (2008) found that most Greek 5–6 y/o did not predict that a smooth ball would roll further than a rough ball over the same surface. In contrast, a sample of English KS2 children appeared to understand what friction is in simple terms even without being prompted to think about friction specifically. When Russell et al. (1998) asked children why it is more difficult to ride a bicycle on grass than the playground, around a half of 8–11 y/o stated it was because there is more friction on grass. A deeper appreciation of friction as a resisting force constantly acting in the opposite direction to another force was not as commonplace. When asked directly whether friction was present when a book slid down a tilted ramp, about a quarter of 8–11 y/o thought that friction was acting only when the book was sliding, although another quarter correctly stated that friction was also acting when the ramp was only slightly tilted and the book was stationary. Children sometimes become confused because friction forces act in an opposing direction to a pulling/pushing force, and believe incorrectly that they are reaction forces (Stead and Osborne, 1980).

Although children understand that friction is present when objects are touching, especially when two surfaces rub together (Osborne et al., 1981), friction created in situations where there is no direct contact between objects is less well understood. Air resistance is a non-contact frictional force that acts to slow down any object travelling through the air. When children were presented with a scenario of a drinks can being dropped through the window of a moving car, none of the 7–11 y/o correctly used the idea of air resistance as a retarding force that would slow down the speed of the can (Russell et al., 1998). However, a small number of the 7–11 y/o could explain that air resistance was a force acting backwards on the can. About half of the 10–11 y/o and a quarter of the 8–9 y/o children described a 'wind' as something that blew the can backwards (Russell et al., 1998: 104). There are similar issues in understanding water resistance, including the idea that friction cannot occur with liquids (Stead and Osborne, 1980).

Forces on moving objects

In some respects, forces on stationary objects are simpler to understand than those on moving objects, for example, two tug of war teams pull with an equal force and there is no movement either way. The reason why a moving object moves in the first place can be explained by considering the forces involved. Newton proved that in order to make a stationary object start to move, a force must first be applied; this became the basis for his first law of motion. In the act of throwing a ball, you apply an accelerating, pushing force to the ball that stops as soon as the ball leaves your hand. Therefore, when the ball is in flight, there is no longer any forward pushing force on the ball. So why does the ball continue to travel forwards? Because you have thrown it, you have applied a force to the ball, which means that it will continue on its present path until acted upon by another force – this is one aspect of Newton's first law of motion. This idea is very counterintuitive and most people instead imagine that you impart some kind of internal moving force or 'impetus' when you throw the ball that is constantly pushing the ball's flight but gradually runs out and then the ball falls to the ground (Driver et al., 1994). In Ioannides and Vosniadou's (2002) Greek study, most primary children believed this idea. If you threw a ball in deep space, unless it collided with something it would carry on in a straight line for eternity because no other force would act on it to change its state of motion. On Earth, a thrown ball is pulled by gravity and slowed by air resistance, which have the combined effect of making the ball fly in an arc and eventually hit the ground. Therefore, as soon as the ball leaves your hand and you have stopped accelerating it, the ball is being constantly decelerated – that is, its speed is slowing down all the time until finally it stops. The motion of the ball is therefore a product of the interaction of two bodies – the ball and the Earth; however, Reiner et al. (2000) explain that learners tend to think of a force as a property of the moving object only, disregarding the influence of external factors.

When a driver in a stationary car pushes down on the accelerator pedal, the engine applies a force to the wheels and the car begins to move forward, and we can say the car is accelerating because it is increasing its speed. If the pedal is pressed harder, more force is applied to the wheels and the car's speed increases further – the car continues to accelerate. However, the engine force that pushes the car forwards is opposed by frictional forces that act to slow the car down. These frictional forces include air resistance on the car's body, wheel bearings that rub together and tyres pushing against the road's surface. When the forward engine force is equal to the sum of these backward frictional forces, this is a balanced system and the car maintains a constant speed. Learners have difficulty accepting that a car travelling in a forward direction has balanced forces acting upon it and instead think that there must be a dominant forward engine force, otherwise the car will come to a stop (Twigger et al., 1994). Only from about 10 years of age, children's understanding of friction is such that they begin to develop a proper grasp of how objects decelerate due to friction (Taylor-Tavares et al., 2009). Indeed, when Russell et al. (1998) asked 5–11 y/o what they needed to do to make a bicycle start moving, only a small proportion mentioned ideas about forces, all of them 10–11 y/o. When asked what an astronaut must do to stop a moving spacecraft in space, around a third of 5–11 y/o thought that turning off the engine would be effective, though just over a quarter of 10–11 y/o stated that a stopping force needs to be applied such as reverse thrust, which is the correct response. These ideas are beyond the KS2 POS but nevertheless are fundamental for a proper understanding of motion and so some schools do teach them, usually as enrichment exercises for able learners.

Magnetic forces

A few empirical studies have focused on primary children's ideas about magnetism; the findings of this work show that the same ideas about magnets emerge in geographically widespread samples. Piaget and Chollet (1973) found that children under 7 years understand that objects either stick to magnets or blow away from them. However, Barrow (1987) contends that children in this age group in the USA tend not to know which materials are magnetic and which are not. Some explain magnetic attraction as the effect of unseen glue on the magnet's surface, or see the effect as a magic trick (Barrow, 1987), although most younger children cannot explain the phenomenon (Erickson, 1994).

Older children aged 7–9 years are able to explain magnetic attraction as being caused by forces, pushes and pulls (Barrow 1997) or streams of energy-like rays that pull objects in (Piaget and Chollet, 1973; Erickson, 1994; Cheng and Brown, 2010). Most Israeli children of this age group believed air is necessary for magnets to work (Bar et al., 1997). Finley (1986) found that 7–8 y/o in the USA knew that magnets attracted metals but overgeneralized and assumed all metals are magnetic. They also thought the bigger the magnet, the stronger it is, and magnets can only influence objects they are in direct contact with (i.e. they cannot exert their effects over a distance). Christidou et al. (2009) assessed which materials Greek 5–6 y/o thought a magnet would stick to, finding that they did not generally know about which materials are magnetic; for instance, they included iron (correct), copper, gold, aluminium, wood and cloth (all incorrect). Fewer, though still significant numbers of children believed that paper, plastic, wood and glass were magnetic. Meyer's (1991) sample of Canadian 9–10 y/o thought that placing a thin barrier in between a magnet and an object would block magnetism, and that a magnetic field has a distinct cut-off boundary outside which there is no influence (magnetic field strength actually falls off gradually with distance). They also tended not to appreciate that the poles are the areas of highest magnetic field strength.

Primary children understand attraction better than repulsion (Barrow, 1987) and also sometimes equate gravity with magnetism (e.g. the force due to gravity is a kind of magnetism), or think that magnets will not work in the absence of gravity (Barrow, 1987; Bar et al., 1997). Although magnetism is traditionally taught alongside electricity in secondary schools because the two phenomena are closely interlinked, understanding these links is well beyond the KS2 POS, so magnetism is taught as a particular type of force and year 3 children encounter magnetic phenomena integrated within a forces topic.

Drawing force arrows

Although forces are invisible, we can represent them diagrammatically in school science by drawing force arrows. By convention, these arrows are drawn using a ruler, point in the direction in which the force is acting, and must touch the object that is being acted upon. Larger forces are drawn with longer arrows and smaller forces with shorter arrows. Thus, force arrows are representations of the size and direction of a force. Ivowi (1986) found learners generally have problems deciding which direction the arrows should face. Russell et al. (1998) presented a diagram of a bottle being lifted up in a person's hand, with two opposing force arrows showing unbalanced forces – that is, the upward 'lifting force' arrow was longer than the downward 'weight of bottle' arrow. When the researchers asked children to explain what the arrows told them about the forces, around three-quarters of 5–7 y/o did not say what the direction of the arrows meant, and hardly any could explain the size of the arrows.

The best ways to teach forces and magnets

POS Year 3 – Forces and magnets (compare how things move on different surfaces; notice that some forces require contact between two objects, but some magnetic forces can act at a distance)

	Typically 5–7 years	Typically 8–9 years	Typically 10–11 years
Pushes and pulls	*Push* is movement away from the body; *pull* is movement towards the body.	*Push* is movement away from the body; *pull* is movement towards the body.	*Push* is movement away from the body; *pull* is movement towards the body.
Pulleys			The mass that is hanging the lowest in a simple pulley system is the heaviest.
Gravitational forces	Objects fall because their support has been removed. Gravity only acts on heavy things because they alone possess the property of weight. Heavy objects fall more quickly than light objects. There is no gravity on the Moon or anywhere else in space.	Objects fall because their support has been removed. Gravity only acts on heavy things because they alone possess the property of weight. Heavy objects fall more quickly than light objects. There is no gravity on the Moon or anywhere else in space. Gravity does not act on objects travelling upwards. Gravity only acts on objects that travel downwards. Gravity does not act on stationary objects.	Objects fall because they are heavy. Gravity acts on an object giving it an internal force that makes it fall. Heavy objects fall more quickly than light objects. There is no gravity on the Moon or anywhere else in space. Gravity does not act on objects travelling upwards. Gravity only acts on objects that travel downwards. Gravity does not act on stationary objects. A minority of children give 'gravity' as the reason when directly asked why an object falls. Gravity does not act in a particular direction; it is a general phenomenon that just causes things to fall.

Figure 11.2 How learning progresses: Forces and magnets

150

	Typically 5–7 years	Typically 8–9 years	Typically 10–11 years
Friction forces	Do not recognize the retarding effects of a rough surface on motion.	Friction is recognized as acting in some everyday situations, e.g. riding a bicycle on grass. Friction acts on moving objects, but not stationary objects.	Friction is recognized as acting in some everyday situations, e.g. riding a bicycle on grass. Friction acts on moving objects, but not stationary objects. Air resistance is like a wind that blows on moving objects.
Forces on moving objects	A constant pushing force keeps a ball in flight. This force gradually runs out until finally the ball falls to the ground.	A constant pushing force keeps a ball in flight. This force gradually runs out until finally the ball falls to the ground.	A constant pushing force keeps a ball in flight. This force gradually runs out until finally the ball falls to the ground. A minority of children understand that a freewheeling object is constantly decelerating due to friction.
Magnetic forces	Magnetic attraction is better understood than magnetic repulsion. Magnets will not work in the absence of gravity. Very limited knowledge of which materials are magnetic. Objects stick to magnets or blow away from them.	Magnetic attraction is better understood than magnetic repulsion. Magnets will not work in the absence of gravity. All metals are magnetic. Bigger magnets are more powerful. Magnets work due to mysterious, invisible forces. Magnets only attract objects in direct contact with them. A thin barrier will block magnetism.	Magnetic attraction is better understood than magnetic repulsion. Magnets will not work in the absence of gravity. A thin barrier will block magnetism. Starts to appreciate that only certain metals are magnetic.

Figure 11.2 (continued)

A 7–8 y/o English child (incorrectly) describes why there is gravity on the Earth and the Moon. This is despite having some scientifically appropriate ideas about the gravitational interaction between the Earth and the Moon.

Child: The Earth spins at a very fast speed and the spinning pulls objects down … Earth has a very strong pull and the Moon has a light pull. The Earth's gravity holds the Moon where it is and [the Moon] can only move slowly because the Earth's gravity stops it moving.
Researcher: Why does the Moon have less gravity?
Child: The Earth's gravity holds the Moon in orbit and stops the Moon spinning fast and that's why it has less spin and less gravity.

Figure 11.3 What children have to say: Forces and magnets (Russell et al., 1998: 87)

As stated previously, at the start of a forces topic the word force is defined for children as being a push or a pull. Children in year 3 can carry out 10 actions of their own choice and decide whether they are pushes or pulls: opening a door, closing a door, throwing a bean bag, sucking through a straw, blowing a ping pong ball across a table, etc. A twist action to open a screw top bottle lid can be described as both a push and a pull. Keeley (2011: 29) suggests taking the class on a 'push and pull walk' around the school where children make note of the forces at work in their immediate environment. Year 3 children can be introduced to forces concepts using story books such as *Oscar and the Cricket* (Waring, 2007), although bear in mind that in general reading books need to be vetted for accuracy, since not all explain forces in a scientifically appropriate way (Barrow, 2000).

Friction forces are probably the simplest for children to understand. Children naturally appreciate the basics of friction as a retarding force in everyday contexts, so these initial ideas can make useful halfway houses and jumping-off points for more scientific explanations. Burton (2012) advises introducing the idea of friction as something that produces heat and allowing children to feel frictional heat for themselves. Start by getting children to rub their hands together and say that friction forces are opposing the movement of your hands, and this opposition makes heat. Then, using different grades of sandpaper, they can determine which sandpaper creates the most friction by rubbing their hands (lightly) across the samples and determining which sample produces the most heat. A common experiment is to run a toy car down slopes made of different materials and measure how far it travels across the floor, with the surfaces that make the car travel the least having the most friction. These activities are important for year 3 children, as those at the early stage of the learning progression may not initially be aware that roughness increases friction. King (2000) describes an innovative way to teach friction – build toy cars out of vegetables and use the results to discuss why some cars travel further than others when released down a slope. Air resistance can be demonstrated by having a race in the playground with open umbrellas. Parachutes or card spinners of different sizes are used as a basis for investigating how air resistance can affect the speed of falling (see below). Water resistance experiments include timing different plasticine shapes as they fall though a tall measuring cylinder of water, oil, etc., and pulling boats across the surface of water with a Newton meter.

POS Year 5 – Forces (explain that unsupported objects fall towards the Earth because of the force of gravity acting between the Earth and the falling object; identify the effects of air resistance, water resistance and friction, that act between moving surfaces)

Primary children can explore the effects of the gravitational attraction of the Earth, or gravity forces, by dropping different objects and comparing how long they take to reach the floor. Different factors can be changed, like the width of parachutes, how heavy each object is, and the material a parachute is made from. A template for making card spinners can be downloaded free from the Internet. Spinners resemble sycamore seeds and they can be made in different blade lengths, different blade widths, and their mass altered by adding paper clips. The common idea that heavy objects fall faster than light objects is quite difficult to address experimentally because unless a vacuum can be generated, heavy objects actually do fall faster (see the final section of this chapter for more explanation). However, if two differently sized marbles are dropped side-by-side in the classroom, then the fact that the larger marble hits the ground first is usually irrelevant, as any differences are visually imperceptible and require datalogger light gates that measure exact falling speeds by means of electronic sensors (Allen, 2010). Children at the early or mid-points of the learning progression can think that gravity works on only heavy things because they alone have the property of weight; some of the teaching approaches outlined in Chapter 5 concerning the properties of materials could be used in order to dispel this idea. Explain that properties depend on the type of material, not how heavy or light it might be.

POS Year 3 – Forces and magnets (observe how magnets attract or repel each other and attract some materials and not others; compare and group together a variety of everyday materials on the basis of whether they are attracted to a magnet, and identify some magnetic materials; describe magnets as having two poles; predict whether two magnets will attract or repel each other, depending on which poles are facing)

Magnet experiments and activities are engaging for children and are accessible to younger age groups. The learning progression usually starts with the belief that practically anything can be attracted to a magnet, proceeding to the idea of all metals being magnetic, ending with an appreciation that only a few metals can be attracted by a magnet. Children can test a tray of different objects with a magnet to see if they are magnetic, although it should be made clear that it is the material that the object is made from and not the object itself that makes it magnetic. The children will quickly notice that only metallic objects are magnetic, but not all metals, only iron (including steel), nickel and cobalt (although there are non-metallic ceramic magnets which are mainly oxides of iron). Wilcox and Richey (2012) describe a mystery box activity where a magnet is taped to the lid of a sealed cardboard shoebox. A variety of objects can be placed on the lid and the box is turned over and the object sticks, then it is made from a magnetic material. Children can devise ways to test magnets to see which one is the strongest, such as which magnet picks up the most paper clips. A simple compass can be made by stroking a sewing needle with a magnet, then attaching it to a plastic bottle top with a little Blue Tack or glue. When floated in a bowl of water, the compass will point to the Earth's magnetic north pole. A classic way to 'see' a magnetic field is to cover a magnet with card, sprinkle iron filings on the card and then tap gently – it becomes obvious that the poles are the areas of greatest magnetic field strength. Children can easily study the effect of unlike poles attracting and like poles repelling by moving a variety of magnetic poles towards each other. Magnets come in different shapes and sizes and children should experience a variety of these different types, which include bar, horseshoe, disc magnets and compass needles. A magnet hunt involves the teacher hiding a magnet somewhere in the room (e.g. inside a cupboard) and the children using plotting compasses to try and find its location.

POS Year 5 – Forces (recognize that some mechanisms, including levers, pulleys and gears, allow a smaller force to have a greater effect)

The effect of levers can be demonstrated in the classroom by the teacher showing how less effort is needed to shift an object such as piece of furniture using a rigid steel rod, crowbar or section of steel pipe. Block-and-tackle type pulleys can be ordered from educational suppliers and are usually customizable, so that different arrangements can be set up to give differing amounts of mechanical advantage. A bicycle gear system shows how one turn of the pedals is magnified by more than one turn of the rear wheel and so the bicycle travels further, with the smaller rear cogs (higher gears) having a greater magnifying effect. Bicycles can also be used to show how a gear system can transmit force over a distance (i.e. the force at the pedals is transmitted via the chain to the rear cogs). A circus of activities can be devised so that the class can experience different aspects of levers, pulleys and gears.

Research exemplar: Marble drop

I carried out a study (Allen, 2010) focusing on the common idea that heavy objects fall more quickly than light objects. The aim was to investigate the effect of a particular intervention that had been devised to encourage conceptual change in children who held this erroneous idea. The intervention was taught to three classes from the South East of England, two of them in a middle school

(10–11 y/o) and the other in a secondary school (11–12 y/o). The rationale behind the intervention was constructivist in nature, allowing learners to discover the scientific theory that explains a phenomenon by testing three hypotheses (only one of which is correct) against practical evidence they themselves have gathered during the lesson. Participants must judge which hypothesis best fits the evidence in the search for a scientific explanation. This approach illustrates the essence of real science – not as a body of facts to be rote-learned, but as trying out your ideas using empirical data directly gathered while observing natural phenomena. The phenomenon in question involved dropping two marbles of different sizes and judging which was falling the fastest (see Figure 11.4 for details).

In certain circumstances, professional scientists can be disposed to biased experimenting if they allow prior expectations about phenomena to influence their actions during experiments. Personal biases can lead to results that agree with what the scientist expected would happen, a kind of self-fulfilling prophesy. These prejudiced results often bear little similarity with what really happened during the experiment and have been termed *expectation-related observations* (EROs). Such actions can take the form of experimenters knowingly manipulating events so that the desired data are collected, though sometimes these actions are carried out subconsciously. The desire to confirm one's expectations with supportive experimental results can be so strong that at times EROs take the form of illusions, whereby observers think they see something that in fact is not there. The fact that schoolchildren can similarly be influenced by expectations and generate biased results during experiments is often not considered by teachers and is an under-researched aspect of school practical science. Children can come to science lessons with their own ideas about the concepts we are about to teach them, ideas that may be regarded by conventional science as being incorrect (i.e. misconceptions). If a learner's expectations are based on these non-scientific ideas, this can lead to the biased collection of data that confirm the misconceptions, and the subsequent failure of a lesson's learning objectives.

The intervention takes into account students' natural biases for the collection of confirmatory data. As discussed, making an ERO can be viewed as an improper experimental approach where unwanted outcomes are the result; however, during the activities, children are actually encouraged to make EROs. They are permitted free rein to allow their natural biases to influence their actions and record observations that did not really happen. At the end of the lesson when the scientific answer is revealed, children experience emotional responses that may facilitate meaningful learning of correct science, and subsequent successful recall at a later date. The lesson format is meant to play like a game, where participants compete with each other to try to guess what the scientific answer is going to be. The game culminates in the scientific revelation of the 'right answer' at the end of the lesson, which elicits feelings of surprise, awe, mild embarrassment, joy or amusement, as does the conclusion of any game when winners and losers are determined. This method is an elaboration of the so-called bluff approach that experienced teachers will be familiar with, where the teacher plays devil's

Research exemplar: Marble drop

Main learning outcome (for ages 8–11 years)
Know that heavy and light objects free-fall at the same speed.

Preamble
The idea that heavier objects will fall faster than lighter ones can be very difficult for children to refute. This lesson will allow children to test their ideas by comparing the dropping speeds of two marbles of different sizes.

Predictions
Simultaneously drop two marbles of different sizes. Say, *which marble is falling the faster, the big, the small, or do they fall at equal speed?* Children work in pairs and have one minute to discuss the problem with their partners and decide which response they think is scientifically correct. They record these predictions on paper. Write the names of the pairs onto a spreadsheet on the interactive whiteboard while children discuss the prediction – you will be recording children's decisions here in the form of a table as the lesson progresses. You may want to guide children's thinking by encouraging misconceptions by overtly stating red herrings:

- *The marbles might appear to be landing together, but look very closely.*
- *If a toy car and a real car are pushed off a cliff, which would be travelling the faster when they hit the ground?*
- *If you throw a golf ball and a ping pong ball high into the air, which comes down first?*

Verbal reporting of predictions
At this point children verbally report which marble they predicted would fall the faster – big, small or same. Record their responses on the interactive whiteboard.

Activities
Children will be dropping two marbles, one large one small, in attempts to test their predictions. They will carry out four activities in a set order. Children' observations will help them to discover the scientific answer. Demonstrate the first activity, then say, *let's go and discover the answer.* Children are given around 5 minutes to carry out this first activity, and write down their observation.

Activity A: Which looks faster? Children drop each marble singly, one at a time, not simultaneously, and assess which appears to be travelling the faster. Children write down their observation on a record sheet.

Verbal reporting of result for activity A. Bring the class back to their seats and ask children, *ok, what have you discovered?* At this point children verbally report to the whole class the marble that looked the faster – big, small or same. Make

Figure 11.4 Lesson outline for Forces and magnets (adapted from Allen, 2010)

it clear that they should only state which theory is supported by their observation, and not what they think the scientific answer is going to be. Record their responses on the interactive whiteboard. Repeat the same procedure with the rest of the activities, first briefly demonstrating each activity before allowing around 5 minutes for data collection, and then bringing the class back to their seats for verbal reporting of results each time.

Activity B: Marble race. The two marbles are dropped simultaneously this time, from around eye level, onto the table. The child in each pair not dropping the marbles can don safety glasses and place their head close to the table surface, so gaining a good view as to which one lands first.

Activity C: More marble races. Repeat the marble race activity but this time from a higher point, with children standing on a chair or table top (with care) and dropping marbles onto the floor. Drop the two marbles simultaneously for a total of five times, noting and recording the winner of the race each time.

Intermediate choice. Children examine their data so far and write down which of the three theories they think best represents the scientific answer.

Activity D: Card tunnel. Activity C is repeated, though to create a fairer test, the marbles are dropped from a 'card tunnel', which is a cut-down cardboard kitchen roll (see Figure 11.5). Hold the tunnel about 30–40 cm from the table top. Line the marbles up as shown in the figure, holding them in place with a flat surface (e.g. a CD case), and when both children in each pair are ready, one of them removes the CD case sharply in a downward arc to release the marbles. Ask children to *listen* when the marbles hit the table – if there is a single sound, they must be landing together; if there are two distinct sounds, then one must be landing before the other, so look closely to see which one it is.

Final choice. Children examine their total data and write down which of the three theories they think represents the scientific answer.

Revealing the science. The teacher plays a brief video clip that has been shot in advance that shows the two marbles landing simultaneously. Show the video in slow motion and then advance it frame-by-frame to prove the case.

Figure 11.4 (continued)

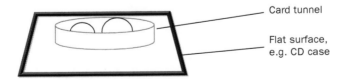

Figure 11.5 Activity D card tunnel

advocate, leading learners initially 'down the garden path' and purposely offering an incorrect explanation about a phenomenon. Later, when the correct, scientific explanation is revealed, the surprise, excitement and even any slight awkwardness students experience help engagement with the science, and thus learning.

The research was conducted as an educational experiment, with each of the three lessons taught alongside a control lesson that was more traditional, and involved a circus of activities that focused on gravity forces, one of which was comparing the speed of fall of two marbles of different sizes. Whether children believed that heavy objects fall more quickly was assessed by pre-test and a number of post-tests: immediately following the lesson, then six weeks, two years and three years later. All of the intervention groups achieved statistically more significant gains in knowledge than the control groups at the time of the post-tests (even three years after the lessons). Additionally, as part of the post-tests, children were asked to indicate the particular emotions they had experienced during the lessons, and the more emotional participants from one of the intervention groups achieved statistically more significant gains in knowledge than those who had reported being less emotionally affected at the time. I recommend that teachers try to access children's emotions such as awe, surprise, joy, anticipation and (even) disappointment during science lessons with the view to enhancing learning.

12
Light

Light is one of those topics in science where we ask children to think about familiar things in a slightly different way. To a layperson, light is a motionless but measurable quality that is present at a particular locality, with different places having varying levels of available light, for example: *I can't see what I'm doing because there isn't enough light in here*. To a scientist, light can also be considered something that is measurable and related to a specific location, for instance, how light intensity inside a greenhouse affects plant growth. Fundamentally, however, light is a type of energy that travels from one place to another, very quickly (nearly a million kilometres every three seconds).

The primary science programme of study (POS) aims to progress children's thinking towards understanding light as travelling rays that have a source, can bounce off some objects (reflection) and pass through others almost unchanged (transmission), be bent (refraction), and split up into its constituent parts (dispersion). Children also need to understand that people see things because light rays from a source such as the Sun reflect from the surface of an object before entering their eyes. The idea that light always travels in straight lines is a key concept that helps explain all these phenomena. (However, light rays can sometimes travel in curved paths in space as they become attracted to large objects such as planets and stars. For further information, study the ideas behind *gravitational lensing*.) Since well before the inception of the National Curriculum in 1988, simple shadow experiments have been used in primary schools as an engaging way of demonstrating light phenomena, alongside other, similar hands-on pedagogies (see later). Light concepts are also included in the POS as part of other topics, such as year 2 *Plants*, in the context of light being needed for plants to grow and stay healthy.

Children's ideas about light

Sources of light

Osborne et al. (1990) explored English 8–11 y/o's ideas about luminous sources (i.e. objects that produce their own light). They found that children could name a variety of different things that 'give off light', including genuine sources of light such as the Sun (the most commonly mentioned), light bulbs, heaters, televisions, stars and fires. The children also mentioned other things that are non-luminous as 'giving off light', including the Moon, the ceiling, windows and the sky – are merely good reflectors of light (Osborne et al., 1990: 15). The authors comment that the phrase they used, whether something 'gives off light', might have been misinterpreted by some children as meaning any bright object, regardless of it being a luminous source. Despite the Sun being the most frequently cited source of light in this study, French primary children instead tended to name only electrical sources and did not include the Sun (Guesne, 1984). The idea that the Moon makes its own light is very common (Philips, 1991) and ways to address this were discussed in Chapter 10.

How light travels

In accordance with the everyday understanding of light described above, before experiencing science lessons primary children tend not to think of light as something that travels at all. Instead, it is a static quality of a particular location. For instance, when French 10–11 y/o were asked about how light spreads out from a source such as a candle in a room, they frequently imagined that its glow reaches only as far as the furthest illuminated object and does not extend into the dark corners of the room (Guesne, 1985). This tendency to only associate light with areas that are visibly lit also explains why when children shine a torch onto a wall, they think that light is only present at the torch and on the illuminated part of the wall where the beam lands (Ravanis et al., 2013). These ideas have been found repeatedly in samples of children from a variety of countries (e.g. Gallegos Cázares et al., 2008; Ravanis and Boilevin, 2009). Because light is not seen as something that moves from place to place, but merely bathes its surroundings, children find it difficult to comprehend scientific ideas such as that light rays reflect from objects, or travel from source to object, then from object to eye, and so on.

Similarly, Osborne et al. (1990) found that hardly any of their 8–11 y/o understood the idea that light travels from the Sun to the Earth, comparable to how children do not appreciate that sound is a travelling entity (see Chapter 13). This is indicative of the *general illumination model* whereby light does not travel but simply floods its immediate area (Settlage, 1995). Around half of the children in the Osborne et al. study drew solid lines to represent light on a picture, although many were merely short, hatched lines surrounding sources such as the Sun or a

bulb to show that is was glowing, which provides little evidence of an appreciation that the light was travelling from one place to another. Another representation drawn by a few of the 8–9 y/o was a 'sea of light', where the whole drawing
was shaded to indicate an extensive presence of light (Osborne et al., 1990: 43),
which may also indicate a general illumination model. That said, more of the
older children (10–11 y/o) drew light as lines or rays, sometimes with arrows, suggesting an awareness that light is travelling and moving in a particular direction.
Erroneous ideas about light are resistant to change and can last well beyond the
school years. For instance, Heywood (2005) found that although English under-
graduate primary school teachers knew that light travels, some still thought it
filled up a space similar to how a gas fills an empty container, which is a variant
of the general illumination model.

Although Guesne's (1985: 19) French 10–11 y/o understood that a mirror
'reflects' light, they related this to the mirror reproducing an image and not to
light travelling and bouncing off the mirror's surface. However, when asked how
objects are seen, the diagrams of some English 10–11 y/o suggested that they
understood that light was reflected from a mirror or some other surface as a ray
(Osborne et al., 1990).

Shadows

Young children are aware of phenomenological aspects of their own shadows
such as they follow you around when you walk and copy what you do (Segal
and Cosgrove, 1993), or even their shadow acts timidly and hides when afraid
(Eschach, 2003). Children throughout the primary age range appear to understand that a shadow is associated with a specific object, even 'belonging' to that
object (Segal and Cosgrove, 1993: 282), sometimes to the extent that the shadow is
inside the object and is released when the object is exposed to strong light (Feher
and Rice, 1988). This has been called the *trigger model*, or *Peter Pan model*. Light
intensity is sometimes thought to affect the shape of a shadow. For instance, Galili and Hazan (2000) found that some adults believed that the stronger the source
of light, the bigger the shadow, while Watts and Gilbert (1985) uncovered the idea
that shadows are only produced in bright light, never dim light.

Piaget and Inhelder (1967) found that 5–7 y/o could not accurately predict the
orientation of shadows. Predictions can be elicited from children's drawings of
their own shadows in relation to the position of the Sun – the shadows are usually
placed in a random direction instead of opposite the Sun. They also found it difficult
to predict how the shape of a shadow may change if light hits an object from a different angle (Piaget and Inhelder, 1967). These problems can be related to younger
children being more egocentric and not being able to judge a pictured scene from
a perspective that is different to their own. Feher and Rice (1988) similarly found
that US 8–11 y/o had problems predicting the shape of a shadow. Guesne's (1985)
10–11 y/o commonly thought that a shadow was a reflection from an object, as
did Feher and Rice's (1988) 8–11 y/o. For instance, children can draw a person's

facial features and details of clothing within the shadow, as if the shadow was a clear reflection of that person in a pool of water. As was the case with the general illumination model, these concepts have been demonstrated more recently, and in diverse populations (e.g. Dedes and Ravanis, 2007; Resta-Schweizer and Weil-Barais, 2009).

How people see things

When asked to explain how they see a book, over a third of English 8–9 y/o could provide no explanation (Osborne et al., 1990). The 10–11 y/o were more able to answer the question, although few of their descriptions were scientifically accurate. Many of the children correctly drew light as travelling lines or rays that linked the object to the eye (more of the older than younger children did this), although around a half of these diagrams had arrows erroneously going from eye to object, with only a small number drawing a scientifically acceptable diagram that shows rays travelling from object to eye (see Figure 12.1) When the researchers added a source of light to the problem, children commonly drew one light ray going from source to object (correct), and another going from eye to object (incorrect). Only a few drew light as travelling first from source to object, then from object to eye, with some evidence that the older age group had more of an inclination to do this. However, children drew more scientifically appropriate diagrams when asked to depict how they can see a source in a mirror, than how they see a book. Gonzalez-Espada (2003) found that American university undergraduates believed that the pupil in the eye is merely a black spot, and not a hole where light enters, suggesting that people in general might not understand the path taken by light rays that enables objects to be seen.

The tendency of learners to draw light travelling away from the eye is long established and very common, and was probably first characterized by Guesne in 1978. The reasons why learners of all ages habitually draw light rays this way include the idea that light needs first to illuminate the eye so that objects can be seen (Galili and Hazan, 2000), and the possible linguistic influence of phraseology such as 'I am looking *at* this object', where vision is expressed as an active process that originates in the eye and targets an object. Another reason is the assumption that vision does not require an external light source (Settlage, 1995), thus humans can see objects in total darkness (Fetherstonhaugh and Treagust, 1990).

The best ways to teach light

POS Year 3 – Light (recognize that light is needed to see things and that dark is the absence of light; notice that light is reflected from surfaces)

	Typically 5–7 years	Typically 8–9 years	Typically 10–11 years
Examples of light sources	The Sun, light bulbs, heaters, televisions, stars, fires, the Moon, the ceiling, windows, the sky.	The Sun, light bulbs, heaters, televisions, stars, fires, the Moon, the ceiling, windows, the sky.	The Sun, light bulbs, heaters, televisions, stars, fires, the Moon, the ceiling, windows, the sky. Starts to distinguish between sources and reflectors.
General illumination model	Common.	Common.	Common.
Drawing light on diagrams		Short lines surrounding a source, indicating a glow. Non-directional.	Short lines surrounding a source, indicating a glow. Sometimes directional.
Reflection of light from a mirror			Reflection as bouncing rays not generally understood. Can sometimes draw lines linking source-eye or mirror-source-eye.
Shadows	Your shadow copies your actions. A shadow is within an object and is released when strong light hits the object (trigger model). Problems predicting the correct orientation of shadows. Difficulties predicting the changing shape of a shadow with changing position of light source.	A shadow is within an object and is released when strong light hits the object (trigger model). Difficulties predicting the changing shape of a shadows with changing position of light source. Shadows are reflections.	A shadow is within an object and is released when strong light hits the object (trigger model). Difficulties predicting the changing shape of a shadow with changing position of light source. Shadows are reflections. Early ideas about shadows being produced when opaque objects block light.
How we see an object such as a book		Not commonly understood.	Some can explain how light travels from source to book to eye.

Figure 12.1 How learning progresses: Light

Some Australian 4-5 y/o's ideas about shadows.

Michelle: They copy you ... they don't sleep.
David: They go to sleep with us ... you can't see them at night ... they climb the trees when we climb the trees.
Leanne: They follow us ... you can see a shadow on the ground.
Jenny: They're invisible ... they do what we do ... they have no eyes ... they have no noses.

Figure 12.2 What children have to say: Light (Segal and Cosgrove, 1993: 278–280)

Typically, a year 3 light topic might begin by reading a story book such as *Here Comes Frankie* (Hopgood, 2009) or *Can't You Sleep Little Bear?* (Waddle, 2013). This initial orientation can be followed by discussions about how to define a light source. Children must know that only luminous objects (those that can produce their own light) can be counted as sources. Anything that we can see that is not a source is a reflector of light. Examples of sources are the Sun, the stars, light bulbs, fireworks, bioluminescent organisms such as glow-worms and the luminous hands of a clock. Children at the lower and mid-points of the learning progression may think that bright reflectors such as the Moon, glitter balls and the reflective safety strips found on clothing are light sources. One way to elicit these ideas is to ask the children whether an object would still light up in a dark cupboard, and if they say yes, then they believe that object is a source. Children can test their predictions using a suitably dark walk-in store cupboard, or a commercially available 'dark den' (a light-proof tent that can be erected indoors). Ashbrook (2012) describes how a cardboard shoe box can be made into a light-proof container by cutting a hole the shape of a pair of safety goggles into the side, then inserting the goggles in such a way that when children press their face into the goggles no light can enter the box. Toys that glow-in-the-dark are engaging examples of sources that children can test. Another term used in the literature for a reflector is 'secondary source', while luminous sources are 'primary sources'. I advise that this distinction be avoided because it can cause confusion and teachers should stick with just calling anything luminous 'a source'; everything else that can be seen is 'a reflector'.

A general illumination model is apparent throughout the learning progression, except for a minority of children at the upper end. Most year 3 children will therefore think that a light source merely bathes its surroundings with its glow, and they do not see light as a travelling entity. To address this, light a candle in a darkened room and ask children the following questions: *Where is the light? Where does the light end? Where is there no light? How far does the light reach?* The same can be done with a torch shone on a wall. The children need to appreciate that light is not only present in bright areas but actually fills the entire room, even the darkest corners (Allen, 2014). Challenge children by asking, *Why are we able to see distant stars that are millions of kilometres away if light does not travel very far away from the source?* For these children, light is inextricably connected to its source and the aim for teachers is to help them think about light as a disconnected entity in its own right. One analogy is that when a train leaves a station, it is no longer part of that station but can travel long distances independently without any further assistance from the station.

> POS Year 3 – Light (recognize that shadows are formed when the light from a light source is blocked by a solid object)

The fact that light can pass through some objects but not others is typically taught by defining the concepts *transparent*, *translucent* and *opaque*. A variety of objects can be tested to see how well light can travel through them using a datalogger light sensor, or more simply, a mobile phone application that senses light intensely. Children can bring their own sunglasses into class to be tested for opaqueness in the same way. Links can be made with the properties of materials (Chapter 5); for example, different bottled liquids can be tested for transparency by the ease with which children can read a printed text when the bottles are placed over it. Ashbrook (2009) outlines an activity for use with young children where a torch is shone through squares of different materials in a dark room in order to judge transparency. Children need to know that opaque objects block light in order to properly understand how shadows are made.

POS Year 6 – Light (recognize that light appears to travel in straight lines; use the idea that light travels in straight lines to explain that objects are seen because they give out or reflect light into the eye; explain that we see things because light travels from light sources to our eyes or from light sources to objects and then to our eyes)

In year 6, the idea that light travels in straight lines can be effectively demonstrated by careful use of a laser pen beam shone onto walls, ceilings and a handheld mirror. The beam can be made visible by sprinkling flour into its path, which also shows that light is present in places that are not normally seen as bright areas (Allen, 2014). Following on from learning that light travels in a straight line, children can draw the path that light takes (as rays) on a diagram using a ruler (Figure 12.1 shows some ray diagrams). These activities will help children appreciate that light does not just stay in one place, close to the source, but moves around at very high speeds and sometimes for very long distances. People (and animals) can see objects for these reasons. Year 6 children are capable of drawing ray diagrams to show light rays linking a source to a human eye, but commonly (for the reasons given previously) they reverse the direction of travel, thinking that light travels from the eye towards the source. One way to overcome this is to ask them the question, *Why is it easier to see a torch in a dark room if I turn it on?* Further complications occur with ray diagrams where light travels from a source, illuminates an object, and then travels into the eye; children may instead draw light travelling from the source towards the eye, then from the eye towards the object (see Figure 12.1). This is indicative of the idea that the eye needs to absorb light from the source in order to see the object. You could say to the children, *When we go into a dark room with a torch, we do not shine the torch beam directly into our eyes to help us to see.*

POS Years 3 and 6 – Light (find patterns that determine the size of a shadow; use the idea that light travels in a straight line to explain why shadows have the same shape as the objects that cast them)

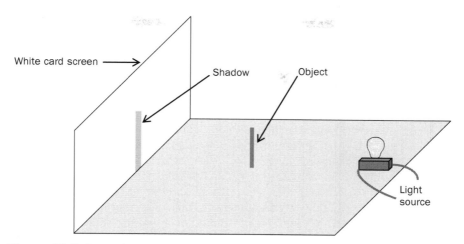

Figure 12.3 Investigating shadows

In year 3, shadows can be introduced with an activity that requires children to make their own shadow puppets, and if time allows having the puppets perform in a short play. Explain that shadows are formed when an opaque object blocks the path of light. Taking the class out into the playground on a sunny day will help children to correctly orient shadows (i.e. they are always on the opposite side to the Sun). Measuring the shadows of their friends will show that a shadow is not always the same size as the object, or exactly the same shape as the object, as it becomes distorted due to the angle of the Sun in the sky (e.g. late afternoons produce long, thin shadows). In year 6, children can carry out a shadow investigation where the relationships between the positions of a source, an object and its shadow are explored (Figure 12.3). Barrow (2007) suggests some interesting variations on this investigation and suggests that an inverted golf tee makes a good object for shadow experiments, while Trundle and Hilson (2012) suggest linking in the Earth and space activity, where the shadow of a stick is tracked throughout the course of a sunny day (described in Chapter 10), to general concepts about what a shadow is and how it is formed.

Research exemplar: Refuting the general illumination model

Ravanis et al. (2013) tested the effects of two brief teaching interventions to help young primary children better understand some fundamental light concepts. Specifically, they chose to challenge the general illumination model. The theoretical framework they used for the interventions was based on recent socio-cognitive approaches to teaching early years science (e.g. Venville et al., 2003). The socio-cognitive tradition is linked with Vygotsky's (1978) work and sees learning as something that is both an individual and social process (see Chapter 1). The interventions involve children making predictions at the start of an activity about what they think might happen, together with reasoned explanations. The data from the activity may conflict with their predictions, so creating cognitive conflict, and an important part of the reconstruction of their ideas is discussion and collaboration with peers and adults in the class. During these social interactions, the role of the teacher is to move children's thinking away from what they personally believe to be happening during the activity (subjective thinking) to what is actually, physically happening (objective thinking), so effecting conceptual change.

One of the interventions used metaphors to help children connect their familiar, existing concepts with unfamiliar, and sometimes counterintuitive, scientific concepts. This approach used the principles of socio-cognitive teaching, as described above. The other intervention was a more typical approach that was teacher-centred, focused on conveying facts and not taking into account children's prior knowledge, which the researchers called 'empiricist' (Ravanis et al., 2013: 2260). Both interventions, however, were devised to help children conceptually change the general illumination model.

The two interventions were taught alongside each other to two groups of 5–6 y/o children in Greece; there were 85 children in each group. Children in the sample were randomized in order to create two groups of equivalent abilities and prior experiences. As discussed in previous chapters, randomization is a particularly powerful method of reducing the effect of confounding variables such as one class having been previously taught by a more effective teacher. In order to assess their knowledge, all children underwent one pre-test two months before the intervention and two post-tests, two and four months after the intervention. For these tests, children were interviewed for 10 minutes and asked questions about where they thought light was present in three different instances (e.g. a torch beam projecting onto a wall), which were devised to elicit both the general illumination model as well as appropriate scientific models. The interventions themselves took place in the children's kindergartens and lasted 15–20 minutes. Children were taught in small groups of three to five by teachers who had been briefed in detail by the researchers. Full details of the metaphor intervention are given in Figure 12.4.

Both groups made some overall progress as a result of the teaching, although the children who underwent the metaphor intervention generally experienced greater gains in knowledge compared with children in the empiricist intervention, to a degree that was statistically significant. Although the metaphor intervention was carried out with KS1-aged children, I believe that it is quite appropriate for use during a year 3 or even year 6 light topic because it is likely that a good number of children will be at the lower end of the learning progression and so initially aligned with a general illumination model.

Research exemplar: Refuting the general illumination model

Main learning outcome (for ages 5–11 years)
To help children replace the general illumination model with a more scientific model that considers light to be a travelling entity.

Activity one – Destabilization of the general illumination model

- Bring a powerful torch into a darkened room. Before switching the torch on and shining the beam onto a wall, ask children to predict where in the room light will be once the torch is on. Encourage discussion and debate. This elicits the general illumination model, and a typical response is light will only be found in visibly lit areas – at the source and at the wall.
- Switch the torch on and ask children where the light actually is now. They compare their responses with their earlier predictions. Children walk around the darkened room (with care) and physically show each other where the light is.
- Turn the room lights on while still keeping the torch on. Initiate discussion by asking children where the light from the torch is now. A typical response is the light is still there but cannot be seen any more.

Activity two – construction of a scientific model of travelling light
Start a new discussion by asking how the Earth is lit by the Sun, with children having to provide reasons for their answers. Typically, children will simply say that rays come from the Sun. Praising these particular answers, explain that light does indeed travel from space, from the Sun towards the Earth. This provides a metaphor that would be familiar to many children because they already understand that the Sun produces rays of light. This should help children mentally isolate light from its source, and appreciate that light is an entity that can travel quite readily through space independently of its source.

Returning to the torch problem, ask children where the light actually comes from, and how light gets from the torch to their eyes. Emphasizing the metaphor, explain that light comes from a source such as the Sun or a torch (or a lamp, fire, etc.) and has to travel to get to our eyes.

Activity three – reinforcement
To reinforce the concepts, show children a diagram of the Sun's visible rays travelling through space towards the Earth, and a number of photographs that clearly show beams of light, for instance, sunbeams passing into a wood clearing, or searchlights shining up into the night sky. The aim is to visually show light travelling from one place to another, and once it has left its source, it no longer needs the source in order to travel.

Figure 12.4 Lesson outline for Light (adapted from Ravanis et al., 2013)

13
Sound

As for light, primary children need to learn the fundamental fact that sound is something that travels from one place to another. This may be at odds with their natural understanding of sound as something intrinsically connected with its source. For instance, the statement *that car is really noisy*, although perfectly acceptable in everyday conversation, could be more scientifically expressed as *that car is producing high-energy sound waves that are travelling into my ear*.

Sounds can differ in loudness and pitch, and in year 4 children learn the reasons for these differences. When an object such as a metal bell is struck with a hammer, the bell starts to shake very rapidly, or vibrate. These vibrations are not restricted to the metal of the bell, but spread out away from the bell (propagate), causing the layer of air immediately next to the bell to vibrate in unison. The propagation continues, as the next layer of air beyond the first layer also starts to vibrate, and so on. As a result, vibrations pass quickly through the air travelling at a speed of about one kilometre every three seconds – this is a *sound wave*. When a sound wave reaches the human ear, it causes apparatus within the ear also to vibrate, with these vibrations being passed to the brain as electrical impulses making us conscious of 'a sound'.

Sound waves can travel quite long distances, although they become weaker the further they travel from the source because they lose energy to the surroundings. This is why if we are far from its source, a sound will be perceived to be quiet if it is heard at all – once it reaches the ear, there is very little energy left to make our hearing apparatus vibrate. The energy of a sound wave depends on how far the layers of air particles move back-and-forth when they are vibrating; this is called the *amplitude* of the wave. High-amplitude waves carry lots of energy that create relatively large movements in our hearing apparatus and so we perceive them as loud sounds; for low-amplitude waves, the opposite is the case. Sound waves with very high amplitudes are associated with powerful shock waves, which are typically destructive; for example, demolition explosives such as TNT generate shock waves that carry enormous amounts of energy that can easily flatten buildings.

Sounds also differ in another perceived quality – their pitch. An example of a sound perceived as high pitched is a robin in full song, while an example of a low-pitched sound is the beating of a base drum. Pitch nearly always depends on how quickly the source is vibrating when first producing the sound wave. The throat of the singing robin vibrates extremely quickly at around 2500 times per second, or 2500 Hertz (Hz). This is the *frequency* of the vibration. The sound wave that reaches our ears will still be vibrating at around this speed, which causes our hearing apparatus also to vibrate as quickly, and we perceive these tiny, very rapid movements within the ear as a high-pitched sound. The skin of a bass drum only vibrates at around 60 times per second (60 Hz) and so we perceive the sound as being of a low pitch.

Children's ideas about sound

Sources of sound

Although the phenomena of light (Chapter 12) and sound share similar scientific qualities, such as being propagated as a wave, there have been comparatively fewer research studies on primary children's concepts of sound. A fundamental concept that children first need to comprehend is that sound is produced when a source vibrates. This idea is less well appreciated by younger children. For example, while around 40% of English 8–11 y/o knew that a rubber band made a sound because it was vibrating or wobbling, only 6% of 5–7 y/o gave this response (Watt and Russell, 1990). These younger children thought instead that objects make a sound because of the material they are made from or because of the action that made the sound (e.g. the rubber band was flicked). There may be difficulties with younger children understanding the general concept of a vibrating object. When asked why rice placed on a drum shakes when the drum is struck, nearly half of 10–11 y/o understood that the drum skin was vibrating, but hardly any of the 5–7 y/o gave this answer. Similarly, Mazens and Lautrey (2003) established that hardly any French 5–6 y/o understood that sound involved vibration, compared with nearly a third of 9–10 y/o. Asoko and colleagues' (1991a) sample of English primary children in general had problems conceptualizing that sound sources vibrate, unless the source was something that was vibrating noticeably, such as a guitar string. The researchers also uncovered the view that the sound inside a musical instrument is always there, waiting to be released by humans (Asoko *et al.*, 1991a).

Sound propagation

When Watt and Russell (1990) asked primary children how sound reaches the listener through a string telephone, most 8–11 y/o correctly deduced that the sound travelled through the string. Nearly half of 10–11 y/o also understood that sound travels through the string as vibrations, perhaps because they were able to physically feel the vibrating string during the activity. The 5–7 y/o were less inclined to think the string was involved in sound propagation and gave answers such as the sound escaped through holes in the yogurt pot, and sound needed open spaces to travel through. Shin and Kim (2013) repeated aspects of Watt and Russell's earlier work with Korean primary children and obtained similar findings, highlighting problems in correctly understanding general sound propagation. However, they note that that when using a string telephone, even 5 y/o children could explain sound propagation in a more scientific way. With Mazens and Lautrey's (2003) French sample, three-quarters of 6–7 y/o stated that sound is unable to travel through solid objects, although it can pass through gaps or unseen holes in such objects. The belief that sound cannot propagate through objects can reflect an idea that sound is not a wave but a semi-material entity and so cannot pass through a solid material. This manifests itself in the common though incorrect idea that sound travels as a mass of moving air like a wind (Sözen and Bolat, 2011), and so this wind requires gaps in order to pass through objects (West and Wallin, 2013). An extension of this view is that this 'sound material' has hardness and can break through softer materials like cardboard but not harder materials like metal (Mazens and Lautrey, 2003). Similarly, if a sound source is muffled, children can think that sound waves have been trapped inside the muffler, instead of being absorbed by the muffling material, though sound can still be heard due to leakage through gaps in the muffler (Asoko et al., 1991b).

How people hear sounds

When asked how sounds such as a plucked elastic band or beating drum reaches the listener, Watt and Russell's (1990) 8–11 y/o understood that the sound travels towards you, and a few had even correctly deduced that sound travels via the air. However, the 5–7 y/o instead gave responses that described characteristics of the listener, such as the sound reaches you because you listen carefully, you have ears, or you simply hear it. The 5–7 y/o also gave similar responses when asked how more everyday sounds reach a listener. Therefore, the younger children tended to think that sound is a phenomenon that only requires a listener, and if a sound is not actively concentrated upon by the listener, it cannot be heard – this is the *active listener model* (see Figure 13.1). They did not see sound as an entity that travels outwards away from a source in all directions – it only travels to the people who are listening, an example of anthropocentric thought. Conversely, Piaget (1971) found that 4–5 y/o did not think anything at all passes between a source and the human ear. By 7 years, Piaget's children did begin to think of sound as something that travels outwards from a source and by 11 years they understood air acted as a medium during propagation. More recently, the early active listener model was confirmed when it was reported that most French 5–6 y/o understood that sound did travel outwards from a source, but only towards people, while over three-quarters of 9–10 y/o thought sound travelled to people and elsewhere (Mazens and Lautrey, 2003). There has been little research on primary children's awareness that sound has a particular speed, although Scott and Asoko (1990) note that the concept of sound having a velocity is usually absent prior to its introduction in formal school science lessons.

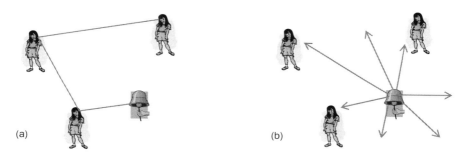

Drawing (a) shows sound travelling from the source and then being passed in a sequential way from listener to listener (this depiction was relatively rare, only being drawn by a few 5–6 y/o and a single 7–8 y/o)

Drawing (b) shows a more accurate depiction of sound travelling simultaneously in all directions away from the source (this was common in 7–10 y/o, but far less so in 5–6 y/o)

Figure 13.1 Swedish primary children's depictions of how sound travels away from a central source (adapted from Mazens and Lautry, 2003: 10)

How children consider the direction that sound travels in compared with light is worthy of comment. As discussed in Chapter 12, it is common for children to erroneously draw light rays travelling from the eye to a source; however, it is more usual for them to correctly draw sound as moving away from a source towards a listener. Even young children understand that the distance from a source is a factor that affects how well they can hear a sound (Watt and Russell, 1990); it is thus easier to recognize that something (i.e. a wave) must be moving away from a sound source, and as it moves away it becomes weaker. Also, compared with light, children accept from a younger age that sound is a travelling entity, since the general illumination model of light is common even at 11 years.

The best ways to teach sound

POS Year 4 – Sound (identify how sounds are made, associating some of them with something vibrating)

	Typically 5–7 years	Typically 8–9 years	Typically 10–11 years
How is a sound made?	Sources make a sound because they are made from a particular material, or because something is done to make them produce a sound.	Sources vibrate to make a sound.	Sources vibrate to make a sound.
Sound propagation through solids	Sound is a material itself and so cannot freely pass through a solid material (unless there are holes).	Sound can pass freely through solid materials.	Sound can pass freely through solid materials, as vibrations.
How we are able to hear sounds	We need to listen carefully before we can hear a sound (active listener model). There is something travelling between source and listener but it only goes to the listener and nowhere else (active listener model). Some believe that there is nothing travelling between source and listener.	Sound travels outwards from a source to different locations (not just to a listener). A sound wave is a mass of air travelling like 'a wind'.	Sound travels outwards from a source to different locations (not just to a listener). A sound wave is a mass of air travelling like 'a wind'. Starts to understand sound is a wave that moves through the air as vibrations.

Figure 13.2 How learning progresses: Sound

A 9–10 y/o Swedish boy was asked whether sound is able to pass through different materials. His responses suggest he probably believes that sound is a material entity that can only pass if gaps exist in obstacles.

(A flute note travelling through the air): *Sound waves are formed from the flute to the brain.*
(Swimmers under water): *No, the water hinders the sound to go through.*
(Wooden door): *No, I do not think that sound can travel through doors. But through narrow openings in the door.*
(Through a vacuum room): *No, nothing stops the sound from going through.*

Figure 13.3 What children have to say: Sound (West and Wallin, 2013: 993)

A year 4 sound topic might begin with a 'sound walk'. The class is taken on a walk to different locations around the school premises where they try to mimic the sounds they can hear at each location. Back in the classroom, they discuss the qualities of each sound, including loudness and pitch, identify the source of the sound, and describe exactly how each sound was made. A fun activity is listening to audio recordings of everyday sounds, which the children then have to identify (e.g. breaking glass, a cow's moo, a pedestrian crossing). A variety of interesting sound bites can be downloaded free from the Internet as audio files. Story books that serve to introduce basic sound concepts include *Oscar and the Bat* (Waring, 2007) and *The Bear Who Wouldn't Share* (Allen, 2000).

Children need to understand that to make a sound, a source must first vibrate, particularly those at the lower end of the learning progression who may not understand the concept of vibration *per se*. Show a series of sources where the vibrations are easy to see and ask children what they have in common. For example, flicking a ruler on the edge of a desk, beating a drum with rice on the skin, hitting a cymbal (the vibrations can also be felt), striking a tuning fork and placing the prongs on the surface of a beaker of water, and (gently) holding your larynx as you speak. Extend this exercise by playing musical instruments and asking the children which part of each instrument vibrates to produce the sound: guitar (strings), recorder (column of air), piano (strings) and maracas (shell). Another way is highlighted by Brown and Boehringer (2007) and involves how homemade musical instruments such as a rubber band guitar can stimulate engagement and used to explore sound phenomena in the classroom. Children can also explore how to increase the volume of a sound produced by a musical instrument by increasing the strength of the vibrations, such as plucking a guitar harder or beating a drum with more force. Ashbrook (2014) provides instructions on how to make a homemade harp from a block of wood, some screw-in metal hooks and elastic bands.

POS Year 4 – Sound (recognize that vibrations from sounds travel through a medium to the ear; find patterns between the volume of a sound and the strength of the vibrations that produced it; recognize that sounds get fainter as the distance from the sound source increases)

Understanding how sound propagates through the air is a difficult idea for learners at the lower end and mid-points on the learning progression. However, they naturally appreciate that when they hear a sound there is 'something' travelling between source and listener, which represents a good halfway house concept from which to extend to more scientific models. Visualizing a sound wave is beyond the KS2 programme of study but schools frequently include it as part of a sound topic in a simple form. If children are able to appreciate what a sound wave is, then clearly they will have understood that sound is a travelling entity that moves outwards from a source. Sound waves are traditionally demonstrated using a slinky spring stretched out over a desk and a wave sent down the spring by flicking the wrist. With practice, slinkys can be used to model different aspects of sound, including how the strength of a wave (and so the volume of a sound) diminish with distance from the source. How different sounds can have different volumes can be explored using a sound meter to measure the intensity (volume) of everyday sounds, and smartphone applications are available that can perform the same function. Children can conduct investigations to find out which is the crunchiest biscuit, the noisiest place in the school, and so on. Hendrix and Eick (2014) describe how children can act out the behaviour of sound waves as drama activities. All this said, Driver et al. (1994) have suggested that children preferably need to understand a particle model of matter before being taught how sound waves propagate through the air, an idea which lies at the top of the learning progression.

Although not part of the curriculum, including activities that show that sound is able to pass through solid (and liquid) barriers will help dispel the idea at the lower reaches of the learning progression that a sound wave is a material thing. A simple demonstration is to have the children gently scratch their desk with a fingernail. The sound will be barely perceptible, but if they place an ear on the desk the sound becomes quite loud, demonstrating that sound can easily travel through solids. String telephones are a traditional way to demonstrate these phenomena.

> POS Year 4 – Sound (find patterns between the pitch of a sound and features of the object that produced it)

The fact that different sounds can have different pitches can be introduced by simply striking the bars of a xylophone. Demonstrate that the longer bars have the lowest pitch and relate this to vibrations – because the longer bars have the most mass, they vibrate more slowly. This principle applies generally, for example, thicker guitar strings, wider drum skins and longer recorders all produce lower pitched sounds because they vibrate more slowly. Note that with the recorder, it is the column of air inside that vibrates and one can change the length of this column by covering the finger holes. Snyder and Johnson (2010) show how pitch can be explored using rubber bands of different thicknesses attached to plastic cups. They used the book *Horton Hears a Who!* by Dr Suess (Geisel, 1954) in order to engage the children in the first place.

A fun activity is to test the upper limit of children's hearing with respect to the pitches of sounds they can perceive (these tests can be freely accessed on the Internet). Humans are typically able to hear sounds in the frequency range 20–20,000Hz, although there are individual differences, with some children able to perceive higher frequencies than others. The upper range for perception diminishes with age, and I have found the younger children in the class can sometimes have a measurably higher frequency range, even though there is less than a year's difference in their ages. This can be related to ultrasound, which is sound pitched above 20,000Hz, and many animals such as dogs, cats and bats can hear very high-frequency sounds that we cannot. This is why domestic cats can be seen stalking something in the garden that is hidden to us because they can hear the high-frequency squeaks that small mammals such as mice and shrews use for communication. Further ideas for investigating pitch and other sound phenomena in the classroom are described in detail in the article by Merwade et al. (2014).

Research exemplar: Using a teaching–learning sequence

West and Wallin's (2013) paper details an intervention devised to address Swedish primary children's erroneous sound concepts. They call the intervention a *teaching–learning sequence* (TLS) whose aim is to improve 'students' understanding of the properties of sound, the function of the ear and hearing, and how to maintain auditory health' (ibid., p. 986). The authors see the role of primary teachers as moving children's thinking away from sound propagation as the transport of matter (e.g. as a moving wind) to sound propagation as a transmission of wave motion which uses matter to carry the wave. As discussed previously, primary children can think of a sound wave as a material thing and so cannot pass through another material like metal unless there are gaps or holes present. However, no material is ever transported in a sound wave. When sound travels through air, the air molecules vibrate from side-to-side for a short distance but eventually return to their original positions. The air does not move *en masse* like a wind; when a sound wave travels, what moves away from the source is just the wave itself. Imagine a crowd doing a Mexican wave in a sports stadium: the people doing the wave do not run around the stadium, the wave does – the wave just uses the people as a medium so it can travel. The medium carries the wave; the medium does not get carried itself.

The intervention was informed by a methodological approach known as design research. The methodology assumes a constructivist view of learning with the teacher as a purveyor of scientific knowledge who is aware of the misconceptions that children could potentially construct. Children have the opportunity to construct appropriate scientific concepts by undertaking constructivist activities in small groups such as peer discussion and writing collaborative reports. The teacher formatively assesses children's progress frequently during the process. Each lesson presents tasks in a planned, deliberate and systematic way in order that learners' thinking is directed along specific pathways (West and Wallin, 2013).

The sample consisted of 48 Swedish children aged 10–11 years from the same school. The teachers who delivered the lessons were probably the children's usual teachers, although this was not absolutely clear from the information given. The teachers planned the lessons themselves in accordance with the Swedish National

Curriculum but used a 'Teachers' Guide' document as a basis (West, 2008), which had been previously tested extensively in the classroom. Figure 13.4 gives specific details of the teaching sequence.

Research exemplar: Using a teaching–learning sequence (TLS)

Main learning outcome (for ages 8–11 years)
See individual 'goals' as set out below.

Preamble
The six topic areas are not individual lessons, they are meant to be worked through at the teacher's and children's own pace.

1. *Sounds around us*
   - Goal: Being aware of the fact that we live in an environment full of sounds and that sound is important for people and animals in different ways.
   - Listen to and discuss different everyday sounds. Categorize sounds into different groups. Why is sound useful for people and animals?

2. *Sound arises when objects vibrate*
   - Goal: Understanding that all sounds arise by means of vibrations.
   - Children make different sounds using an elastic band, a ruler, a wire stretched across two nails, or homemade musical instruments. They should preferably arrive at the conclusion by themselves that vibrations are producing the sounds, although the teacher must introduce the word *vibration* to them.

3. *What substances transmit sound?*
   - Goal: Know that sound is transmitted via matter in gaseous, liquid and solid substances.
   - Let children listen to an engaging sound, e.g. play a song from a CD, then ask them *how does the sound get to your ears? What is there between the sound and your ears?* Encourage discussion around sound as being something travelling through the air (called a wave) and that air is made of particles. Introduce a simple model of particle theory to the class if it has not previously been covered. Explain that the sound wave travels through air because particles bump into each other, similar to how when people are stood closely together in a queue and someone pushes at one end.
   - Get children to think of activities that would show that sound travels in liquids. For example, at the swimming pool, when underwater you can hear somebody knocking on a ladder. Banging two spoons together in a beaker of water can be heard quite clearly (try this with different liquids, e.g. cooking oil, honey). Similarly, ask them to think of ways to show that sound travels in solids, e.g. knocking on a desk or radiator with your ear pressed against it. Make string telephones.

Figure 13.4 Lesson outline for Sound (adapted from West, 2008; West and Wallin, 2013)

4. *How is sound transmitted?*
   - Goal: To be able to describe the transmission of sound with the help of different models and reflect on the merits and limitations of the models.
   - Children construct drawings – simply ask them to 'draw sound'. Use these as a lead-in to connect together all the previous concepts that have been covered. Children will use different models or ways of pictorially representing sound – discuss the merits and limitations of each one. End by explaining that sound travels as a wave that is carried by matter (solid, liquid or gas).

5. *Why do sounds sound different?*
   - Goal: To know that sound has different properties: pitch (frequency) and sound level (sound volume).
   - Use materials that have been previously constructed (e.g. wire stretched across two nails) to try to change the sound that is produced. Direct activities towards making sounds of differing pitch and sounds of differing volume. Try to get children to consider these two variables one at a time. Carry out a class activity that tests the range of frequencies that can be heard. Children find out the ranges of hearing of different animals and compare them with human hearing (which is generally quite poor in comparison). Ask where could there be loud sounds in the school? Measure the sound intensity at different locations using a sound meter or smartphone application.

6. *The sound strikes different surfaces*
   - Goal: Experiencing that a sound that strikes the surface of a material can be transmitted, absorbed or reflected.
   - Ask *which materials are good for muffling sound?* Children plan and carry out activities to investigate this question. Sound sources that can be used include a digital stopwatch where the alarm has been set to sound continuously, an MP3 player, or mobile phone. Conclude that materials can absorb sound waves, and this reduces the loudness of the noise. Sound waves that are not absorbed can be reflected from a material. When a sound wave is not absorbed or reflected from a material, it can pass straight through (be transmitted).

Figure 13.4 (continued)

The children underwent a pre-test before the intervention followed by two post-tests, the first of which was performed immediately after the intervention and the second one year later. The children made statistically significant progress after the intervention, constructing more scientifically acceptable concepts and appearing to shed erroneous ideas. Specifically, children were less inclined to view sound propagation as the transmission of matter, replacing this view with one of sound as transmission of wave motion that uses matter to carry the wave. One limitation to this research is that it used a single group only, no control group was used as a comparison, so it might be argued that the children could have made equivalent progress with a different intervention that focused on the same content.

References

Chapter 1   Introduction

Adey, P., Shayer, M. and Yates, C. (1989) *Thinking Science: The Curriculum Materials of the CASE Project.* London: Thomas Nelson.

Alonzo, A. C. and Gotwals, A. W. (2012) *Learning Progressions in Science: Current Challenges and Future Directions.* Rotterdam: Sense.

Ault, C. R., Jr. (1984) Intelligently wrong: Some comments on children's misconceptions, *Science and Children,* 21(8): 22–24.

Blake, A. (2004) Helping young children to see what is relevant and why: Supporting cognitive change in earth science using analogy, *International Journal of Science Education,* 26(15): 1855–1873.

British Educational Research Association (BERA) (2014) *Research and the Teaching Profession: Building the Capacity for a Self-improving Education System.* London: BERA and RSA.

Claxton, G. (1985) Teaching and acquiring scientific knowledge, in T. Keen and M. Pope (eds) *Kelly in the Classroom: Educational Applications of Personal Construct Psychology.* Montreal: Cybersystems.

Department for Education (DfE) (2013) *Science Programmes of Study: Key Stages 1 and 2.* DFE-00182-2013. London: Crown Copyright.

DiCenso, A., Cullum, N. and Ciliska, D. (1998) Implementing evidence-based nursing: Some misconceptions, *Evidence Based Nursing,* 1(2): 38–40.

diSessa, A. A. (2006) A history of conceptual change research: Threads and fault lines, in K. Sawyer (ed.) *Cambridge Handbook of the Learning Sciences.* Cambridge: Cambridge University Press.

Duncan, R. G. and Rivet, A. E. (2013) Science learning progressions, *Science,* 339: 396–397.

Eimas, P. D. (1994) Categorisation in early infancy and the continuity of development, *Cognition,* 50: 83–93.

Goldacre, B. (2013) *Building Evidence into Education.* London: Crown Copyright.

Gorard, S. (2013) *Research Design: Robust Approaches for the Social Sciences.* London: Sage.

Goswami, U. (2014) *Cognition in Children.* Abingdon: Psychology Press.

Jofili, Z., Geraldo, A. and Watts, M. (1999) A course for critical constructivism through action research: A case study from biology, *Research in Science and Technological Education*, 17(1): 5–17.

Miller, R. (2011) *Vygotsky in Perspective*. New York: Cambridge University Press.

National Research Council (NRC) (2012) *A Framework for K-12 Science Education: Practices, Crosscutting Concepts, and Core Ideas. Committee on a Conceptual Framework for New K-12 Science Education Standards*. Board on Science Education, Division of Behavioral and Social Sciences and Education. Washington, DC: National Academies Press.

Piaget, J. (1972) *The Psychology of the Child*. New York: Basic Books.

Plummer, J. D. and Krajcik, J. (2010) Building a learning progression for celestial motion: Elementary levels from an earth-based perspective, *Journal of Research in Science Teaching*, 47(7): 768–787.

Posner, G., Strike, K., Hewson, P. and Gertzog, W. (1982) Accommodation of a scientific conception: Towards a theory of conceptual change, *Science Education*, 66: 211–227.

Smith, M. U. (2010) Current status of research in teaching and learning evolution: II. Pedagogical issues, *Science and Education*, 19(6/8): 539–571.

Suzuki, K., Yamaguchi, E. and Hokayem, H. (2015) Learning progression for Japanese elementary students' reasoning about ecosystems, *Procedia-Social and Behavioral Sciences*, 167: 79–84.

Swan, M. (2001) Dealing with misconceptions in mathematics, in P. Gates (ed.) *Issues in Mathematics Teaching*. London: RoutledgeFalmer.

Tracana, R. B., Varanda, I., Viveiros, S. and Carvalho, G. S. D. (2012) Children's conceptions about respiration before and after formal teaching: Identification of learning obstacles. In *Proceedings of the XV International Organisation for Science and Technology Education (IOSTE) Symposium: 'The Use of Science and Technology Education for Peace and Sustainable Development'*, Hammamet, Tunisia.

Vygotsky, L. (1978) *Mind in Society: The Development of Higher Psychological Processes*. Cambridge, MA: Harvard University Press.

Chapter 2   Animals including humans

Allen, M. (2015) Preschool children's taxonomic knowledge of animal species, *Journal of Research in Science Teaching*, 52(1): 107–134.

Althea and O'Neill, C. (2006) *Lunch Boxes*. Bradfield: Happy Cat Books.

Arnaudin, M. W. and Mintzes, J. J. (1985) Students' alternative conceptions of the human circulatory system: A cross-age study, *Science Education*, 69(5): 721–733.

Barrow, L. H. (2002) What do elementary students know about insects?, *Journal of Elementary Science Education*, 14(2): 53–60.

Bell, B. F. (1981) When is an animal, not an animal?, *Journal of Biological Education*, 15: 213–218.

Braund, M. (1991) Children's ideas in classifying animals, *Journal of Biological Education*, 25: 103–110.

Brinkman, F. and Boschhuizen, R. (1989) Preinstructional ideas in biology: A survey in relation with different research methods on concepts of health and energy, in M. T. Voorbach and L. G. M. Prick (eds) *Teacher Education 5: Research and Developments on Teacher Education in the Netherlands*. London: Taylor & Francis.

Cakici, Y. (2005) Exploring Turkish upper primary level pupils' understanding of digestion, *International Journal of Science Education*, 27: 79–100.

Caravita, S. and Falchetti, E. (2005) Are bones alive?, *Journal of Biological Education*, 39(4): 163–170.

Caravita, S. and Tonucci, F. (1987) How children know biological structure–function relationships. Paper presented at the Second International Seminar: 'Misconceptions and Educational Strategies in Science and Mathematics', 26-29 July, Cornell University. Ithaca, NY.

Carey, S. (1985) *Conceptual Change in Childhood*. Cambridge, MA: MIT Press.

Carvalho, G., Silva, R., Lima, N. and Coquet, E. (2004) Portuguese primary school children's conceptions about digestion: Identification of learning obstacles, *International Journal of Science Education*, 26: 1111–1130.

Chen, S. H. and Ku, C. H. (1998) Aboriginal children's alternative conceptions of animals and animal classification, *Proceedings of the National Science Council (Part D)*, 8: 55–67.

Cinici, A. (2013) From caterpillar to butterfly: A window for looking into students' ideas about life cycle and life forms of insects, *Journal of Biological Education*, 47(2): 84–95.

Contento, I. (1981) Children's thinking about food and eating – A Piagetian-based study, *Journal of Nutrition Education*, 13(1): S86–S90.

Croshaw, C. and Willis, A. (2011) Puppets: A science teacher's best friend?, *Primary Science*, 119: 12–13.

Cubero, R. (1998) La construcción del conocimiento del proceso digestivo, in E. Banet and A. De Pro (eds) *Un Studio Longitudinal. Un Investigación e Innovación en la Enseñanza de las Ciencia*s. Murcia: DM.

Davies, D. (2013) Taking a 'giant tour' to explore the human body, *Primary Science*, 127: 26–28.

Dempster, E. and Stears, M. (2014) An analysis of children's drawings of what they think is inside their bodies: A South African regional study, *Journal of Biological Education*, 48(2): 71–79.

Endreny, A. H. (2006) Children's ideas about animal adaptations: An action research project, *Journal of Elementary Science Education*, 18(1): 33–42.

Garcia-Barros, S., Martínez-Losada, C. and Garrido, M. (2011) What do children aged four to seven know about the digestive system and the respiratory system of the human being and of other animals?, *International Journal of Science Education*, 33: 2095–2122.

Gellert, E. (1962) Children's conceptions of the content and functions of the human body, *Genetic Psychology Monographs*, 65: 293–405.

Gelman, S. A. and Opfer, J. E. (2002) Development of the animate–inanimate distinction, in U. Goswami (ed.) *Blackwell Handbook of Childhood Cognitive Development*. Oxford: Blackwell Publishing.

Giordan, A. and Vecchi, G. (1988) *Los Orígenes del Saber*. Sevilla: Ed. Diada.

Hachey, A. C. and Butler, D. (2012) Creatures in the classroom: Including insects and small animals in your preschool gardening curriculum, *Young Children*, 67(2): 38–42.

Hmelo, C. E., Holton, D. L. and Kolodner, J. L. (2000) Designing to learn about complex systems, *Journal of the Learning Sciences*, 9(3): 247–298.

Inagaki, K. and Hatano, G. (1987) Young children's spontaneous personification as analogy, *Child Development*, 58: 1013–1021.

Kattmann, U. (2001) Aquatics, flyers, creepers and terrestrials: Students' conceptions of animal classifications, *Journal of Biological Education*, 35: 141–147.

Mafra, P., Lima, N. and Carvalho, G. S. (2015) Experimental activities in primary school to learn about microbes in an oral health education context, *Journal of Biological Education*, 49(2): 190–203.

Margett, T. E. and Witherington, D. C. (2011) The nature of preschoolers' concept of living and artificial objects, *Child Development*, 82(6): 2067–2082.

McShane, J. B. (1991) Dental detectives: The trial of the toothpastes presents no problems for the tooth sleuths, *Science and Children*, 28(4): 12–15.

Myers, O. E., Jr., Saunders, C. D. and Garrett, E. (2004) What do children think animals need? Developmental trends, *Environmental Education Research*, 10(4): 545–562.

Nurettin, Y., Sahin, M. and Aydin, H. (2009) Are animals 'more alive' than plants? Animistic-anthropocentric construction of life concept, *Eurasia Journal of Mathematics, Science and Technology Education*, 5(4): 369–378.

Opfer, J. E. and Gelman, S. A. (2001) Children's and adults' models for predicting teleological action: The development of a biology-based model, *Child Development*, 72: 1367–1381.

Opfer, J. E. and Siegler, R. S. (2004) Revisiting preschoolers' living things concept: A microgenetic analysis of conceptual change in basic biology, *Cognitive Psychology*, 49: 301–332.

Osborne, J. F., Wadsworth, P. and Black, P. J. (1992) *SPACE Research Report: Processes of Life*. Liverpool: Liverpool University Press.

Óskarsdóttir, G., Stougaard, B., Fleischer, A. et al. (2011) Children's ideas about the human body: A Nordic case study, *Nordic Studies in Science Education*, 7(2): 179–188.

Piaget, J. (1929) *The Child's Conception of the World*. London: Routledge & Kegan Paul.

Prokop, P., Kubiatko, M. and Fančovičová, J. (2007a) Why do cocks crow? Children's concepts about birds, *Research in Science Education*, 37: 393–405.

Prokop, P., Prokop, M. and Tunnicliffe, S. D. (2008) Effects of keeping animals as pets on children's concepts of vertebrates and invertebrates, *International Journal of Science Education*, 30(4): 431–449.

Prokop, P. A., Prokop, M. A., Tunnicliffe, S. D. and Diran, C. (2007b) Children's ideas of animals' internal structures, *Journal of Biological Education*, 41(2): 62–67.

Reiss, M. J., Tunnicliffe, S. D., Bartoszeck, A. et al. (2002) An international study of young people's drawings of what is inside themselves, *Journal of Biological Education*, 36(2): 58–64.

Rowlands, M. (2004) What do children think happens to the food they eat?, *Journal of Biological Education*, 38: 167–171.

Russell, T. and Watt, D. (1990) *SPACE Research Report: Growth*. Liverpool: Liverpool University Press.

Ryman, D. (1974) Children's understanding of the classification of living organisms, *Journal of Biological Education*, 8: 140–144.

Schauble, L., Klopfer, L. E. and Raghavan, K. (1991) Students' transition from an engineering model to a science model of experimentation, *Journal of Research in Science Teaching*, 28(9): 859–882.

Shepardson, D. P. (1997) Of butterflies and beetles: First graders' ways of seeing and talking about insect life cycles, *Journal of Research in Science Teaching*, 34(9): 873–889.

Shepardson, D. P. (2002) Bugs, butterflies, and spiders: Children's understandings about insects, *International Journal of Science Education*, 24: 627–643.

Teixeira, F. M. (1998) What happens to the food we eat? Children's conceptions of the structure and function of the digestive system. In *Proceedings of the Second Conference of European Researchers in Didaktik of Biology (ERIDOB): 'Research in Didaktik of Biology'*, 18–22 November, University of Göteborg, Göteborg, Sweden.

Tracana, R. B., Varanda, I., Viveiros, S. and Carvalho, G. S. D. (2012) Children's conceptions about respiration before and after formal teaching: Identification of learning obstacles. In *Proceedings of the XV International Organisation for Science and Technology Education (IOSTE) Symposium: 'The Use of Science and Technology Education for Peace and Sustainable Development'*, Hammamet, Tunisia.

Trowbridge, J. E. and Mintzes, J. (1985) Students' alternative conceptions of animal classification, *School Science and Mathematics*, 85: 304–316.

Trowbridge, J. and Mintzes, J. (1988) Alternative conceptions in animal classification: A cross-age study, *Journal of Research in Science Teaching*, 25: 547–571.

Tunnicliffe, S. D. and Reiss, M. J. (1999) Students' understandings about animal skeletons, *International Journal of Science Education*, 21(11): 1187–1200.

Tunnicliffe, S. D., Gatt, S., Agius, C. and Pizzuto, S. A. (2008) Animals in the lives of young Maltese children, *Eurasia Journal of Mathematics, Science and Technology Education*, 4: 215–221.

Yen, C. F., Yao, T. W. and Chiu, Y. C. (2004) Alternative conceptions in animal classification focusing on amphibians and reptiles: A cross-age study, *International Journal of Science and Mathematics Education*, 2: 159–174.

Yen, C. F., Yao, T. W. and Mintzes, J. J. (2007) Taiwanese students' alternative conceptions of animal biodiversity, *International Journal of Science Education*, 29: 535–553.

Chapter 3 Plants

Alonzo, A. C., Benus, M., Bennett, W. and Pinney, B. (2009) A learning progression for elementary school students' understanding of plant nutrition, in G. Cakmakci and M. F. Taser (eds) *Contemporary Science Education Research: Learning and Assessment*. Ankara: Pegem Akademi.

Anderson, J. L., Ellis, J. P. and Jones, A. M. (2014) Understanding early elementary children's conceptual knowledge of plant structure and function through drawings, *CBE-Life Sciences Education*, 13(3): 375–386.

Barman, C. R., Stein, M., McNair, S. and Barman, N. S. (2006) Students' ideas about plants and plant growth, *The American Biology Teacher*, 68(2): 73–79.

Bell, B. F. (1981) What is a plant? Some children's ideas, *New Zealand Science Teacher*, 31: 10–14.

Bianchi, L. and Feasey, R. (2011) *Science Beyond the Classroom Boundaries for 3-7 Year Olds*. Maidenhead: Open University Press.

Bruce, L. (2000) *Fran's Flower*. London: Bloomsbury.

Cañal, P. (1999) Photosynthesis and 'inverse respiration' in plants: An inevitable misconception?, *International Journal of Science Education*, 21(4): 363–371.

Cid, M. and Fialho, I. (2013) Making sense of the natural world: Seeds and plant germination, *Journal of Emergent Science*, 5: 22–28.

Gatt, S., Dale Tunnicliffe, S., Borg, K. and Lautier, K. (2007) Young Maltese children's ideas about plants, *Journal of Biological Education*, 41(3): 117–122.

Hershey, D. R. (2004) Avoid misconceptions when teaching about plants. Available at: http://www.actionbioscience.org/education/hershey.html (accessed 17 November 2015).

Kinchin, I. M. (1999) Investigating secondary-school girls' preferences for animals or plants: A simple 'head-to-head' comparison using two unfamiliar organisms, *Journal of Biological Education*, 33: 95–99.

Kolb, D. A. (1984) *Experiential Learning: Experience as the Source of Learning and Development*. Englewood Cliffs, NJ: Prentice-Hall.

Lewis, J. and Wood-Robinson, C. (2000) Genes, chromosomes, cell division, and inheritance: Do students see any relationship?, *International Journal of Science Education*, 22: 177–195.

Margett, T. E. and Witherington, D. C. (2011) The nature of preschoolers' concept of living and artificial objects, *Child Development*, 82(6): 2067–2082.

Mayhew, J. (2001) *Katie and the Sunflowers*. London: Hachette Children's Books.

McNair, S. and Stein, M. (2001) Drawing on their understanding: Using illustrations to invoke deeper thinking about plants. Presented at the Association for the Education of Teachers of Science Annual Meeting, 18-21 January, Costa Mesa, CA.

Nurettin, Y., Sahin, M. and Aydin, H. (2009) Are animals 'more alive' than plants? Animistic anthropocentric construction of life concept, *Eurasia Journal of Mathematics, Science and Technology Education*, 5(4): 369–378.

Opfer, J. E. and Siegler, R. S. (2004) Revisiting preschoolers' living things concept: A microgenetic analysis of conceptual change in basic biology, *Cognitive Psychology*, 49: 301–332.

Orbach, R. (2015) *Apple Pigs*. London: National Trust Books.

Osborne, R. J. and Freyberg, P. (1985) *Learning in Science*. London: Heinemann.

Patrick, P. and Tunnicliffe, S. D. (2011) What plants and animals do early childhood and primary students' name? Where do they see them?, *Journal of Science and Educational Technology*, 20: 630–642.

Powell, K. and Wells, M. (2002) The effectiveness of three experiential teaching approaches on student science learning in fifth-grade public school classrooms, *Journal of Environmental Education*, 33(2): 33–38.

Russell, T. and Watt, D. (1990) *SPACE Research Report: Growth*. Liverpool: Liverpool University Press.

Schussler, E. E. (2008) From flowers to fruits: How children's books represent plant reproduction, *International Journal of Science Education*, 30(12): 1677–1696.

Schussler, E. and Winslow, J. (2007) Drawing on students' knowledge about plant life cycles, *Science and Children*, 44: 40–44.

Smith, E. L. and Anderson, C. W. (1984) Plants as producers: A case study of elementary science teaching, *Journal of Research in Science Teaching*, 21: 685–698.

Smith, S. M. (2004) A cross-age study of students' conceptual understanding of interdependency in seed dispersal, pollination, and food chains using a constructivist theoretical framework. Unpublished PhD dissertation, North Carolina State University, Raleigh, NC.

Stavy, R. and Wax, N. (1989) Children's conceptions of plants as living things, *Human Development*, 32: 85–94.

Tolman, M. N. and Hardy, G. R. (2000) Teaching plant reproduction, *Science and Children*, 37(7): 16–17.

Villarroel, J. D. and Infante, G. (2014) Early understanding of the concept of living things: An examination of young children's drawings of plant life, *Journal of Biological Education*, 48(3): 119–126.

Western Regional Environmental Education Council and Western Association of Fish and Wildlife Agencies (WREEC/WAFWA) (1992) *Project WILD Activity Guide*. Bethesda, MD: WREEC.

Zangori, L. and Forbes, C. T. (2014) Scientific practices in elementary classrooms: Third-grade students' scientific explanations for seed structure and function, *Science Education*, 98(4): 614–639.

Chapter 4   Ecology, evolution and inheritance

Bravo-Torija, B. and Jiménez-Aleixandre, M. P. (2012) Progression in complexity: Contextualizing sustainable marine resources management in a 10th grade classroom, *Research in Science Education*, 42(1): 5–23.

Chin, C. and Teou, L. Y. (2010) Formative assessment: Using concept cartoon, pupils' drawings, and group discussions to tackle children's ideas about biological inheritance, *Journal of Biological Education*, 44(3): 108–115.

Demetriou, D., Korfiatis, K. and Constantinou, C. (2009) A 'bottom-up' approach to food web construction, *Journal of Biological Education*, 43(4): 181–187.

Dennis, M., Duggan, A. and McGregor, D. (2015) Evolution in action, *Primary Science*, 131: 8–10.

Endreny, A. H. (2006) Children's ideas about animal adaptations: An action research project, *Journal of Elementary Science Education*, 18(1): 33–42.

Engel-Clough, E. and Wood-Robinson, C. (1985a) Children's understanding of inheritance, *Journal of Biological Education*, 19: 304–310.

Engel-Clough, E. and Wood-Robinson, C. (1985b) How secondary students interpret instances of biological adaptation, *Journal of Biological Education*, 19(2): 125–130.

Evans, E. M. (2001) Cognitive and contextual factors in the emergence of diverse belief systems: Creation versus evolution, *Cognitive Psychology*, 42: 217–266.

Evans, E. M. (2008) Conceptual change and evolutionary biology: A developmental analysis, in S. Vosniadou (ed.) *International Handbook of Research on Conceptual Change*. New York: Routledge.

Evans, E. M., Mull, M. and Poling, D. (2001) Confronting the existential questions: Children's understanding of death and origins. Biennial Meeting of the Society for Research in Child Development, 19–22 April, Minneapolis, MN.

Evans, E. M., Rosengren, K. S., Szymanowksi, K. et al. (2005) Culture, cognition, and creationism. Biennial Meeting of the Cognitive Development Society, October, San Diego, CA.

Foreman, M. (2006) *Norman's Ark*. London: Andersen Press.

Gelman, S. A. (2003) *The Essential Child: Origins of Essentialism in Everyday Thought*. Oxford: Oxford University Press.

Gotwals, A. W. and Songer, N. B. (2010) Reasoning up and down a food chain: Using an assessment framework to investigate students' middle knowledge, *Science Education*, 94: 259–281.

Griffiths, A. K. and Grant, B. A. C. (1985) High school students' understanding of food webs: Identification of a learning hierarchy and related misconceptions, *Journal of Research in Science Teaching*, 22(5): 421–436.

Hogan, K. (2000) Assessing students' system reasoning in ecology, *Journal of Biological Education*, 35: 22–28.

Hogan, K. and Fisherkeller, J. (1996) Representing students' thinking about nutrient cycling in ecosystems: Bidimensional coding of a complex topic, *Journal of Research in Science Teaching*, 33: 941–970.

Kampourakis, K. (2013) Teaching about adaptation: Why evolutionary history matters, *Science and Education*, 22(2): 173–188.

Kargbo, D. B., Hobbs, E. D. and Erickson, G. L. (1980) Student beliefs about inherited characteristics, *Journal of Biological Education*, 14: 137–146.

Kelemen, D. (2003) British and American children's preferences for teleo-functional explanations of the natural world, *Cognition*, 88: 201–221.

Leach, J., Driver, R., Scott, P. and Wood-Robinson, C. (1992) *Progression in Conceptual Understanding of Ecological Concepts by Pupils Aged 5-16*. Leeds: Centre for Studies in Science and Mathematics Education, University of Leeds.

McGough, J. and Nyberg, L. (2013) Making connections through conversation, *Science and Children*, 50(6): 42–46.

Munson, B. H. (1994) Ecological misconceptions, *Journal of Environmental Education*, 25(4): 30–34.

Oversby, J. (1996) Knowledge of earth science and the potential for its development, *School Science Review*, 78(283): 91–97.

Powell, D. A., Aram, R. B., Aram, R. J. and Chase, T. L. (2007) We're going on a fossil hunt!, *Science Activities: Classroom Projects and Curriculum Ideas*, 44(2): 61–68.

Rule, A. C., Baldwin, S. and Schell, R. (2008) Second graders learn animal adaptations through form and function analogy object boxes, *International Journal of Science Education*, 30(9): 1159–1182.

Schollum, B. (1983) Arrows in science diagrams: Help or hindrance for pupils?, *Research in Science Education*, 13: 45–49.

Schroeder, M., McKeough, A., Graham, S. A., Stock, H. and Palmer, J. (2007) Teaching preschoolers about inheritance, *Journal of Early Childhood Research*, 5(1): 64–82.

Smith, M. U. (2010a) Current status of research in teaching and learning evolution: I. Philosophical/epistemological issues, *Science and Education*, 19(6/8): 523–538.

Smith, M. U. (2010b) Current status of research in teaching and learning evolution: II. Pedagogical issues, *Science and Education*, 19(6/8): 539–571.

Smith, S. M. (2004) A cross-age study of students' conceptual understanding of interdependency in seed dispersal, pollination, and food chains using a constructivist theoretical framework. Unpublished PhD dissertation, North Carolina State University, Raleigh, NC.

Springer, K. (1995) Acquiring a naïve theory of kinship through inference, *Child Development*, 66: 547–558.

Strommen, E. (1995) Lions and tigers and bears, oh my! Children's conceptions of forests and their inhabitants, *Journal of Research in Science Teaching*, 32: 683–698.

Sundberg, M. D. and Dini, M. L. (1993) Science majors vs. non-majors: Is there a difference?, *Journal of College Science Teaching*, 22: 299–304.

Taber, K. S. (2013) Representing evolution in science education: The challenge of teaching about natural selection, in B. Akpan (ed.) *Science Education: A Global Perspective*. Abuja, Nigeria: Next Generation Education Ltd.

Trend, R. (1998) An investigation into understanding of geological time among 10- and 11-year-old children, *International Journal of Science Education*, 20(8): 973–988.

Weissman, M. D. and Kalish, C. W. (1999) The inheritance of desired characteristics: Children's view of the role of intention in parent–offspring resemblance, *Journal of Experimental Child Psychology*, 73: 245–265.

Wood-Robinson, C. (1994) Young people's ideas about inheritance and evolution, *Studies in Science Education*, 24(1): 29–47.

Chapter 5 Properties of everyday materials

Bouma, H., Brandt, I. and Sutton, C. (1990) *Words as Tools in Science Lessons*. Amsterdam: Chemiedidactiek, University of Amsterdam.

Engineering is Elementary (2011) *Solid as a Rock: Replicating an Artifact*. Boston, MA: Museum of Science.

Galili, I. and Bar, V. (1997) Children's operational knowledge about weight, *International Journal of Science Education*, 19(3): 317–340.

Jones, B. L. and Lynch, P. P. (1989) Children's understanding of the notions of solid and liquid in relation to some common substances, *International Journal of Science Education*, 11(4): 417–427.

Krnel, D., Glažar, S. S. and Watson, R. (2003) The development of the concept of 'matter': A cross-age study of how children classify materials, *Science Education*, 87(5): 621–639.

Krnel, D., Watson, R. and Glažar, S. A. (1998) Survey of research related to the development of the concept of 'matter', *International Journal of Science Education*, 20(3): 257–289.

Lachapelle, C. P. and Cunningham, C. M. (2014) *Research and Evaluation Results for the Engineering is Elementary Project, 2004-2014*. Boston, MA: Museum of Boston.

Ling, L. M., Chik, P. and Pang, M. F. (2006) Patterns of variation in teaching the colour of light to Primary 3 students, *Instructional Science*, 34(1): 1–19.

Liu, X. and Lesniak, K. (2005) Students' progression of understanding the matter concept from elementary to high school, *Science Education*, 89: 422–450.

Liu, X. and Lesniak, K. (2006) Progression in children's understanding of the matter concept from elementary to high school, *Journal of Research in Science Teaching*, 43: 320–347.

Monson, D. and Besser, D. (2015) Smashing milk cartons, *Science and Children*, 52(9): 38.

Piaget, J. (1929) *The Child's Conception of the World*. London: Routledge & Kegan Paul.

Roy, K. (2012) Modeling safety in clay use, *Science and Children*, 50(4): 84–85.

Russell, T., Longden, K. and McGuigan, L. (1991) *SPACE Research Report: Materials*. Liverpool: Liverpool University Press.

Sargianis, K., Lachapelle, C. P., Cunningham, C. M. et al. (2012) Limestone or wax?, *Science and Children*, 50(4): 54–61.

Skamp, K. (2011) Teaching chemistry in primary science: What does the research suggest?, *Teaching Science*, 57(4): 37–43.

Smith, C. L., Wiser, M., Anderson, C. W. and Krajcik, J. (2006) Focus article: Implications of research on children's learning for standards and assessment: A proposed learning progression for matter and the atomic-molecular theory, *Measurement: Interdisciplinary Research and Perspective*, 4(1/2): 1–98.

Varelas, M., Pappas, C. C., Kane, J. M., et al. (2008) Urban primary-grade children think and talk science: Curricular and instructional practices that nurture participation and argumentation, *Science Education*, 92(1): 65–95.

Vogelezang, M. J. (1987) Development of the concept 'chemical substance': Some thoughts and arguments, *International Journal of Science Education*, 9(5): 519–528.

Wiser, M. and Smith, C. (2008) Learning and teaching about matter in grades K-8: When should the atomic-molecular theory be introduced?, in S. Vosniadou (ed.) *International Handbook of Research on Conceptual Change*. New York: Routledge.

Chapter 6   States of matter

Adams, B. (2006) All that matters, *Science and Children*, 44(1): 53–55.

Barcus, S. and Patton, M. M. (1996) What's the matter?, *Science and Children*, 34(1): 49–51.

Brook, A., Briggs, H. and Driver, R. (1984) *Aspects of Secondary Students' Understanding of the Particulate Nature of Matter*. Children's Learning in Science Project. Leeds: Centre for Studies in Science and Mathematics Education, University of Leeds.

Brook, A. and Driver, R., in collaboration with Hind, D. (1989) *Progression in Science: The Development of Pupils' Understanding of Physical Characteristics of Air Across the Age Range 5-16 Years*. Leeds: Centre for Studies in Science and Mathematics Education, University of Leeds.

Galili, I. and Bar, V. (1997) Children's operational knowledge about weight, *International Journal of Science Education*, 19(3): 317–340.

Geisel, T. S. (1949) *Bartholomew and the Oobleck*. New York: Random House.

Harrison, A. and Treagust, D. (1996) Secondary students' mental models of atoms and molecules: Implications for teaching chemistry, *Science Education*, 80(5): 509–534.

Jones, B. L. and Lynch, P. P. (1989) Children's understanding of the notions of solid and liquid in relation to some common substances, *International Journal of Science Education*, 11(4): 417–427.

Krnel, D., Glažar, S. S. and Watson, R. (2003) The development of the concept of 'matter': A cross-age study of how children classify materials, *Science Education*, 87(5): 621–639.

Krnel, D., Watson, R. and Glažar, S. A. (2005) The development of the concept of 'matter': A cross-age study of how children describe materials, *International Journal of Science Education*, 27: 367–383.

Lee, K. and Tan, S. (2004) Atoms and molecules: Do they have a place in primary science?, *Primary Science Review*, 82: 21–23.

Metz, K. (2004) Children's understanding of scientific inquiry: Their conceptualization of uncertainty in investigations of their own design, *Cognition and Instruction*, 22: 219–290.

Novick, S. and Nussbaum, J. (1978) Junior high school pupils' understanding of the particulate nature of matter: An interview study, *Science Education*, 62(3): 273–281.

Opfer, J. E. and Siegler, R. S. (2004) Revisiting preschoolers' living things concept: A microgenetic analysis of conceptual change in basic biology, *Cognitive Psychology*, 49: 301–332.

Oversby, J. (2004) Science knowledge: Representing liquids, *Primary Science Review*, 83: 27.

Purvis, D. (2006) Fun with phase changes, *Science and Children*, 43(5): 23–25.

Royce, C. A. (2015) Understanding matter and energy, *Science and Children*, 52(6): 16.

Russell, T., Longden, K. and McGuigan, L. (1991) *SPACE Research Report: Materials*. Liverpool: Liverpool University Press.

Sere, M. G. (1985) The gaseous state, in R. Driver, E. Guesne and Tiberghien, A. (eds) *Children's Ideas in Science*. Milton Keynes: Open University Press.

Skamp, K. (1999) Are atoms and molecules too difficult for primary school children?, *School Science Review*, 81(295): 97–96.

Skamp, K. (2009) Atoms and molecules in primary science: What are teachers to do?, *Australian Journal of Education in Chemistry*, 69: 5–10.

Skamp, K. (2011) Teaching chemistry in primary science: What does the research suggest?, *Teaching Science*, 57(4): 37–43.

Smith, C. L., Wiser, M., Anderson, C. W. and Krajcik, J. (2006) Focus article: Implications of research on children's learning for standards and assessment: A proposed learning progression for matter and the atomic-molecular theory, *Measurement: Interdisciplinary Research and Perspective*, 4(1/2): 1–98.

Stavy, R. (1991) Children's ideas about matter, *School Science and Mathematics*, 91(6): 240–244.

Stavy, R. (1994) States of matter: Pedagogical sequence and teaching strategies based on cognitive research, in P. J. Fensham, R. F. Gunstone and R. White (eds) *The Content of Science*. London: Falmer Press.

Stavy, R. and Stachel, D. (1985) Children's ideas about 'solid' and 'liquid', *European Journal of Science Education*, 7: 407–421.

Tytler, R., Peterson, S. and Prain, V. (2006) Picturing evaporation: Learning science literacy through a particle representation, *Teaching Science: The Journal of the Australian Science Teachers Association*, 52(1): 12–17.

Varelas, M., Pappas, C. C., Kane, J. M., Arsenault, A., Hankes, J. and Cowan, B. M. (2008) Urban primary-grade children think and talk science: Curricular and instructional practices that nurture participation and argumentation, *Science Education*, 92(1): 65–95.

Zoehfeld, K. W. (1998) *What is the World Made of? All about Solids, Liquids, and Gases*. New York: HarperCollins.

Chapter 7   Reversible and irreversible changes

Ahtee, M. and Varjola, I. (1998) Students' understanding of chemical reaction, *International Journal of Science Education*, 20(3): 305–316.

Ashbrook, P. (2006) The matter of melting, *Science and Children*, 43(4): 18–21.

Bar, V. (1989) Children's views about the water cycle, *Science Education*, 73(4): 481–500.

Bar, V. and Galili, I. (1994) Stages of children's views about evaporation, *International Journal of Science Education*, 16(2): 157–174.

Ben-Zvi Assaraf, O., Eshach, H., Orion, N. and Alamour, Y. (2012) Cultural differences and students' spontaneous models of the water cycle: A case study of Jewish and Bedouin children in Israel, *Cultural Studies of Science Education*, 7(2): 451–477.

Ben-Zvi Assaraf, O. and Orion, N. (2010) System thinking skills at the elementary school level, *Journal of Research in Science Teaching*, 47: 540–563.

Bouma, H., Brandt, I. and Sutton, C. (1990) *Words as Tools in Science Lessons*. Amsterdam: Chemiedidactiek, University of Amsterdam.

Chang, J. (1999) Teachers college students' conceptions about evaporation, condensation and boiling, *Science Education*, 83(5): 511–526.

Cross, A. and Board, J. (2015) Playground science, *Primary Science*, 136: 26–28.

Dove, J. (1998) Alternative conceptions about the weather, *School Science Review*, 79(289): 65–69.

Driver, R., Squires, A., Rushworth, P. and Wood-Robinson, V. (eds) (1994) *Making Sense of Secondary Science: Research into Children's Ideas*. London: Routledge.

Gabel, D. L., Keating, T. M. and Petty, M. (1999) Children's perceptions of chemical and physical change. Paper presented at the Annual Meeting of the National Association for Research in Science Teaching, March, Boston, MA.

Gabel, D. L., Stockton, J. D., Monaghan, D. L. and MaKinster, J. G. (2001) Changing children's conceptions of burning, *School Science and Mathematics*, 101(8): 439–451.

Johnson, P. (2005) The development of children's concept of a substance: A longitudinal study of interaction between curriculum and learning, *Research in Science Education*, 35(1): 41–61.

Kingir, S., Geban, O. and Gunel, M. (2013) Using the science writing heuristic approach to enhance student understanding in chemical change and mixture, *Research in Science Education*, 43(4): 1645–1663.

Liu, X. and Lesniak, K. M. (2005) Students' progression of understanding the matter concept from elementary to high school, *Science Education*, 89(3): 433–450.

Löfgren, L. and Helldén, G. (2008) Following young students' understanding of three phenomena in which transformations of matter occur, *International Journal of Science and Mathematics Education*, 6(3): 481–504.

Lott, K. and Jensen, A. (2012) Changes matter!, *Science and Children*, 50(2): 54–61.

Meheut, M., Saltiel, E. and Tiberghien, A. (1985) Pupils' (11-12-y/o) conceptions of combustion, *European Journal of Science Education*, 7(1): 83–93.

Nieswandt, M. (2001) Problems and possibilities for learning in an introductory chemistry course from a conceptual change perspective, *Science Education*, 85(2): 158–179.

Norris, S. and Phillips, L. (2003) How literacy in its fundamental sense is central to scientific literacy, *Science Education*, 87: 224–240.

Osborne, R. J. and Cosgrove, M. M. (1983) Children's conceptions of the changes of state of water, *Journal of Research in Science Teaching*, 20(9): 825–838.

Paik, S. H., Kim, H. N., Cho, B. K. and Park, J. W. (2004) K-8th grade Korean students' conceptions of 'changes of state' and 'conditions for changes of state', *International Journal of Science Education*, 26(2): 207–224.

Papageorgiou, G., Grammaticopoulou, M. and Johnson, P. M. (2010) Should we teach primary pupils about chemical change?, *International Journal of Science Education*, 32: 1647–1664.

Papageorgiou, G. and Johnson, P. (2005) Do particle ideas help or hinder pupils' understanding of phenomena?, *International Journal of Science Education*, 27(11): 1299–1317.

Parker, S. (2015) Adventure on the Thames, *Primary Science*, 138: 5–6.

Pfundt, H. (1982) Pre-instructional conceptions about transformations of substances, *Chimica Didactica*, 8: 2–25.

Philips, W. C. (1991) Earth science misconceptions, *The Science Teacher*, 58(2): 21–23.

Ross, K. (2013) Let the children talk: The power of talk in promoting understanding, *Primary Science*, 129: 31–33.

Ross, K. and Law, E. (2003) Children's naive ideas about melting and freezing, *School Science Review*, 85: 99–102.

Russell, T., Bell, D., Longden, K. and McGuigan, L. (1993) *SPACE Research Report: Rocks, Soil and Weather.* Liverpool: Liverpool University Press.

Russell, T. and Watt, D. (1990) *SPACE Research Report: Evaporation and Condensation.* Liverpool: Liverpool University Press.

Shepardson, D., Wee, B., Priddy, M. et al. (2009) Water transformation and storage in the mountains and at the coast: Midwest students' disconnected conceptions of the hydrologic cycle, *International Journal of Science Education,* 31: 1447–1471.

Skamp, K. (2009) Atoms and molecules in primary science: What are teachers to do?, *Australian Journal of Education in Chemistry,* 69: 5–10.

Smothers, S. M. and Goldston, M. J. (2010) Atoms, elements, molecules, and matter: An investigation into the congenitally blind adolescents' conceptual frameworks on the nature of matter, *Science Education,* 94(3): 448–477.

Southerland, S., Kittleson, J., Settlage, J. and Lanier, K. (2005) Individual and group meaning-making in an urban third grade classroom: Red fog, cold cans, and seeping vapor, *Journal of Research in Science Teaching,* 42(9): 1032–1061.

Stavridou, H. and Solomonidou, C. (1998) Conceptual reorganization and the construction of chemical reaction concept during secondary education, *International Journal of Science Education,* 20(2): 205–221.

Stavy, R. (1990) Pupils' problems in understanding conservation of mass, *International Journal of Science Education,* 12(5): 501–512.

Stavy, R. and Stachel, D. (1984) *Children's Ideas about Solid and Liquid.* Tel Aviv: Israeli Science Teaching Centre, School of Education, Tel Aviv University.

Tytler, R. (2000) A comparison of Year 1 and Year 6 students' conceptions of evaporation and condensation: Dimensions of conceptual progression, *International Journal of Science Education,* 22(5): 447–467.

Tytler, R., Peterson, S. and Prain, V. (2006) Picturing evaporation: Learning science literacy through a particle representation, *Teaching Science: The Journal of the Australian Science Teachers Association,* 52(1): 12–17.

Watson, J., Prieto, T. and Dillon, J. (1997) Consistency of students' explanations about combustion, *Science Education,* 81(4): 425–444.

Za'Rour, G. I. (1976) Interpretation of natural phenomena by Lebanese school children, *Science Education,* 60(2): 277–287.

Chapter 8   Rocks

Ault, C. R., Jr. (1982) Time in geological explanations as perceived by elementary-school students, *Journal of Geological Education,* 30(5): 304–309.

Barrow, L. and Haskins, S. (1996) Earthquake knowledge and experiences of introductory geology students, *Journal of College Science Teaching,* 26(2): 143–146.

Blake, A. (2004) Helping young children to see what is relevant and why: Supporting cognitive change in earth science using analogy, *International Journal of Science Education,* 26(15): 1855–1873.

Brass, K. and Duke, M. (1994) Primary science in an integrated curriculum, in P. J. Fensham, R. F. Gunstone and R. White (eds.) *The Content of Science.* London: Falmer Press.

Brass, K. and Jobling, W. (1994) Digging into science: A unit developed for a year 5 class, in P. J. Fensham, R. F. Gunstone and R. White (eds) *The Content of Science.* London: Falmer Press.

Cheek, K. A. (2010) Commentary: A summary and analysis of twenty-seven years of geoscience conceptions research, *Journal of Geoscience Education*, 58(3): 122–134.

Christian, P. (2008) *If You Find a Rock*. Orlando, FL: Harcourt.

Dal, B. (2006) The origin and extent of students' understandings: The effect of various kinds of factors in conceptual understanding in volcanism, *Electronic Journal of Science Education*, 11(1): 38–59.

Dove, J. E. (1998) Students' alternative conceptions in Earth science: A review of research and implications for teaching and learning, *Research Papers in Education*, 13(2): 183–201.

Duff, P. M. D. and Duff, D. (eds) (1993) *Holmes' Principles of Physical Geology*. London: Taylor & Francis.

Ford, D. J. (2003) Sixth graders' conceptions of rocks in their local environments, *Journal of Geoscience Education*, 51: 373–377.

Ford, D. J. (2005) The challenges of observing geologically: Third graders' descriptions of rock and mineral properties, *Science Education*, 89: 276–295.

Gulay, H., Yilmaz, S., Gullac, E. T. and Onder, A. (2010) The effect of soil education project on preschool children, *Educational Research and Reviews*, 5(11): 703–711.

Happs, J. C. (1982) *Some Aspects of Student Understanding of Rocks and Minerals*. Hamilton, NZ: Science Education Unit Working Paper, University of Waikato.

Kalogiannakis, M. and Violintzi, A. (2012) Intervention strategies for changing preschool children's understandings about volcanoes, *Journal of Emergent Science*, 4: 12–18.

Kusnick, J. (2002) Growing pebbles and conceptual prisms: Understanding the source of student misconceptions about rock formation, *Journal of Geoscience Education*, 50(1): 31–39.

Martínez, P., Bannan, B. and Kitsantas, A. (2012) Bilingual students' ideas and conceptual change about slow geomorphological changes caused by water, *Journal of Geoscience Education*, 60(1): 54–66.

Piotrowski, J., Mildenstein, T., Dungan, K. and Brewer, C. (2007) The radish party, *Science and Children*, 45(2): 41–46.

Ramirez, M. (2006) I am a kindergarten vulcanologist, in W.R. Dupré (ed.) *Living with Geologic Hazards*. Houston, TX: Houston Teacher Institute.

Ross, K. and Shuell, T. J. (1993) Children's beliefs about earthquakes, *Science Education*, 77: 191–205.

Russell, T., Bell, D., Longden, K. and McGuigan, L. (1993) *SPACE Research Report: Rocks, Soil and Weather*. Liverpool: Liverpool University Press.

Schoon, K. (1989) Misconceptions in the Earth sciences: A cross-age study. Paper presented at the Annual Meeting of the National Associations for Research in Science Teaching, April, San Francisco, CA.

Sharp, J. G., Mackintosh, A. P. and Seedhouse, P. (1995) Some comments on children's ideas about Earth structure, volcanoes, earthquakes and plates, *Teaching Earth Sciences*, 20(1): 28–30.

Simsek, C. L. (2007) Turkish children's ideas about earthquakes, *Journal of Environmental and Science Education*, 2(1): 14–19.

Smith, M. (2010) Creative soil conservation, *Science and Children*, 47(6): 44–46.

Trend, R. (1998) An investigation into understanding of geological time among 10- and 11-year-old children, *International Journal of Science Education*, 20(8): 973–988.

Trundle, K., Miller, H. and Krissek, L. (2013) Digging into rocks with young children, *Science and Children*, 50(8): 46–51.

Whitburn, N. (2007) Earth science in the classroom, *Primary Science Review*, 96: 30–34.

Chapter 9   Electricity

Allen, M. (2014) *Misconceptions in Primary Science* (2nd edn). Maidenhead: Open University Press.

Armitage, R. (2007) *The Lighthouse Keeper's Lunch*. London: Scholastic Books.

Aydeniz, M., Cihak, D. F., Graham, S. C. and Retinger, L. (2012) Using inquiry-based instruction for teaching science to students with learning disabilities, *International Journal of Special Education*, 27(2): 189–206.

Azaiza, I., Bar, V., Awad, Y. and Khalil, M. (2012) Pupils' explanations of natural phenomena and their relationship to electricity, *Creative Education*, 3(8): 1354–1365.

Chapman, S. (2014) Teaching the 'big ideas' of electricity at primary level, *Primary Science*, 135: 5–8.

Chiu, M. H. and Lin, J. W. (2005) Promoting fourth graders' conceptual change of their understanding of electric current via multiple analogies, *Journal of Research in Science Teaching*, 42(4): 429–464.

Davies, T. (2014) Tricky circuitry, *Primary Science*, 135: 9–11.

Glauert, E. B. (2009) How young children understand electric circuits: Prediction, explanation and exploration, *International Journal of Science Education*, 31: 1025–1047.

Lee, S. J. (2007) Exploring students' understanding concerning batteries: Theories and practices, *International Journal of Science Education*, 29: 497–516.

Mant, J. and Wilson, H. (2007) Understanding simple circuits, *Primary Science Review*, 98: 29–33.

Osborne, J. F., Black, P. J., Smith, M. and Meadows, J. (1991) *SPACE Research Report: Electricity*. Liverpool: Liverpool University Press.

Osborne, R. J. (1983) Towards modifying children's ideas about electric current, *Research in Teaching and Technological Education*, 1: 73–82.

Peppler, K. and Glosson, D. (2013) Stitching circuits: Learning about circuitry through e-textile materials, *Journal of Science Education and Technology*, 22: 751–763.

Rhoneck, C. von (1981) Students' conceptions of the electric circuit before physics instruction, in W. Jung, H. Pfundt and C. J. von Rhoneck (eds) *Proceedings of the International Workshop on Problems Concerning Students' Representation of Physics and Chemistry Knowledge*, 14-16 September, Pedagogische Hochschule, Ludwigsburg.

Sandifer, C. (2009) Shoe box circuits, *Science and Children*, 47(4): 20–23.

Shen, J. and Linn, M. (2010) A technology-enhanced unit of modeling static electricity: Integrating scientific explanations and everyday observations, *International Journal of Science Education*, 33: 1–27.

Shepardson, D. P. and Moje, E. B. (1994) The nature of fourth graders' understandings of electric circuits, *Science Education*, 78(5): 489–514.

Shipstone, D. M. (1985) Electricity in simple circuits, in R. Driver, E. Guesne and A. Tiberghien (eds) *Children's Ideas in Science*. Milton Keynes: Open University Press.

Tiberghien, A. and Delacote, G. (1976) Manipulations et représentations de circuits électriques simples préexistant à l'enseignement, in G. Delacote (ed.) *Physics Teaching in Schools*. London: Taylor & Francis.

Chapter 10   Earth and space

Baxter, J. (1989) Children's understanding of familiar astronomical events, *International Journal of Science Education*, 11: 502–513.

Chiras, A. (2008) Day/night cycle: Mental models of primary school children, *Science Education International*, 19(1): 65–83.

Davies, R. W. (2002) There's a lot to learning about the Earth in space, *Primary Science Review*, 72: 9–12.

Durant, J. R., Evans, G. A. and Thomas, G. P. (1989) The public understanding of science, *Nature*, 340: 11–14.

Jones, B. L., Lynch, P. P. and Reesink, C. (1987) Children's conception of the Earth, Sun and Moon, *International Journal of Science Education*, 9: 43–53.

Keeley, P. (2013) When is the next full moon? Using K-2 concept cartoons, *Science and Children*, 51(1): 32–34.

Kibble, B. (2002a) Misconception about space? It's on the cards, *Primary Science Review*, 72: 5–8.

Kibble, B. (2002b) Simple sundials, *Primary Science Review*, 72: 23–25.

Lievesley, T. (2009) Focus on: Journeys into space, *Primary Science*, 108: 3.

McDermott, L. (1996) *Physics by Inquiry*. New York: John Wiley.

Nussbaum, J. and Sharoni-Dagan, N. (1983) Changes in second grade children's preconceptions about the Earth as a cosmic body resulting from a short series of audio-tutorial lessons, *Science Education*, 67(1): 99–114.

Osborne, J. F., Wadsworth, P., Black, P. J. and Meadows, J. (1994) *SPACE Research Report: The Earth in Space*. Liverpool: Liverpool University Press.

Piaget, J. (1929) *The Child's Conception of the World*. London: Routledge & Kegan Paul.

Plummer, J. D. (2009) Early elementary students' development of astronomy concepts in the planetarium, *Journal of Research in Science Teaching*, 46: 192–209.

Plummer, J. D. and Krajcik, J. (2010) Building a learning progression for celestial motion: Elementary levels from an earth-based perspective, *Journal of Research in Science Teaching*, 47(7): 768–787.

Sharp, J. G. (1996) Children's astronomical beliefs: A preliminary study of year 6 children in south- west England, *International Journal of Science Education*, 18: 685–712.

Sharp, J. G. (1999) Young children's ideas about the Earth in space, *International Journal of Early Years Education*, 7(2): 159–172.

Sharp, J. G. and Kuerbis, P. (2006) Children's ideas about the solar system and the chaos in learning science, *Science Education*, 90(1): 124–147.

Sharp, J. G. and Sharp, J. C. (2007) Beyond shape and gravity: children's ideas about the earth in space reconsidered, *Research Papers in Education*, 22: 363–401.

Sneider, C. I. and Ohadi, M. M. (1998) Unraveling students' misconceptions about the earth's shape and gravity, *Science Education*, 82(2): 265–284.

Stahly, L. L., Krockover, G. H. and Shepardson, D. P. (1999) Third grade students' ideas about lunar phases, *Journal of Research in Science Teaching*, 36(2): 159–177.

Trundle, K. C., Atwood, R. K. and Christopher, J. E. (2007) Fourth grade elementary students' conceptions of standards-based lunar concepts, *International Journal of Science Education*, 29: 595–616.

Trundle, K. C., Atwood, R. K., Christopher, J. E. and Sackes, M. (2010) The effect of guided inquiry-based instruction on middle school students' understanding of lunar concepts, *Research in Science Education*, 40: 451–478.

Vosniadou, S. and Brewer, W. F. (1990) A cross-cultural investigation of children's conceptions about the Earth, the Sun and the Moon: Greek and American data, in H. Mandl, E. De Corte, N. Bennett and H. F. Friedrid (eds) *Learning and Instruction: European Research in an International Context.* Oxford: Pergamon Press.

Vosniadou, S. and Brewer, W. F. (1992) Mental models of the Earth: A study of conceptual change in childhood, *Cognitive Psychology*, 24: 535–585.

Chapter 11 Forces and magnets

Ahtee, M. and Hakkarainen, O. (2012) Importance of the order of demonstrations in changing pupils' conceptions, *Nordic Studies in Science Education*, 1(1): 31–42.

Allen, M. (2010) Learner error, affectual stimulation and conceptual change, *Journal of Research in Science Teaching*, 47: 151–173.

Bar, V., Zinn, B., Goldmuntz, R. and Sneider, C. (1994) Children's conceptions about weight and free fall, *Science Education*, 78: 149–169.

Bar, V., Zinn, B. and Rubin, E. (1997) Children's ideas about action at a distance, *International Journal of Science Education*, 19(10): 1137–1157.

Barrow, L. H. (1987) Magnet concepts and elementary students' misconceptions, in J. Novak *Proceedings of the Second International Seminar on Misconceptions and Educational Strategies in Science and Mathematics.* Ithaca, NY: Cornell University Press.

Barrow, L. H. (2000) Do elementary science methods textbooks facilitate the understanding of magnet concepts?, *Journal of Science Education and Technology*, 9(3): 199–205.

Burton, B. (2012) Experiencing friction in first grade, *Science and Children*, 50(2): 68–72.

Champagne, A., Klopfer, L. and Anderson, J. (1980) Factors influencing the learning of classical mechanics, *American Journal of Physics*, 48(12): 1074–1079.

Cheng, M.-F. and Brown, D. E. (2010) Conceptual resources in self-developed explanatory models: The importance of integrating conscious and intuitive knowledge, *International Journal of Science Education*, 32(17): 2367–2392.

Christidou, V., Kazela, K., Kakana, D. and Valakosta, M. (2009) Teaching magnetic attraction to preschool children: A comparison of different approaches, *International Journal of Learning*, 16(2): 115–128.

Driver, R., Squires, A., Rushworth, P. and Wood-Robinson, V. (1994) *Making Sense of Secondary Science: Research into Children's Ideas.* London: Routledge.

Erickson, G. (1994) Pupils' understanding of magnetism in a practical assessment context: The relationship between content, process and progression, in P. J. Fensham, R. F. Gunstone and R. White (eds) *The Content of Science.* London: Falmer Press.

Finley, F. N. (1986) Evaluating instruction: the complementary use of clinical interviews, *Journal of Research in Science Teaching*, 23(7): 635–650.

Gunstone, R. F. and White, R. T. (1981) Understanding of gravity, *Science Education*, 65(3): 291–299.

Hakkarainen, O. and Ahtee, M. (2005) Pupils' mental models of a pulley in balance, *Journal of Baltic Science Education*, 8: 26–34.

Halloun, I. and Hestenes, D. (1985) Common sense concepts about motion, *American Journal of Physics*, 53(11): 1056–1065.

Hast, M. (2011) Explicit versus tacit knowledge in early science education: The case of primary school children's understanding of object speed and acceleration. Unpublished doctoral dissertation, University of Cambridge, Cambridge.

Ioannides, C. and Vosniadou, S. (2002) The changing meanings of force, *Cognitive Science Quarterly*, 2(1): 5–62.

Ivowi, U. M. O. (1986) Students' misconceptions about conservation principles and fields, *Research in Science and Technological Education*, 4(2): 127–137.

Keeley, P. (2011) Pushes and pulls, *Science and Children*, 49(2): 28.

King, M. D. (2000) Rev up your veggies!, *Science and Children*, 38(1): 20–25.

McCloskey, M. (1983) Naive theories of motion, in D. Gentner and A. L. Stevens (eds) *Mental Models*. Hillsdale, NJ: Lawrence Erlbaum.

Meyer, K. (1991) Children as experimenters: Elementary students' actions in an experimental context with magnets. Unpublished doctoral dissertation, University of British Columbia, Vancouver.

Osborne, R., Schollum, B. and Hill, G. (1981) *Learning in Science Project: Force, Friction and Gravity (Notes for Teachers)*. Hamilton, NZ: University of Waikato.

Palmer, D. (2001) Students' alternative conceptions and scientifically acceptable conceptions about gravity, *Australian Science Teachers Journal*, 23(7): 691–706.

Piaget, J. and Chollet, M. (1973) Le problème de l'attraction à propos des aimants, in J. Piaget (ed.) *La Formation de la Notion de Force*. Paris: Presses Universitaire de France.

Ravanis, K., Koliopoulos, D. and Boilevin, J. M. (2008) Construction of a precursor model for the concept of rolling friction in the thought of preschool age children: A sociocognitive teaching intervention, *Research in Science Education*, 38(4): 421–434.

Reiner, M., Slotta, J. D., Chi, M. T. H. and Resnick, L. B. (2000) Naive physics reasoning: A commitment to substance-based conceptions, *Cognition and Instruction*, 18: 1–34.

Reynoso, E., Fierro, E., Torres, G. et al. (1993) The alternative frameworks presented by Mexican students and teachers concerning the free fall of bodies, *International Journal of Science Education*, 15: 127–138.

Russell, T., McGuigan, L. and Hughes, A. (1998) *SPACE Research Report: Forces*. Liverpool: Liverpool University Press.

Stead, K. and Osborne, R. (1980) Friction. LISP Working Paper 19. Hamilton, NZ: Science Education Research Unit, University of Waikato.

Taylor-Tavares, J., Howe, C. and Devine, A. (2009) Children's conceptions of horizontal motion: Tacit and explicit understanding in middle childhood. Poster presented at the Biennial Meeting of the Society for Research on Child Development, Denver, CO.

Twigger, D., Byard, M., Driver, R. et al. (1994) The conception of force and motion of students aged between 10 and 15 years: An interview study designed to guide instruction, *International Journal of Science Education*, 16(2): 215–229.

Viennot, L. and Rozier, S. (1994) Pedagogical outcomes of research in science education: Examples in mechanics and thermodynamics, in P. J. Fensham, R. F. Gunstone and R. White (eds) *The Content of Science*. London: Falmer Press.

Waring, G. (2007) *Oscar and the Cricket*. London: Walker Books.

Watts, D. M. (1982) Gravity: Don't take it for granted, *Physics Education*, 17: 116–121.

Wilcox, J. and Richey, L. R. (2012) May the magnetic force be with you, *Science and Children*, 50(2): 62–67.

Chapter 12   Light

Allen, M. (2014) *Misconceptions in Primary Science* (2nd ed.). Maidenhead: Open University Press.

Ashbrook, P. (2009) Does light go through it?, *Science and Children*, 46(7): 16–18.

Ashbrook, P. (2012) Shining light on misconceptions, *Science and Children*, 50(2): 30–31.

Barrow, L. H. (2007) Bringing light onto shadows, *Science and Children*, 44(9): 43–45.

Dedes, C. and Ravanis, K. (2007) Reconstruction des représentations spontanées des élèves: La formation des ombres par des sources étendues, *Skholê (HS)*, 1: 31–39.

Department for Education (DfE) (2013) *Science Programmes of Study: Key Stages 1 and 2*. DFE-00182–2013. London: DfE.

Eschach, H. (2003) Small-group interview-based discussions about diffused shadow, *Journal of Science Education and Technology*, 12(3): 261–275.

Feher, E. and Rice, K. (1988) Shadows and anti-images: Children's conceptions of light and vision II, *Science Education*, 72(5): 637–649.

Fetherstonhaugh, T. and Treagust, D. F. (1990) *Students' understanding of light and its properties following a teaching strategy to engender conceptual change*. Paper presented to the Annual Meeting of the American Educational Research Association, 16–20 April, Boston, MA.

Galili, I. and Hazan, A. (2000) Learners' knowledge in optics: interpretation, structure and analysis, *International Journal of Science Education*, 22(1): 57–88.

Gallegos Cázares, L., Flores Camacho, F. and Calderón Canales, E. (2008) Aprendizaje de las ciencias en preescolar: La construcción de representaciones y explicaciones sobre la luz y las sombras, *Revista Iberoamericana de Educación*, 47: 97–121.

Gonzalez-Espada, W. J. (2003) A last chance for getting it right: Addressing alternative conceptions in the physical sciences, *The Physics Teacher*, 41: 36–38.

Guesne, E. (1978) Lumière et vision des objets: Un example de represéntation des phénomènes physiques chez les enfants de 7 à 12 ans, *Revue Française de Pedagogie*, 34: 32–44.

Guesne, E. (1984) Children's ideas about light, in E. J. Wenman (ed.) *New Trends in Physics Teaching, Vol. IV*. Paris: UNESCO.

Guesne, E. (1985) Light, in R. Driver, E. Guesne and A. Tiberghien (eds) *Children's Ideas in Science*. Milton Keynes: Open University Press.

Heywood, D. (2005) Primary teachers' learning and teaching about light: Some pedagogic implications for initial teacher training, *International Journal of Science Education*, 27: 1447–1475.

Hopgood, T. (2009) *Here Comes Frankie*. London: Macmillan Children's Books.

Osborne, J. F., Black, P. J., Smith, M. and Meadows, J. (1990) *SPACE Research Report: Light*. Liverpool: Liverpool University Press.

Philips, W. C. (1991) Earth science misconceptions, *Science Teacher*, 58: 21–23.

Piaget, J. and Inhelder, B. (1967) *The Child's Conception of Space*. New York: Norton.

Ravanis, K. and Boilevin, J. M. (2009) A comparative approach to the representation of light for five-, eight- and ten-year-old children: Educational perspectives, *Journal of Baltic Science Education*, 8(3): 182–190.

Ravanis, K., Christidou, V. and Hatzinikita, V. (2013) Enhancing conceptual change in pre-school children's representations of light: A sociocognitive approach, *Research in Science Education*, 43(6): 2257–2276.

Resta-Schweizer, M. and Weil-Barais, A. (2009) Initiation scientifique et développement intellectuel de l'enfant à l'âge pré-scolaire, *Dossiers des Sciences de l'Education*, 21: 101–113.

Segal, G. and Cosgrove, M. (1993) 'The sun is sleeping now': Early learning about light and shadows, *Research in Science Education*, 23(1): 276–285.

Settlage, J. (1995) Children's conceptions of light in the context of a technology-based curriculum, *Science Education*, 79 (5): 535–553.

Trundle, K.C. and Hilson, M. P. (2012) Shadow play: Linking shadows to learning about seasons, *Science and Children*, 49(5): 31–35.

Venville, G., Adey, P., Larkin, S. and Robertson, A. (2003) Fostering thinking through science in the early years of schooling, *International Journal of Science Education*, 25(11): 1313–1331.

Vygotsky, L. (1978) *Mind in Society: The Development of Higher Psychological Processes*. Cambridge, MA: Harvard University Press.

Waddle, M. (2013) *Can't You Sleep Little Bear?* London: Walker Books.

Watts, D. M. and Gilbert, J. K. (1985) *Appraising the Understanding of Science Concepts: Light*. Guilford: Department of Educational Studies, University of Surrey.

Chapter 13   Sound

Allen, J. (2000) *The Bear Who Wouldn't Share*. Harlow: Rigby.

Ashbrook, P. (2014) Becoming attuned to sound, *Science and Children*, 51(6): 26–27.

Asoko, H. M., Leach, J. and Scott, P. H. (1991a) Classroom research as a basis for professional development of teachers: A study of students' understanding of sound, in J. H. C. Vonk, J. H. G. I. Giesbers, J. J. Peters and Th. Wubbels (eds.) *New Prospects for Teacher Education in Europe II*. Amsterdam: VU Press.

Asoko, H. M., Leach, J. and Scott, P. H. (1991b) A study of students' understanding of sound 5-16 as an example of action research. Paper prepared for the symposium on 'Developing Students' Understanding in Science' at the Annual Conference of the British Educational Research Association, 2 September, Roehampton Institute, London.

Brown, T. and Boehringer, K. (2007) Breaking the sound barrier, *Science and Children*, 44(5): 35–39.

Driver, R., Rushworth, A., Squires, P. and Wood-Robinson, V. (1994) *Making Sense of Secondary Science*. London: Routledge.

Geisel, T. S. (1954) *Horton Hears a Who!* New York: Random House.

Hendrix, R. and Eick, C. (2014) Creative sound dramatics: Dramatic models of sound travel extend inquiry learning for fourth graders, *Science and Children*, 51(6): 37–43.

Mazens, K. and Lautrey, J. (2003) Conceptual change in physics: Children's naive representations of sound, *Cognitive Development*, 18(2): 159–176.

Merwade, V., Eichinger, D., Harriger, B. et al. (2014) The sound of science, *Science and Children*, 51(6): 30–36.

Piaget, J. (1971) *Les Explications Causales*. Paris: Presses Universitaire France.

Scott, P. H. and Asoko, H. M. (1990) A study of students' understanding of sound, 5-16, as an example of action research. Paper presented to the Conference of the British Educational Research Association, London.

Shin, E. and Kim, E. (2013) The development of concepts on sound propagation of children, *Korean Journal of Child Studies*, 34(4): 19–36.

Snyder, R. and Johnson, J. (2010) Do you hear what Horton hears?, *Science and Children*, 48(2): 68–70.

Sözen, M. and Bolat, M. (2011) Determining the misconceptions of primary school students related to sound transmission through drawing, *Procedia-Social and Behavioral Sciences*, 15: 1060–1066.

Waring, G. (2007) *Oscar and the Bat*. London: Walker Books.

Watt, D. and Russell, T. (1990) *SPACE Research Report: Sound.* Liverpool: Liverpool University Press.

West, E. (2008) *Teaching about Sound, Hearing and Health – Knowledge Base: Suggestions for Teaching and Copying Material.* Gothenburg: University of Gothenburg

West, E. and Wallin, A. (2013) Students' learning of a generalized theory of sound transmission from a teaching–learning sequence about sound, hearing and health, *International Journal of Science Education*, 35(6): 980–1011.

Index

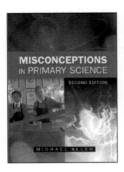

MISCONCEPTIONS IN PRIMARY SCIENCE
2/e

Michael Allen

February 2014
9780335262663 – Paperback

eBook also available

Most pupils start their scientific learning with previously formed ideas, based on prior reasoning or experience, but these ideas are often founded on common misconceptions, which if left unexplained can continue into adulthood. The new edition of this bestselling book offers advice on how to recognize and challenge such misconceptions. This book offers coverage of the most common scientific misconceptions that you may come across and, in addition to background theoretical and research material, offers appropriate teaching strategies to help you seek out and challenge misconceptions during your primary science teaching.

This handy book has been expanded to offer even more support and practical advice for dealing with the common misconceptions encountered in the primary science classroom. Michael Allen describes over 100 common misconceptions and their potential origins, and then offers creative activities to help you grasp the underlying scientific concepts and bring them alive in the classroom, as well as practical strategies to improve pupil learning.

Highlights of the second edition include:

- Updated in line with the new primary science National Curriculum Programme of Study
- Incorporates the latest research findings
- Covers the new National Curriculum elements and other more advanced material including Drugs, Energy, the Environment and Evolution
- Includes new boxed features: Did you Know?, Famous Scientists, and Be Safe

This easy to navigate and friendly guide is a superb toolkit to support you as you prepare to teach in the primary school, irrespective of your training route.

www.openup.co.uk

ENHANCING PRIMARY SCIENCE
Developing Effective Cross-Curricular Links

Lois Kelly and Di Stead

9780335247042 (Paperback)
2012

eBook also available

This book gives helpful insights into why making effective cross-curricular links enriches science and discusses when and how to make effective and authentic links between science and other subjects. Each chapter tackles a particular subject and considers how it can enhance science learning through a variety of approaches and a wealth of ideas for the classroom.

Key features:

- Includes contributions from a range of expert practitioners
- Provides a good balance between theory and practice
- Includes practical advice and tasks to help develop your confidence and skill in cross-curricular teaching

www.openup.co.uk

OPEN UNIVERSITY PRESS
McGraw - Hill Education